An Outline of the Origins of Money

HAU
Books

Director
Frédéric Keck

Editorial Collective
Deborah Durham
Casey High
Nora Scott

Managing Editor
Hannah Roberson

Hau Books are published by the
Society for Ethnographic Theory (SET)

www.haubooks.org

An Outline of the Origins of Money

Heinrich Schurtz

Translated and annotated, with an introduction by
Enrique Martino and **Mario Schmidt**

Foreword by **Michael Hudson**

Hau Books
Chicago

ISBN: 978-1-914363-07-8 [paperback]
ISBN: 978-1-914363-27-6 [PDF]
ISBN: 978-1-914363-28-3 [e-book]

LCCN: 2024933339

Hau Books
Chicago Distribution Center
11030 S. Langley Ave.
Chicago, IL 60628
www.haubooks.org

Hau Books publications are marketed and distributed by
The University of Chicago Press.
www.press.uchicago.edu

Printed in the United States of America on acid-free paper.

In memory of Jane Guyer (1943–2024) and Felix Brandl (1983–2024)

Contents

Contents

List of Figures

Acknowledgments

In 2021, I (Martino) scrolled through the *Grundriss einer Entstehungs-geschichte des Geldes* completely unaware of its author, Heinrich Schurtz. I was struck by its intellectual originality, and surprised to find that it had barely been cited in the past half-century—with the exception of a brief but appreciative footnote by Mario Schmidt in his PhD thesis. We got in touch, but pitching a new edition to publishers without funds for a translator proved difficult, and we eventually decided to translate it ourselves while I was on a Juan de la Cierva postdoctoral fellowship, financed by the Spanish State Research Agency, at the Departamento de Historia, Teorías y Geografía Políticas of the Complutense University of Madrid, and Mario was employed as a Senior Research Fellow at the Department of the Anthropology of Economic Experimentation at the Max Planck Institute for Social Anthropology in Halle. We wish to thank Catherine Howard, and then Debbie Durham, editors at Hau Books, as well as Anne-Christine Taylor, who saw promise in this piece of fin de siècle anthropology.

Much of the foundation for the publication was laid during Martino's fellowship at the Freiburg Institute for Advanced Studies (FRIAS) in 2021, which was funded by the Balzan Prize for Global History awarded to Jürgen Osterhammel. Martino held presentations on Schurtz's *Grundriss* at the FRIAS Humanities and Social Sciences Colloquium in April 2021 ("When economics met ethnology: The concepts of 'commercial' and 'social' money around 1900"), and at the Research Colloquium of the Department of Economic History of the Humboldt University of Berlin in November 2021 ("'Primitive' money, commercial capitalism and the intellectual and ethnological legacy of the German historical school of economics, with special reference to Central Africa and the Western Pacific"), and wishes to thank Bernd Kortmann, Alexander Nützenadel, and Marie Huber for the invitations and also Sven Beckert, Günther Schulze, and Nikolaus Wolf for their encouraging comments.

At the final stages of completing the translation and introduction, Martino joined Schmidt as a Guest Researcher at the Max Planck Institute for Social Anthropology in Halle for several months in late 2023, and we are grateful for the discussion and especially the more detailed comments by Balázs Gosztonyi, Richard Pfeilstetter, and Ghassan Hage. Special thanks to Biao Xiang, the director of the department, for providing this opportunity and additional funds to support part of the editorial expenses and the image licensing rights. In Madrid, Martino also presented a draft of the introductory study at the Seminario de Historia Santos Juliá, and wishes to thank Juan Aranzadi and Javier Moreno Luzón for organizing the presentation and for discussing the work in detail.

We wish to thank Jürgen Osterhammel, André Orleans, Carlotta Santini, Keith Hart, Dmitri van den Bersselaar, and Felix Brandl for providing invaluable advice helping us to complete our introduction. For help on specific aspects of the translation and annotations, we want to thank Sabine Scheuring, Adam Jones, Lukas Wissel, William Clarence-Smith, David Mayer, Jan Delaeter, Romain Tiquet, Kerem Duymus, Tiago Guidi, Reda Mokhtar El Ftouh, and Alessandro De Cola. For valuable insights into Schurtz's former workplace and some of the museological collections as well as images, we also want to thank Jan Wassmann at the Übersee-Museum Bremen, Julien Volper at the Royal Museum for Central Africa, Mark R. Dickerson at the Pitt Rivers Museum, Travis Stansel at the Spurlock Museum of World Cultures, and Esther Rimer at the Department of Anthropology, Smithsonian Institution.

The Institutional-Systemic Origins of Money

Michael Hudson

The late nineteenth century saw economists, mainly German and Austrian, create a mythology of money's origins that is still repeated in today's textbooks. Money is said to have originated as just another commodity being bartered, with metal preferred because it is nonperishable
(and hence amenable to being saved), supposedly standardized (despite
fraud if not minted in temples), and thought to be easily divisible, as if
silver could have been used for small marketplace exchanges, which was
unrealistic given the rough character of ancient scales for weights of a
few grams.[1] This mythology does not recognize government as having
played any role as a monetary innovator, sponsor, or regulator, or as giving
money its value by accepting it as a vehicle to pay taxes, buy public services, or make religious contributions. Also downplayed is money's function as a standard of value for denominating and paying debts.[2] Although
there is no empirical evidence for the commodity-barter origin myth, it

---

1. Menger 1892. The barter theory has been refuted by modern research
    uncovering the Bronze Age Near Eastern institutional origins of money,
    which I discuss in chapters 1 and 3 of *Temples of Enterprise* (Hudson 2024).
    My criticisms of this theory are in "Origins of Money and Interest: Palatial
    Credit, not Barter" (Hudson 2020).
2. See the papers collected in Wray 2004.

has survived on purely hypothetical grounds because of its political bias that serves the anti-socialist Austrian school and subsequent "free market" creditor interests opposing government money creation.

Schurtz's Treatment of Money as Part of the Overall Social System

As one of the founders of economic anthropology, Heinrich Schurtz approached the origins of money as being much more complex than the "economic" view that it emerged simply as a result of families going to the marketplace to barter. Surveying a wide range of indigenous communities, his 1898 *An Outline of the Origins of Money* described their trade and money in the context of the institutional system within which members sought status and wealth. Schurtz described these monetary systems as involving a wide array of social functions and dimensions, which today's "economic" theorizing excludes as external to its analytic scope. Placing money in the context of the community's overall system of social organization, Schurtz warned that anyone who detaches "sociological and economic problems from the environment in which they emerged ... their native land ... only carries away a part of the whole organism and fails to understand the vital forces that have created and sustained it" (p. 163).

Looking at indigenous communities as having preserved presumably archaic traditions, Schurtz viewed trade with outsiders as leading wealth to take an increasingly monetary form that eroded the balance of internal social relations. Schurtz deemed the linkage between money, debt, and land tenure to lie beyond the area on which he focused, nor did he mention contributions to group feasts (which Bernard Laum would suggest as the germ from which Greek obols and drachmas may have evolved).[3]

The paradigmatic forms of indigenous wealth were jewelry and other items of personal adornment, decorations, and trophies, especially foreign exotic products in the form of shells and gemstones or items with a long and prestigious history that gave their wearers or owners status. Thorstein Veblen would call the ownership and display of such items conspicuous consumption in his 1899 *Theory of the Leisure Class*. They had an exchange value, as they do today, but that did not make them monetary means of exchange. Schurtz saw many gray areas in their

---

3.   Mauss (1925) 2016; Laum 1924. Schurtz mentions spit-money in passing but finds trade in food relatively unimportant.

monetization: "Beads made of clay and stone are also crafted by indige-nous people and widely used as ornaments but rarely as money" (p. 119). At issue was how a money economy differs from barter, and from the circulation and exchange of useful and valued items in a social economy. Was indigenous exchange and wealth pre-monetary, an archaic seed that led to money's "more ideal forms" (p. 34)?

Schurtz's Distinction between Inside-Money and Outside-Money

Exchange with outsiders typically was conducted by political leaders as the face of their communities to the outside world. Trade (and also payment of tribute) involved fiscal and social relations whose monetary functions differed from those of the domestic economy but ended up dovetailing with them to give money a hybrid character. Schurtz distin-guished what he called outside-money from inside-money, with outside-money ultimately dominating the inside monetary system. "The concept of money," he wrote, originated

> from two distinct sources: What functions as the foundation of wealth and measure of value for property and serves social ends within a tribe is, in its origins, something entirely different from the means of exchange that travels from tribe to tribe and eventually transforms itself, as a universally welcomed commodity, into a kind of currency. (p. 35)

Inside-money was used within communities for their own exchange and wealth. Outside-money derived from transactions with outsiders. And what was "outside" was a set of practices governing trade outside the jurisdiction of local governance.[4] Schurtz's distinction emphasized a characteristic of trade that has continued down through today's world: the contrast between domestic payments subject to checks and balances to protect basic needs and navigating status hierarchies but (ideally) lim-iting sharp wealth disparities, and exchange with outsiders, often con-ducted on islands, quay areas, or other venues socially outside the com-munity's boundaries, subject to more impersonal standardized rules.

---

4. I discuss this in "From Sacred Enclave to Temple to City" (Hudson 1999) and chapter 10 of *Temples of Enterprise* (Hudson 2024).

Throughout the ancient world we find offshore island entrepots wherever these are conveniently located for conducting trade with outsiders. They kept foreign contact at arm's length so as to prevent mercantile relations from disturbing local economic balance. Egypt restricted foreign contacts to the Delta region where the Nile flowed into the Mediterranean. For the Etruscans, the island of Ischia/Pithekoussai became the base for Phoenician and Greek merchants to deal with the Italian mainland in the eighth and seventh centuries BCE. North Germans seem to have conducted the Baltic amber trade by way of the sacred island of Helgoland.

"The emergence of specific internal monetary systems is always supported by the inclination to transform outside-money into inside-money, and to employ money not to facilitate external trade, as one might assume according to common theories, but rather to obstruct it," Schurtz concluded (p. 155). And in his earlier chapter "Metal as Ornament and Money," he pointed out that it was foreign trade that led metal to become the primary form of money. "While most varieties of ornament-money gradually lose their significance, one of them, *metal-money*, asserts its ground all the more and finally pushes its competitors out of the field" (p. 123). He added that: "Metal-money made from noble metals is not a pure sign-money, it is at the same time a valuable commodity, the value of which depends on supply and demand. In its mature form, it therefore in itself embodies the fusion of inside-money with outside-money, of the sign of value and valuable property with the means of exchange" (p. 124).[5]

This merging of inside- and outside-money is documented already in the third millennium BCE in the Near East. Silver-money was used for long-distance trade and came to be used for domestic enterprise as well, while grain remained the monetary vehicle for denominating agrarian

---

5. Schurtz cited as an example of how monetary authorities could substitute sign-money for metal-money the case of "Kublai Khan, the ruler of the Mongolian empire, [who] drove out metal-money with sign-money, specifically stamped pieces of paper, evidently following the Chinese example; Marco Polo's accounts indicate that the endeavor must have temporarily succeeded only because of the tremendous power and authority of the ruler, with the result of a vast accumulation of gold and silver in the Khan's residence" (p. 57). But he made disparaging remarks about the French government's paper money assignats and called John Law a "swindler" (p. 139), dismissing government money creation.

production, taxes and debt service on the land, and for distribution to dependent labor in Mesopotamia's temples and palaces.

Schurtz also posed the question of whether the dominance of metallic money emerged spontaneously in many places, or whether there was a diffusion from a singular origin, that is, "whether a cultural institution has grown in situ or whether it has been transferred from other regions through migration and contact between societies" (p. 163). The diffusion of Mesopotamian weights associated with silver points to its diffusion from that region, as does the spread of the region's practice of setting interest rates simply for ease of calculation in terms of the local fractional arithmetic system (60ths in Mesopotamia for a shekel per mina a month, 10ths or percentages in decimalized Greece, and 12ths in Rome for a troy ounce per pound each year).

Checks and Balances to Prevent the Selfish Concentration of Wealth

What do seem to have developed spontaneously were social attitudes and policies to prevent the concentration of wealth from injuring economic balance. Wealth concentration, especially when achieved by depriving cultivators of their means of livelihood, would have violated the ethic of mutual aid that low-surplus economies need as a condition for their resilience.

Viewing money as part of the overall social context, Schurtz described "the social transformation brought about by wealth" as a result of monetizing trade and its commercial "pursuit of profit" [*Erwerbssinn*]:

> [E]veryone is now compelled to join in the competition for property or he will be pulled into the vortex created by one of the newly emerging centers of power and property, where he will need to work hard to be able to live at all. For the property owner, no temporal limit constrains his view on the perpetual increase of his wealth. (p. 66)

Schurtz characterized the economic mentality as a drive for "the unlimited accumulation of movable property" (p. 69), to be passed on to one's children leading to the creation of a wealthy hereditary class. If archaic societies had this ethic, could ancient civilizations have taken off? How did they prevent the growth of wealth from fostering an oligarchy seeking to increase its wealth at the expense of the community at large and its resilience?

Schurtz reviewed how indigenous communities typically avoided that fate by shaping a social value system that would steer wealth away from being used to achieve predatory power over others. He cited numerous examples in which "immense treasures often accumulate without reentering the transactions of daily life" (p. 66). One widespread way to do this was simply to bury wealth. "The primitive man," he wrote, "believes that he will have access to all the goods given to him in the grave, even in the afterlife. Thus, he too knows no bounds to acquisition" (p. 66). Taking his greed and wealth with him to use in the hereafter prevents hoarded wealth from being inherited "and growing into a dangerous instrument of power" by becoming dynastic; ultimately operating "on the belief that the deceased does not give up his rights of ownership but jealously guards over his property to ensure that no heir makes use of it" (p. 70).

A less destructive removal of wealth from its owners was to create an ethic of peer pressure in which individuals gained status and popular acclaim by accumulating wealth to give away. Schurtz wrote,

> remnants of the ancient communism remain alive enough for a long time to effectively block attempts to amass as many assets as possible in a single hand. And *in places without an actual system of debt and interest*, the powerful individual, into whose house the tributes of the people flow, has indeed little choice but to "represent" by way of his wealth: in other words, to allow the people to participate in his indulgences. (p. 67, italics added)

Such an individual achieves philanthropic renown by generously distributing his possessions to "his friends and followers, winning their hearts and thereby establishing real power based on loyal devotion" (p. 67). One widespread practice was to celebrate marriages, funerals, and other rites of passage by providing great feasts. This "extraordinary ... destruction and squandering of valuable property, particularly livestock and food, during those grand festivals of the dead that evolved out of sacrifices and are, among some peoples, not only an effective obstacle to the accumulation of wealth but have turned into economic calamities" when families feel obliged to take on debt to host such extravagant displays (p. 71). Religious officials and temples often played a role in such rituals. Noting that "money, trade, and religion had a good relationship with one another in antiquity" (p. 64), Schurtz cited the practice of donating wealth to temples or their priesthoods. But he recognized that this might enable them to "gain dominance through the ownership of money" under their control (p. 66).

"The communist countermeasures against wealth generally do not endure," Schurtz wrote. "Certain kinds of property seem to favor greed directly, especially cattle farming, which can literally turn into a hoarding addiction" (p. 69). And he described communalistic values of mutual aid as tending to break down as economies polarized with the increase in commercial wealth. Schurtz also noted that the social checks on personal wealth-seeking that he described did not apply to economies that developed a "system of debt and interest" (see p. 67 cited above). Wealth in the form of monetary claims on debtors was not buried, and hardly could be redistributed to the population at large, whose members typically were debtors to the rising creditor interest.

The only way to prevent such debts from polarizing society was to cancel them. That is what Near Eastern rulers did, but Schurtz's generation had no way of knowing about their Clean Slate proclamations. Starting with the very outset of debt records ca. 2500 BCE in Sumer, and continuing down through Babylonia, Assyria, and their neighbors and on through the early first millennium BCE, rulers annulled financial claims on agrarian debtors. That prevented creditors from concentrating money and land in their own hands. One might say that these debt cancellations and land redistributions were the Near Eastern alternative to destroying material wealth to preserve balance. These royal acts did not destroy physical wealth, but simply wiped out the debt overhead so as to maintain widespread land tenure and liberty for the population at large. Canceling agrarian debt was politically feasible because most personal debts were owed to the palace sector and its temples or their officials.

Royal Clean Slates seemed so unthinkable when they began to be translated around the turn of the last century that early readers hardly could believe that they actually were enforced in practice. Thureau-Dangin's French translation of the Sumerian ruler Enmetena's (ca. 2400 BCE) proclamation in 1905 was believed by many observers to be too utopian and socially disruptive to have been followed in practice, as was the Biblical Jubilee Year of Leviticus 25.[6] But so many such proclamations have been found, extending so continuously over thousands of years—along with lawsuits in which judges upheld their increasing detail—that there

---

6.   Thureau-Dangin (1905: 86–87) translated the Sumerian term for justice (*amargi*) to mean specifically that officials and wealthy individuals ("the powerful") would have no legal claims for debt foreclosure.

is no doubt that these acts did indeed reconcile the accumulation of monetary wealth with social resilience by blocking the creation of predatory oligarchies such as would emerge in classical Greece and Rome and indeed survive into today's world.

Monetary Innovations in the Bronze Age Near Eastern Palaces and Temples

Economic documentation in Schurtz's day was able to trace monetary practice only as far back as classical Greece and Rome. There was a general belief that their practices must have evolved from indigenous Indo-European speakers. Marcel Mauss would soon treat the gift exchange of the Kwakiutl tribe of the Canadian Pacific Northwest (with their competitive one-upmanship) as the prototype for the idea of charging interest. But monetary interest has a specific stipulated rate, with payments due on specific periodic dates set by written contracts. That practice stems from Sumer in the third millennium BCE, along with silver (and grain) money and related financial innovations in the economic Big Bang that has shaped subsequent Western economic evolution.

Money's function as a standard of valuation did not play a big role in Schurtz's survey. But subsequent archeological research has revealed that money's emergence as part of an overall institutional framework cannot be understood without reference to written account-keeping, denominating debt accruals and fiscal relations. Money, credit/debt, and fiscal obligations have all gone together since the origins of written records in the ancient Near East (Hudson 2004).

Near Eastern fiscal and financial records describe a development of money, credit, and interest-bearing debt that neither the barter theory nor Schurtz's ethnographic studies had imagined. Mesopotamia's "more ideal" (p. 83) money evolved out of the fiscal organization of account-keeping and credit in the palaces and temples of Sumer, Babylonia, and their Bronze Age neighbors (3200–1200 BCE). These Near Eastern economies were larger in scale and much more complex and multi-layered than most of the indigenous communities surveyed by Schurtz. In contrast to largely self-sufficient communities, southern Mesopotamia was obliged to engage in large-scale long-distance trade, because the region's river-deposited soil lacked metal, stone, and even hardwood. The region's need for raw materials was far different from the trade and "monetization" of luxuries by the relatively small-scale and self-sufficient communities studied by Schurtz and hypothesized by economists imagining individuals bartering at their local market. In these communities, he noted: "The amount of metal shaped into ornaments almost always far outweighs the amount transformed into practical tools" (p. 123). Mesopotamia's trade had to go far beyond personal decorative luxuries and prestige commodities or trophy items.

An entrepreneurial merchant class was needed to obtain these raw materials, along with a specialized labor force, which was employed by the temples and palaces that produced most export handicrafts, provisioned corvée labor to work on public infrastructure, served as mints and overseers of weights and measures, and mediated most monetary wealth and debt. Their large scale required forward planning and account-keeping to feed and supply labor (war widows, orphans, and slaves) in their weaving and other handicraft workshops, and to consign their output to merchants for export. Calculating the cost of distributing food and raw materials within these large institutions and valuing their consignment of goods to merchants required designing standard weights and measures as the basis for this forward planning. Selecting monetary units was basically part of this standardization of measuring costs and value. This made possible the calculation of expected rental income or shortfalls, along with profit-and-loss statements and balance sheets. The typical commodity to be distributed was grain, which served as a standard of value for agrarian transactions and credit balances that mounted up during the crop year for advances to sharecroppers, consumption such as beer from ale-women, and payments to priests for performing ceremonial functions. Their value in grain was to be paid at harvest time. Calculation of food rations for distribution to the various grades of labor (male, female, and children) enabled the costs to be expressed in grain or in workday equivalents.

Schurtz would have called this grain "inside-money," and regarded as "outside-money" the silver minted by temples for dealing with foreign trade and as the basic measure of value for business transactions with the palace economy and for settling commercial obligations. A mina (60 shekels) of silver was set as equal to a corresponding unit of grain as measured on the threshing floor. That enabled accounts to be kept simultaneously in silver and grain. The result was a bimonetary grain-silver standard reflecting the bifurcation of early Mesopotamian economies between the agrarian families on the land (using grain "inside-money") and the palatial economy with its workshops, foreign trade, and associated commercial enterprise (using silver "outside-money"). Prices for market transactions with outsiders might vary, but prices for debt payments, taxes, and other transactions with the large institutions were fixed.

Schurtz's conclusion, that the rising dominance of commercial money tended to break down domestic checks and balances protecting the indigenous communities that he studied, is indeed what happened when commercial debt practices were brought from the Near East to the Aegean and Mediterranean lands around the eighth century BCE. Having no tradition of royal debt cancellations as had existed in the Near East ever since the formative period of interest-bearing debt, the resulting decontextualization of credit practices fostered financial oligarchies in classical Greece and Rome. After early debt cancellations and land redistribution by populist "tyrants" in the seventh and sixth centuries BCE, the ensuing classical oligarchies resisted popular revolts demanding a revival of such policies.

The dynamics of interest-bearing debt and the pro-creditor debt laws of classical antiquity's creditor oligarchies caused economic polarization that led to five centuries of civil warfare. These upheavals were not the result of the coinage that began to be minted around the eighth century BCE, as many nineteenth-century observers believed, mistakenly thinking that Aegean coinage was the first metallic money. Silver-money had been the norm for two millennia throughout the Near East, without causing disruption like that experienced by classical antiquity. What polarized classical antiquity's economies were pro-creditor debt laws backed by political violence, not money as such.

Conclusion and Discussion

Schurtz's starting point was how communities organized the laws of motion governing their distribution of wealth and property. He viewed money as emerging from this institutional function with a basically communalistic ethic. A key characteristic of indigenous economic resilience was social pressure expecting the wealthy to contribute to social support. That was the condition set by unwritten customs for letting some individuals and their families become rich. Schurtz and subsequent ethnologists found a universal solution for reconciling wealth-seeking with community-wide prosperity to be social pressure for wealthy families (that was the basic unit, not individuals) to distribute their wealth to the citizenry by reciprocal exchange, gift-giving, mutual aid, and other forms of redistribution, and providing large feasts, especially for rites of passage.

This was a much broader view than the individualistic economic assumption that personal gain-seeking and indeed selfishness was the driving force of overall prosperity. The idea of monetizing economic life under communalistic mutual aid or palace direction was and remains anathema to mainstream economists, reflecting the worldview of modern creditors and financial elites. Schurtz recognized that mercantile wealth-seeking required checks and balances to prevent economies from impoverishing their members. The problem for any successfully growing society to solve was how to prevent the undue concentration of wealth obtained by exploitative means that impaired overall welfare and the ability of community members to be self-supporting. Otherwise, economic polarization and dependency would lead members to flee from the community, or perhaps it simply would shrink and end up being defeated by outsiders who sustained themselves by more successful mutual aid.

As noted above, Schurtz treated the monetization of wealth in the form of creditor claims on debtors as too post-archaic to be a characteristic of his ethnographic subjects. But what shaped the context for monetization and led "outside-money" to take priority over inside-money were wealth accumulation by moneylending and the fiscal and military uses of money. Schurtz correctly rejected (p. 34) Bruno Hildebrand's characterization of money as developing in stages, from small-scale barter to monetized economies becoming more sophisticated as they evolved into financialized credit economies.[7] And in fact the actual historical sequence was the reverse. From Mesopotamia to medieval Europe, agrarian economies operated on credit during the crop year. Monetary payment occurred at harvest time to settle the obligations that had accumulated since the last harvest and to pay taxes. This need to pay debts was a major factor requiring money's development in the first place. Barter became antiquity's final monetary "stage" as Rome's economy collapsed after its creditor oligarchy imposed debt bondage and took control of the land. When emperors were unable to tax this oligarchy, they debased the coinage, and life throughout the Empire devolved into local subsistence production and quasi-barter. Foreign trade was mainly for luxuries brought by Arabs and other Near Easterners. The optimistic sequence that Hildebrand imagined not only mistakenly adopted the

---

7.   Bruno Hildebrand (1864) classified economies as passing from *Natural-wirtschaft* ("barter economy") to *Geldwirtschaft* ("gold/commodity money economy") and finally *Kreditwirtschaft* ("credit economy").

barter myth of monetary origins, but failed to take debt polarization into account as economies became monetarized and financialized.

Schurtz described how the aim of preventing the maldistribution of wealth was at the heart of indigenous social structuring. But it broke down for various reasons. Economies in which family wealth took the form of cattle, he found, tended to become increasingly oppressive in order to maintain the polarizing inequality that developed. The same might be said of credit economies under the rising burden of interest-bearing debt. Schurtz noted (p. 45) the practice of charging debtors double the loan value—and any rate of interest indeed involves an implicit doubling time. That exponential dynamic is what polarizes financialized economies. In contrast to Schurtz, mainstream economists of his generation avoided dealing with the effect of monetary innovation and debt on the distribution of wealth. The tendency was to treat money as merely a "veil" of price changes for goods and services, without analyzing how credit polarizes the economy's balance sheet of assets and debt liabilities. Yet the distinguishing feature of credit economies was the use of moneylending as a lever to enrich creditors by impoverishing debtors. That was more than just a monetary problem. It was a political creditor/debtor problem, and ultimately a public/private problem. At issue was whether a ruler or civic public checks would steer the rise in monetary wealth in ways that avoided the creation of creditor oligarchies.

Most nineteenth-century and even subsequent economic writers shied away from confronting this political context, leaving the most glaring gap in modern economic analysis. It was left to the discovery of cuneiform documentation to understand how money first became institutionalized as a vehicle to pay debts. This monetization was accompanied by a remarkable success in sustaining rising wealth while preventing its concentration in the hands of a hereditary oligarchy. That Near Eastern success highlights what the smaller and more anarchic Western economies failed to achieve when interest-bearing debt practices were brought to the Mediterranean lands without being checked by the tradition of regular cancellation of personal nonbusiness debt. Credit and monetary wealth were privatized in the hands of what became an increasingly self-destructive set of classical oligarchies culminating in that of Rome which fought for centuries against popular revolts seeking protection from impoverishing economic polarization.

The devastating effects of transplanting Near Eastern debt practices into the Mediterranean world's less communalistic groupings shows the need to discuss the political, fiscal, and social-moral context for money and debt. Schurtz placed monetary analysis in the context of society's political institutions and moral values, and explained how money is a product of this context, and indeed, how monetization tends to transform it—in a way that tends to break down social protection. His book has remained relatively unknown over the last century largely because his institutional anthropological perspective is too broad for an economics discipline that has been narrowed by pro-creditor ideologues who have applauded the "free market" destruction of social regulation aimed at protecting the interests of debtors. That attitude avoids recognizing the challenges that led the indigenous communities studied by Schurtz, and also the formative Bronze Age Near East, to protect their resilience against the concentration of wealth, a phenomenon that has plagued economics ever since classical antiquity's decontextualization of Near Eastern debt practices.

References

Hildebrand, Bruno. 1864. "Naturalwirthschaft, Geldwirthschaft und Creditwirthschaft." *Jahrbücher für Nationalökonomie und Statistik* 2: 1–24.

Hudson, Michael. 1999. "From Sacred Enclave to Temple to City." In *Urbanization and Land Ownership in the Ancient Near East*, edited by Michael Hudson and Baruch Levine, 117–46. Cambridge, MA: Peabody Museum of Archaeology and Ethnology, Harvard University.

———. 2004. "The Development of Money-of-Account in Sumer's Temples." In *Creating Economic Order: Record-Keeping, Standardization and the Development of Accounting in the Ancient Near East*, edited by Michael Hudson and Cornelia Wunsch, 303–29. Bethesda, MD: CDL Press; Republished by Dresden: ISLET, 2023.

———. 2018. "Origins of Money and Interest: Palatial Credit, Not Barter." In *Handbook of the History of Money and Currency*, edited by Stefano Battilossi, Youssef Cassis, and Kazuhiko Yago, 45–66. Berlin: Springer.

———. 2024. *Temples of Enterprise: Creating Economic Order in the Bronze Age Near East*. Dresden: ISLET.

Laum, Bernard. 1924. *Heiliges Geld: Eine historische Untersuchung über den sakralen Ursprung des Geldes*. Tübingen: Mohr.

Mauss, Marcel. (1925) 2016. *The Gift: Expanded Edition*. Translated by Jane Guyer. Chicago: Hau Books.

Menger, Carl. 1892. "On the Origins of Money." *Economic Journal* 2: 238–55.

Thureau-Dangin, François. 1905. *Les Inscriptions de Sumer et d'Akkad*. Paris: Leroux.

Wray, L. Randall. 2004. *Credit and State Theories of Money: The Contributions of A. Mitchell Innes*. Cheltenham: Edward Elgar Publishing.

Heinrich Schurtz's Anthropology of Money

Enrique Martino and Mario Schmidt

> Even in a brief conversation, he unfolded a treasure trove of observations, from which it became evident that he was one of the few possessing an eye for everything and yet viewing all things in their own, unique way.
> Friedrich Ratzel, *In Memoriam Dr. Heinrich Schurtz* (1903: 52)

It is not clear whether the object on the cover of this book is an ornament, a standardized metal ingot, or a counterweight for a scale. Donated to The Metropolitan Museum of Art by an American banker who organized loans to the Chinese government from his office in Shanghai in 1928, it is described as a "bronze coin" from the Han dynasty period. Most likely, it circulated after the political fragmentation of the Warring States period had come to an end in the second century BCE. Alongside a range of other bronze objects, such as imitations of cowrie shells and miniaturized agricultural tools, it preceded the iconic round *qian* or "cash" coin that circulated for over two thousand years and was minted on a large scale by early Han Dynasty officials to prevent that "different designs of the coins will cause great confusion" (Vissering 1877: 33;

Chen 2005). We did not choose this artifact as the cover of our translation of Heinrich Schurtz's *Grundriss einer Entstehungsgeschichte des Geldes* (1898a, hereafter *Grundriss*) to fulfill the common expectation of a coin-themed cover for books about money. Rather, we chose it because of its aesthetic ambivalence and historical inconclusiveness and because Schurtz was fascinated by the monetary history of China which he describes as displaying the "most remarkable experiments" (p. 161).

Peppered with global and epoch-spanning observations that avoid demarcating types of money into strict regional areas or temporal stages, the *Grundriss* was published during a peak of the *Methodenstreit* ("methods dispute") in German economics, heightened by Vienna-based Carl Menger's contentious entry on "money" in the *Handwörter-buch der Staatswissenschaften* ("Handbook of Political Science," 1892). The *Methodenstreit* polarized the adherents of the neoclassical doctrines of Menger and the large profession of economist-historians at German universities, many of whom were loosely connected with what came to be known as the Historical School of Economics (Schefold 1996; Hodgson 2001). Schurtz viewed these academic disputes as vicious cycles where "one-sidedness" begets more "one-sidedness," leading to intellectual stagnation rather than conceptual development (p. 163). Schurtz would "often refer to the fundamental problem plaguing all the contemporary works of economists" as being a "lack of perspective" (quoted in Ratzel 1903: 55).

Some of the questions proponents of the different sides tried to answer were how and where money originated, and whether economic actors had universally given rise to rudimentary forms of it before adopting the most efficient metals to overcome the problems of barter, or whether well-organized government institutions of antiquity managing complex societies were needed as well. These discussions of the origin of money were so vehement because they signaled the divergent starting points of two opposing types of economic theory: on the one hand the idea of a utility-seeking actor conceived of as an anthropological constant and projected backwards in time, and, on the other, a historically oriented, largely empirical approach trying to condense the written and archaeological data into a theory of bounded but progressing historical economic stages. Bypassing theories built on the "alarmingly narrow basis" of the "records of ancient and modern civilized people" alone, Schurtz's intention was to provide an ethnographically saturated and theoretically sound alternative to these "warring interests" of the discipline (p. 32). Joseph Schumpeter (1954: 754) most probably thought of this characteristic Schurtzian sensibility when he suggested that economics should turn to "ethnology" when encountering problems of "origins" and "economic foundations."[1]

Widely read in the decades after his early death in 1903, Schurtz was "well-known to a large part of the German audience" who consulted his work to inform themselves about the "latest scientific perspectives on the origins of trade and commerce" (Lasch 1906: 621). Described in one of Germany's premier academic journals edited by Max Weber and Werner Sombart as a "highly gifted man, whose richness of thought, mastery of form, and scholarly depth were unparalleled" (Schlüter 1906: 630), Schurtz quickly became a scholarly household name across disciplines and political attitudes. By the end of the twentieth century, however, only a few German-speaking scholars explicitly remembered him as "probably the most progressive thinker in German anthropology of his time" (Müller 1981: 213) who wrote with a "complete mastery of language" (Ducks 1996: 3).

While Marcel Mauss (1914: 15), in one of his earliest engagements with money, called the *Grundriss* an "excellent little book by the much-missed Schurtz, so full of facts and ideas," Raymond Firth, one of the founders of anglophone economic anthropology, was probably the last prominent anthropologist to explicitly appreciate Schurtz's economic writings, calling him "the soundest of the older writers," and adding that "considerable value attaches to his detailed studies of economic phenomena in primitive society" (1927: 320, 328). More recently, Schurtz has also been lauded as a prime example of the "good anthropology" of Wilhelmine Germany, the fate of which was to end up as "hidden, and half-forgotten treasures" (Gingrich 2010: 102–103, 61). Before outlining the main economic and anthropological themes and theories of the *Grundriss* and its unique place in the history of ideas on money, the next

---

1.   Schumpeter (1954: 755, 11) adds that looking into the findings of comparative anthropology was necessary not only because these were "infinitely more important and enlightening than anything a mere economist can say" but also because the "fundamental errors" committed by economists were caused by their hesitation to embrace what he called a "historical-prehistorical-ethnological sociology." It is noteworthy that in Menger's revised chapter on money (1936: 16–17), he cites the *Grundriss* as the "latest attempt to solve the problem on an ethnographic basis" and as challenging the "ahistorical" view that money originated from "legislation or a social contract."

section provides an overview of Heinrich Schurtz's intellectual life and work.

Heinrich Schurtz's Life and the Production of the *Grundriss*

Born in Zwickau, Kingdom of Saxony, in December 1863, Camillo Heinrich Schurtz began to study chemistry and mineralogy at the University of Leipzig in 1885 after being discharged from the local infantry regiment for medical reasons. Intrigued by Friedrich Ratzel's popular lectures on anthropological questions, Schurtz ended up writing his PhD thesis under the supervision of Ratzel, a well-known figure of the late nineteenth-century German university system who founded the "anthropogeographic" method that tries to reconstruct the history and migration of human societies through the study of their material culture and their relation to the environment (Ratzel 1894–1895; Osterhammel 1994; Santini 2018). Following this method, Schurtz's thesis focused on the geographical distribution of the throwing knife, characterized by him as an "impractical" and almost entirely "ornamental" weapon (1889: 10). As noted by Ratzel in the ten-page eulogy he dedicated to his student, Schurtz's first academic contributions, such as his thesis and an early article focusing on amulets as both "spiritual weapons" and "ornaments" (1893a: 57), already reveal a shift from a "geographical-anthropological" method towards a unique and more "psychological-aesthetic" paradigm (Ratzel 1903: 53).

During his time at the University of Leipzig, Schurtz also deepened his relationships with Wilhelm Wundt, the founder of experimental and ethnographic psychology who, when he heard about Schurtz's passing, lamented that "his death also means the loss of the best ethnologist we had."[2] Schurtz's affinities for the new psychology explain his attempts to excavate the analytic potential of collective psychological forces in the *Grundriss*, such as the "hoarding drive" (*Sammeltrieb*) and the "mimetic drive" (*Nachahmungstrieb*), that play a pivotal role for the acceptance of new, and even the switch between different, currencies. Schurtz's interest for an emerging psychology was probably also intensified by the fact that his father, also called Heinrich Schurtz, was Saxony's foremost spiritist

---

2. Universitätsbibliothek Leipzig, Nachlass Wilhelm Wundt, NA Wundt/ III/Wundt/Briefe/701-800. Wilhelm Wundt to E. Meumann, June 5, 1903.

and chair of the *Verein für psychische Studien* ("Association for Psychic Studies") who not only had a "popular reputation as a miracle healer" (Birndt 1900: 654) but also a dedicated police file against him for running seance sessions at his home since at least the 1870s when Schurtz was still a child (Steinmetz 2009: 143). In his crucial essay "Skull Cults and the Hoarding Drive" (1896a: 105) published just before he started to prepare the *Grundriss*, Schurtz had conceptually advanced some of these psychological phenomena further in order to use them to explain economic phenomena: "The importance of the hoarding drive for the development of humanity is almost impossible to fully comprehend; the value attributed to money, for example, can be traced back to it in a certain sense."[3]

While Schurtz's focus on the aesthetic is evident in his habilitation thesis (1891a) on the psychological origin of clothing and adornments, his early works also point towards an emerging interest in economic questions. The article *Kleidung als Geld* ("Clothing as Money"), for instance, criticizes the assumption that money is a modern invention: "Amongst less civilized peoples barter prevails as money is unknown—this is a widely held view, but one that is, in this sweeping generality, difficult to have any justification for" (1890a: 891). Schurtz continues with the argument that it was entirely "arbitrary" to think of only "coins and banknotes" as "truly deserving" to be called money, a view he expounded on in his anthropology textbook *Katechismus der Völkerkunde* (1893b: 117) in which he concludes that "measures of value are created everywhere and pure barter dominates almost nowhere."

---

3. He calls the hoarding drive a "compulsion" and "delusion" beyond "logic and reason" and a "deeper current of the human soul that manifests itself in countless ways," finding "among civilized nations, its most frequent representatives, or if you will, its victims." Nevertheless, what is "collected must possess some inherent value" to the hoarder, though the value "can be entirely imaginary for others." The article concludes with a proto-psychoanalytic hypothesis of social change: "Thus, it is not only the individual human being who is partially constructed and dominated by forces alien to the logical and conscious mind; in the life of peoples as well, customs and practices are reshaped and determined by deeper currents than the superficial ripple of rational consideration. To explore and illuminate these dark depths, animated by mysterious forces, with prudence will be the task of those who work on a true history of humanity, a history that, indeed, has almost nothing in common with the historical research of today" (1896a: 105; see also 1896c).

Furthermore, it is interesting to note that during his postdoctoral period, Schurtz published two books (1890b, 1891b) on the longue durée of mining in his home region, the *Erzgebirge*, which had been at the center of an ancient tin and amber trade route between the Mediterranean and the Baltic. The early modern wealth of Saxony was largely built on its silver deposits, but due to the decline of the silver price that began with Germany's adoption of the gold standard in 1871 and the subsequent unprofitability of its silver mining industry (Flandreau 2004: 181; Volckart 2024: 121), the region experienced an economic decline during Schurtz's youth and his father's involvement in various mining enterprises meant that these overarching economic circumstances had direct repercussions on Schurtz's family.

After lecturing in Ratzel's geography department, where Schurtz had given courses on, for instance, medieval Germany and on primitive art (Ducks 1996: 21), he became fully employed in Germany's booming colonial port city Bremen in 1893. Here, he was tasked with reorganizing the collections of the Städtische Museum für Natur-, Völker- und Handelskunde ("Municipal museum for natural science, anthropology and commerce") for the next three years before its grand opening. According to his colleague Johannes Weißenborn (1912: 452), Schurtz still hoped to become a professor although his office at the museum soon became "his real world" from where he "unfolded the dormant forces" of one of the "primary ethnological collections on the continent." Schurtz's main activity was to write and disseminate scholarly works that made use of the museum's extensive collection, most of which had been acquired by the wealthy Free Hanseatic City of Bremen from various merchant associations (Schurtz 1896b, 1896d; Briskorn 2000). The museum's focus on curating artifacts amassed from the various corners of the world visited by German merchants throughout the preceding decades, notably Africa, Oceania, East and Central Asia, and Central America, explains the *Grundriss*'s strong focus on types of money from these regions.

The imperial backdrop of Schurtz's workplace and the concerns of a colonial expansionary Wilhelmine Germany thus had an influence on his scholarship (Mirowski 1994; Steinmetz 2008; Gräbel 2015).[4] He kept a

---

4.   Schurtz (1902b: 561) was a defender of the German colonial empire not only because it would expand the navy and might help develop an independent network of "world trade" in the event of an embargo or a war and "other obstacles" put up by other European imperial powers, but also

constant eye on the accelerating number of ethnographic, missionary, and military reports from Germany's colonial ventures and possessions and had considered the political and economic implications of the early article "Money in Africa" by the aged and eminent German geographer and legionnaire Friedrich Gerhard Rohlfs who became stranded on a Moroccan oasis in the 1860s and eventually disguised himself as a Muslim merchant and crossed the Sahara only to appear at the mouth of the Niger delta several years later. Rohlfs's article tries to understand how colonial powers can issue well-functioning currencies with the political aim in mind to replace the two main currencies that circulated from the Sahel to East Africa, namely the Maria Teresa thaler and cowries that were used as small change but did not continuously circulate because they were hoarded, buried, or used "peculiarly and exclusively as objects for adornment" (Rohlfs 1889: 192). It is therefore unsurprising that emerging colonial currency policies in the early twentieth century explicitly used insights from the *Grundriss* as was the case, for instance, with Karl Helfferich, who was appointed director of the colonial division of the German foreign ministry in 1901 and designed the introduction of the nonconvertible colonial silver German rupee for the German East African colonies to drive out the Indian rupee and imported British commodities that were used as money in local markets (Helfferich [1903] 1923; Krozewski 2022).[5]

---

because of "imponderables that do not lie within the economic domain." Schurtz believed that overseas colonies would change Germany's view on the world, thereby catalyzing his fellow Germans' ambitions to look beyond their immediate surroundings.

5. In the revised edition of his book *Das Geld* ("Money" [1903] 1923: 13–17), which became the "standard" book on money in early twentieth-century German economics (Williamson 2015: 393), Helfferich had not changed his first chapter, "The Origin of Money," which still only contained footnotes to Schurtz and Simmel, and in many instances the citations to Simmel flow directly back to Schurtz. As suggested by David Frisby, the editor and translator of Simmel's *Philosophy of Money*, Simmel's "bewildering, unacknowledged array of ethnographic examples on early exchange and money transactions" were primarily drawn from Schurtz (Simmel [1978] 2004: 530). Helfferich is well known for becoming the head of the German treasury (*Reichsschatzamt*) during World War I, and for creating the *Rentenmark* that successfully halted the creeping and later almost uncontainable Weimar hyperinflation (Williamson 2015: 386–89).

The fact that Schurtz's early works already make use of the African sources cited in the *Grundriss* helps us to understand what influenced his theorizations and choice of empirical examples in the *Grundriss*. On the one hand, Schurtz was surrounded by ethnographic artifacts at the museum, which might have animated his interest in the aesthetic and material qualities of monetary objects. Described by his close friend Viktor Hantzsch (1905: 34) as someone who "did not regard the transcendental as a theoretical aid, but as a real power with which he could establish relationships," and sometimes even believed "that he was in contact with spirits and the departed," we can imagine him wandering around ethnographic artifacts and dioramas, being inspired and touched by their aura. On the other hand, Schurtz, like other so-called armchair anthropologists, relied upon a critical interpretation of primary sources. Of particular importance for his analysis of African monetary systems were travel narratives of the multiple years long expeditions of the scholarly and diplomatic travelers Gustav Nachtigal and Heinrich Barth in West Africa and the Sahel.

Schurtz's professional relocation to Bremen furthermore widened his geographic focus. As the footnotes of the *Grundriss* suggest, he not only immersed himself in the skilled ethnographic works of John Stanislaw Kubary, a Polish long-term resident of various Pacific islands, but also began to closely study the work of Otto Finsch, prolific ethnographer of Oceania, collaborator in the New Guinea Company, and former director of Bremen's ethnological museum (Stocking 1991).

Based upon his intensive work at the museum, Schurtz had already written much of the first half of the *Grundriss* by 1896 and published it as a twenty-thousand-word article in the journal *Deutsche Geographische Blätter* (1897). The article has the same content and similar chapter headings as the first eight chapters of the *Grundriss*. We can thus assume that he added more empirical material to the second half of the book over the course of 1897. Chapter 6 on "countermeasures" against wealth accumulation and the last three chapters on value ratios, ethnological zones, and money and commodities were also new and likely written in 1897. Schurtz also included more references to gift-giving in chapter 8 where he developed the concept of the "obligatory gift" (see also Athané 2008: 332; Magnani 2008: 531). Upon publication, the *Grundriss* impressed reviewers in a variety of journals, for example François Simiand in the second volume of Émile Durkheim's *L'Année sociologique* (1898), Heinrich Cunow in the socialist *Die Neue Zeit* (1900), and Alfred Vierkandt in the anti-Marxist *Zeitschrift für Socialwissenschaft* (1898).

Showcasing his extensive interest in the economies of African societies, Schurtz furthermore finished the book *Das Afrikanische Gewerbe* in 1898 ("African Trade," 1900a). As an ethnological-historical equivalent to the German historical school's detailed studies on social classes, craft industries, guilds, family businesses, labor relations, and the growth and structure of markets and towns, it was not as theoretically ambitious as the *Grundriss*. However, it was awarded the prestigious annual prize by the *Jablonowskische Gesellschaft der Wissenschaften* on Karl Bücher's recommendation, the only anthropological book to have received it (Wagner-Hasel 2011: 257).

In his ten-year tenure at the Bremen museum, Schurtz also helped lay the foundation for academic anthropology as a formal discipline in Germany by publishing two anthropology textbooks (1893b, 1903a) as well as his two most influential works *Urgeschichte der Kultur* ("The History of Culture," 1900b) which impressed with its broad scope and detailed research, receiving over one hundred reviews in various national and international journals, and *Altersklassen und Männerbünde: Eine Darstellung der Grundformen der Gesellschaft* ("Age Sets and Male Associations: A Description of the Fundamental Forms of Society," 1902a) which had a "breath-taking" effect on the contemporary academic world (Reulecke 2001: 40).[6] During a period when the new discipline was rapidly growing in German-speaking Europe, Schurtz had achieved a "remarkable status in modern anthropology" (Koppers 1915: 994), independently from the center of a professionalizing discipline at the Ethnological Museum in Berlin dominated by Adolf Bastian who had initially made efforts to block Schurtz's career. The conceptual formalism and

6. In a review of *Urgeschichte der Kultur* published in the first volume of the anthropological journal *Man*, Northcote W. Thomas (1901: 125), an eminent Fellow of the Royal Anthropological Institute in London, wrote that "Schurtz has written a work which is worthy of his reputation" and that "no man can cover this ground single-handed. Dr. Schurtz has been amazingly industrious." The book *Altersklassen und Männerbünde* is a political anthropology of non-kinship-based male "associations" and the gendered sociability drive (Durkheim 1901; Lowie 1920: 247–48, 394–96). The term *Männerbünde* was coined by Schurtz and subsequently picked up by a variety of German social and political youth movements (Bruns 2008, 2009; Burrell 2023). Schurtz (1902c, 1903c) considered the book as a first step towards a more comprehensive treatise on the origins of the state, which he was working on before his death. However, the draft of this manuscript has been lost (Abel 1969: 81; Ducks 1996).

comparative breadth of Schurtz went against Bastian's empiricist vision for anthropology. Bastian warned that it was not "yet time" to write such a book in his review (1901: 95, 102) of Schurtz's *Urgeschichte*, and expressed fears that anthropology would attract scholars with "metaphysical urges," who might endanger the ongoing fieldwork-based production of "meticulous monographs," a "still barely excavated raw material" that could only eventually deliver a "total survey."

In his short life, Schurtz also published at least a dozen other widely appreciated articles, many of them showing his "great conceptual competency," "interest in socioeconomic matters," and familiarity with the history and ethnography of different world regions (Gingrich 2010: 93). These include articles on the tabu codes of Oceania or the Janissaries of the Ottoman Empire in the journal *Preussische Jahrbücher* (1895b; 1903c), as well as the articles *Wirtschaftliche Symbiose* ("Economic Symbiosis," 1898c), *Die Anfänge des Landbesitzes* ("The Beginnings of Land Ownership," 1900c), and *Das Basarwesen als Wirtschaftsform* ("The Bazaar as an Economic System," 1901a), published in the *Zeitschrift für Socialwissenschaft*, which was founded and edited by Julius Wolf in 1898 in order to conceptually renew the social sciences to pull them away from conservative positivists and left-wing theorists both of which Schurtz distanced himself from. He also published studies about his ethnographic and artifact-gathering trips to Spain, Morocco, Tunisia, and Turkey and contributed several book-length entries on Africa, North Africa, West Asia in the Islamic Period, and Highland Asia and Siberia to the widely consulted *Weltgeschichte* explicitly set up by Hans Helmolt to provide a non- or less Eurocentric world history.

One of his last articles recounts his journey to Santiago de Compostela to where he had traveled after buying artifacts for the museum in Madrid. Probably also a kind of pilgrimage for Schurtz, Santiago appeared to him "most magnificent in the evening light from the southwest" and he describes how the city carries its "massive three-towered cathedral on its shoulders to heaven" and its "yellowish sandstone from which all these structures are built glows in the light of the setting sun like liquid gold" (1903b: 65). After a short illness that had already started while he was in Santiago, Schurtz died from appendicitis on May 2, 1903 at the age of 39 with the "firm belief in the light" of a Christian God (Hantzsch 1905: 34). He was buried next to his parents in the Loschwitz cemetery in Dresden. His mother (b. Camilla Rehm) had died only a few weeks after giving birth to him.

Schurtz's Economic Anthropology and Theory of Money

The title of Schurtz's book suggests that his main goal was to answer a question that his contemporaries had wrestled with for some time: Where does money come from and what are its essential features? Yet, Schurtz was hesitant to take a side in debates about the origins of cultural practices and artifacts that revolved around the question if they are human universals or the result of intercultural borrowing. This question also divided scholars interested in the origin of money. The academically dominant narrative situated money's "birth" in the Greek Mediterranean, where precious metals were first minted into coins. As the classicist Theodor Mommsen wrote in *Das Geld* (1863: 382), money "did not generate itself, no, like the steam engine and the alphabet" it had to be "invented."[7] Alongside this Eurocentric view of the "civilizational" constitution of money, Carl Menger (1871: 260) claimed that "no nation" or people "invented" money but that it emerged as a universal human tool in a number of different forms wherever "economizing individuals" understood that money simplifies trade, thereby setting in motion the teleological movement towards a global commercial society with an ever more efficient medium of exchange. Considering the massive influence of these conflicting visions of money's origin, it is surprising that Schurtz developed a robust alternative to them from the marginal position of a young anthropologist working at the ethnological museum in Bremen.

At first glance, it appears as if Schurtz tried to find a way around the two opposing views on money's origin prevailing in Germany, only to end up recreating the common Victorian practice of endlessly listing empirical examples of different monetary objects from all over the world, such as feathers or shells used to buy goods, and imaginary oxen or slaves giving quantitative value to all other commodities. As shown by the fact that the first part of the *Grundriss*, which contains most of

---

7.   For accessible overviews on the role of money in antiquity, see Eich (2022: chap. 1) and Spread (2022: chap. 11). For broader histories of money that do not focus centrally on coins, see Graeber (2011), Shell (2019), and Kaufman (2020). For an excellent discussion on the history of money in German nineteenth-century thought, see Gray (2008). Over the course of the twentieth century the question unfortunately became more starkly phrased as a matter of which of the three or four functions of money (store of value, medium of exchange, standard of deferred payment, unit of account) had evolutionary or logical priority (Schumpeter 1954; Hart 1986; Orléan 1992; Wray 1993; Ingham 2004; Desan 2013).

Schurtz's theoretical innovations, was written and published before the second part, which adds the empirical examples, however, we should not consider Schurtz's excessive gathering of data as an end in itself. Rather, we suggest viewing it as a means to convince the reader that both theoretically absolute as well as empirically too narrowly focused theories on the origin of money are lopsided.

Schurtz's hesitancy to choose between the alternative to either locate money's origin at a specific moment in time or to propose that it could have been generated anywhere at any time across all human societies and epochs already hints at his unique proto-structuralist position, epitomized in the claim that modern money is an "illusory unity" that emerged out of two historically separate types of money, which became "fused" in volatile ways (p. 34). On the one hand, "inside-money" emerges from the "internal forces of social life" and has the potential to organize and solidify social hierarchies, to reproduce religious beliefs, and to tie members of the same society to one another (p. 172). Thereby inside-money becomes one of the primary guarantors of what Schurtz elsewhere calls (1900b: 8) a society's "outer shell" or "bone," a *Sitte*, that is an inflexible "custom" or cultural institution acting as a boundary to the external, impersonal, commercial world of constant movement.

As "outside-money," on the other hand, money seeks infinite movement, causes boundaries between societies to crumble, undermines internal hierarchies, and animates individual profit-making to become a cultural value. Because of his dual notion of money, Schurtz has sometimes mistakenly been placed into the "diverse group of social scientists including Marx, Schurtz, Buecher, Weber, and Polanyi" who "argued that money as a medium of exchange arises first in the foreign trade sector" (Pryor 1977: 395).[8] In contrast, Schurtz understands money as a circulating medium that fulfills two opposing social functions depending on the location of its circulation, setting in motion a kind of permanent and productive tension between inside- and outside-money that closely

---

8.   If forced to decide between the alternatives of money originating in exchange or in hoarding, Schurtz would probably give conceptual primacy to the hoarding or store of value function of money based on his speculative-historical assumptions, which aligns with, for example, Suzanne de Brunhoff's (1976) interpretation of Marx's ([1859] 1975: 358) theory of money, the main arguments of Schumpeter (1991: 499; see Busch 2003: 196) and Wilhelm Gerloff's theory (1940, 1950; see Taeuber 1945; Höltz 1984: 227; Brandl 2015: 284).

corresponds to Jonathan Parry and Maurice Bloch's (1989) insight about money's dual role in the reproduction of both the "short-term" commercial transactional and the "long-term" social order. Just like the gift, money is a "total social fact" that crystallizes social contradictions in its material embodiments and movements, producing constant social change, development, and tension (Mauss [1925] 2016; Balandier [1961] 2018; Orléan 2013; Schmidt 2014).

Even capitalist money, in other words, has never been modern. Rather, it fused the two separate forms of inside- and outside-money into a fragile hybrid, whereby it became so effective that it often even transformed into the inside-money of other societies. This happened, for instance, when fabrics produced in Manchester and silver Maria Theresa thalers minted in Vienna were exported to West and East Africa as well as the Arabian Peninsula (Hogendorn 1997; Kuroda 2007; Guyer and Pallaver 2018). Such entanglements established global hierarchies of currencies, and by analyzing these examples, Schurtz illustrates that losing the capacity to produce one's own money also increased dependence on and exploitation by the merchants who provided different types of money from abroad, especially if these were relatively overvalued or starting to be manufactured cheaply in Europe. These insights exemplify a nuanced understanding of the imperial nature of the world economy that prefigures the detailed accounting-based analysis of the unequal basis of world trade by Arghiri Emmanuel (1969) and Michael Hudson ([1972] 2003) as well as recent debates about the viability and potential of independent currencies in a global economy (Amin 1990; Ben Gadha et al. 2022).

Schurtz's hypothesis of money as a contradictory social phenomenon also supports our claim that his encyclopedic amassing of monetary objects under specific categories is not a mere classificatory exercise but an attempt to excavate the material agency of different monetary instruments, such as shells, fabrics, or metals, which have different affordances and different geographical distributions, foreshadowing economic anthropology's interest in the materiality of monetary objects (Hogendorn and Johnson 1986; Graeber 1996; Stewart and Strathern 2002). This concrete fact can best be elaborated on by taking into account Schurtz's distinction between "ornament-money" and "use-money." Ornament-money originates in what Schurtz calls "aesthetic" values and is initially used to adorn the body but also encapsulates and channels the values and history of the whole community (see chapters 9 and 10). In contrast, "use-money," which refers to useful and consumable goods such as stimulants or base metals with a value that is acknowledged cross-culturally, emerges as the primary form of outside-money (see chapter 13). An important mediator between the two is "fabric-money" which often, in the form of simple textiles that can easily be quantified, functions as use-money and also, in the form of beautifully decorated textiles, as ornament-money (see chapter 12). This unique consideration of the function, form, geographic origin, and materiality of different types of money is the foundation of what can be described as Schurtz's "non-evolutionary evolutionism," at the beginning of which universal social problems cause unforeseeable monetary developments, catalyzed by money's different material affordances. Due to this theoretical assumption, Schurtz feels compelled to suggest a radically empirical ethnographic turn whose "only correct method is therefore to examine each individual case without prejudice" (p. 164) as money's contradictory double nature combined with the clash of different political, social, and monetary systems cause new developments and produce an unforeseeable surplus of meaning and generative social potential.

Almost an unrecognized blueprint, or *Grundriss*, of later economic anthropology, Schurtz's observations anticipate many of economic anthropology's more recent and fundamental insights such as the exposure of the myth of money's origin in barter (Humphrey and Hugh-Jones 1992; Servet 2001; Graeber 2011), the mechanics of separate spheres of exchange (Bohannan 1959; Godelier 1971; Zelizer 2004), the concept of wealth in people (Guyer and Belinga 1995), and the biographies of commodities (Kopytoff 1986). Quite clearly laid out in the *Grundriss* are also observations on potlatches, gifts, the distinction between alienable and inalienable possessions (Mauss [1925] 2016; Gregory [1982] 2015; Weiner 1992), the intricate nature of multiple currency systems in Melanesia, Atlantic Africa, and China (Akin and Robbins 1999; Guyer 2004; Kuroda 2020), and merchant capitalism's ability to extract local resources by using different currencies (Wolf 1982; Sahlins 1988). It also includes a succinct analysis of the turbulent effects of colonial trade on local communities, bridewealth systems, and social hierarchies (Bourdieu and Sayad 1964; Meillassoux 1964; Rey 1971). In the particularly remarkable chapter on "countermeasures," we see a whole range of practices that preemptively prevent the intensification of hierarchies set forth by the accumulation of money, such as the redistribution and destruction of wealth, intensively discussed during the second golden age of economic anthropology in the 1970s and 1980s, when economic anthropologists increasingly began to rely almost exclusively on the seemingly inexhaustible frameworks provided by Karl Polanyi, Karl Marx,

Georg Simmel, and Marcel Mauss (Sahlins 1972; Shipton 1989; Graeber 2001; Maurer 2006; Dodd 2014; Dodd and Neiburg 2019). This uncanny soundness, scope, and versatility of Schurtz's theory is probably why Woodruff Smith (1991: 75), in his widely appreciated *Politics and the Sciences of Culture in Germany, 1840–1920*, characterizes Schurtz as "Boas's brilliant contemporary" who "developed the outlines of a comprehensive ethnology that in some ways foretold the structuralism of a later era."

Resurfacing a Silenced Classic

Schurtz's book was published during a time when economic history and sociology increasingly merged as subjects of study, resulting in the publication of several classics, such as Georg Simmel's *Philosophy of Money* ([1900] 1978), Max Weber's *The Protestant Ethic and the Spirit of Capitalism* ([1905] 2001), and Thorstein Veblen's *The Theory of the Leisure Class* (1899). Schurtz was part of the same generation of thinkers, born around 1860, who proposed alternatives to the "distressing" way the industrial revolution and the conceptual apparatus of classical and neoclassical economics had been "carving up society" (Mirowski 2000: 923). Schurtz made a specifically anthropological contribution to these discussions that unfolded during the renaissance of the German social sciences in Wilhelmine Germany and were characterized by intensive conceptual debates about money, gifts, exchange, barter, markets, and the psychological, social, and cultural foundations of the economy.[9]

Schurtz's *Grundriss* is just over one hundred pages but contains close to five hundred footnotes citing first-hand ethnographic and historical

---

9. Pre-World War I advanced monetary theory was already detaching itself from the idea that the essence of money was to have an "intrinsic value" (Keynes 1914: 421; see also Mitchell Innes [1913] 2004; and Gesell 1916). In Germany this trend is illustrated by the theoretical economics textbook of Adolph Wagner (1909: 129, 132). Wagner, a well-known professor in Berlin, who explicitly bases his own "general theory of money" on the "cautious generalizations" of Schurtz, notes that the "origin of money as such cannot be traced empirically-historically" because it is determined by "the mental life of the people who use it" and based on the "naturalization and consolidation of confidence," or trust which remains the "decisive factor for the origin, as well as for the concept and nature of money" (see also Martino 2018).

sources from outside of Europe woven together in a contextualized but kaleidoscopic way. Having carefully studied more or less all published ethnographic writing available up to 1897, Schurtz's selection of sources still provides a useful historical overview of monetary objects. The conceptual lesson of Schurtz's analysis of such a great variety of ethnographic observations is that it is not advisable to force these observations into existing theoretical edifices, whether they are universal "historical" stages or the abstract models of the British and Austrian approaches to political economy. Instead of relying on given theories, Schurtz moved forward with a conceptually tenable and original portrayal of money as always concrete, material, multiple, and contradictory.

Although Schurtz wrote clearly and without jargon, his conceptual repertoire entails heuristic categories that are nonrigid, imperfect, and provisional (pp. 32, 35), thereby retaining the potential to accommodate empirical irregularities and understand historical and material combinations of the different traits of money, processes Schurtz further characterizes with the terms *Umbildung* (transformation, p. 75), *Verschmelzung* (fusion, melting, or amalgamation, p. 84), *schwankend* (blurry, fluctuating, and ambivalent, p. 83), or *verwickelt* (intricate, tangled, or threaded, p. 90). Schurtz considered his concepts almost a byproduct of the meticulous arrangements and juxtaposition of polythetic facts, the result of the "intellectual apprehension" (p. 153) of what he elsewhere calls the "manifoldness of reality" (1900b: 297). For him, there was "no need to aid reality with artificial theories," as he summarizes his position in the preface to *Altersklassen und Männerbünde* (1902a: iii), where he also suggests that he "accidentally" created a new theory as "it originally never occurred to" him "to formulate a new theory of the formation of society." With regard to its sometimes broad-ranging essayistic form and dialectical meandering, Schurtz's *Grundriss* thus resembles Marcel Mauss's *The Gift*. The resemblance, however, ends when we look at the two books' intellectual reception. While *The Gift* is probably *the* classic of economic anthropology, the *Grundriss*, which has barely been cited in the past half century, joined the forgotten milieu of a fin-de-siècle German anthropology.

Yet, one can still trace the various ways in which Schurtz was selectively incorporated into economics and economic anthropology in the first half of the twentieth century, which allows us to propose the *Grundriss* as an evident but "silent" foundation for many of the subsequent and still perennial debates around more recent social and ethnographic conceptualizations of the economy. While Schurtz more or less directly influenced and was acknowledged by some of his renowned contemporaries, such as Karl Helfferich, Max Weber, Marcel Mauss, Franz Oppenheimer, and Richard Thurnwald, the borrowing of his conceptual ideas or empirical material by well-known social scientists and economists remained unknown to many contemporary readers because they were often hidden in footnotes or remained implicit, such as in the case of Simmel, Schumpeter, and Polanyi. Starting in the interwar period, the decline of German fluency in international scholarship along with editorial decisions and omissions in several influential translations made it even more difficult for scholars to become acquainted with or even become aware of Schurtz's *Grundriss*.

One example of this is Weber's reception of Schurtz's work and the way in which references to Schurtz have been excluded from some English translations. It is known that Weber "read with pleasure the great work of Heinrich Schurtz" (Radkau 2013: 37), and the *Grundriss* is the only text discussed in-line apart from Ludwig von Mises and Georg Friedrich Knapp in the section on money in Weber's continuously influential *Economy and Society*. While Weber notes that he will not treat "the foundations" of money, he makes several Schurtzian points on inside or "internal money" as an intragroup "payment" system for "social prestige," where money serves as "a mark of social rank" and prices are determined by "custom and convention." Even Schurtz's example of spheres of exchange is noted by Weber when he observes that cowrie shells cannot be used in "exchange for women" (Weber 1922: 40; 1947: 177; 1972: 41; 2019: 163). Weber also meticulously summarized Schurtz's theory of property and Schurtz's distinction between inside- and outside-money in the first seven pages of the chapter "Money and monetary history" in his *General Economic History* (1950: 236–41). However, the citation to Schurtz can only be found in the original German edition (1923: 208) as the translator and editor Franklin Knight excluded the opening bibliography from his popular edition.

Schurtz's influence on Weber seems to have been channeled through several tensions the latter had with the eminent economic historian Karl Bücher who also taught at the University of Leipzig and has been viewed, alongside Marx and Polanyi, as one of the "three Karls" considered the founders of economic anthropology (Hann 2015; see also Hann and Hart 2011: 39–42). After Bücher (1914) had delivered the opening chapter on "economic stages" for Weber's multivolume social and economic history in early 1913, Weber expressed his disappointment with what he considered an evolutionist manuscript "of no use," and wrote to his close friend Johann Plenge, a former student of Bücher, that his own "views on this point are currently undergoing significant change," referring to his upcoming *Economy and Society* that would "offer entirely different things than 'economic stages'" (Weber 2009: 69).[10] Indeed Bücher's text "infuriated Weber" to such a degree that, "if one were to believe Weber's repeated written statements, his entire later sociology could be understood as a replacement for Bücher's mistake" (Bruhns 2006: 169).

In contrast to the largely positive response to the *Grundriss* in the contemporary academic sphere, it might therefore not be surprising that it was Bücher who wrote the only overtly negative review of the *Grundriss*. In this review, Bücher, the German academic authority on "primitive economics," advised Schurtz to treat the "scientific work of modern economists with a bit more respect" (1899: 85). In defense of his already published theory assuming that money is a scarce commodity sourced from external trade (Bücher 1893), Bücher (1899: 86) rejected Schurtz's claim that inside-money is "the main root of the monetary system" and attacked him for his "vague and fluctuating concept of money" that "adversely affects the entire course of the investigation."[11] In a letter to Bücher, Schurtz writes that he had expected his incursion into the field of economics to cause "difficulties," as Schurtz saw Bücher as an "economist who has ventured into ethnology and seeks to use it for his purposes," while he portrayed himself as an "anthropologist who views

---

10. Plenge (1919: xi) did not only consider Schurtz one of the most important scholars of the economy but also criticized Bücher for having "neglected" the "commendable work of Schurtz" and leaving him "unsupported." Plenge even published an anthology, *Die Stammformen der vergleichenden Wirtschaftstheorie* ("The fundamental forms of comparative economic theory"), which places Schurtz alongside Aristotle, Smith, List, Marx, Hildebrand and Schönberg. In his editorial introduction, Plenge (1919: xi) describes the reprint of Schurtz's (1901) article on the bazaar as "a rediscovery of a buried scientific treasure. With each page, you gain new inspiration."

11. Karl Polanyi, who can be considered Bücher's intellectual descendant (Köcke 1979; Schrader 1980; Mirowski 1994; Hudson 2000), was also critical of Schurtz and rejected the distinction between inside- and outside-money. Polanyi's selection of essays, posthumously published as *Primitive, Archaic, and Modern Economies*, however, contains the interesting but neglected section "Primitive Money" as an appendix to his most programmatic and widely cited "The Semantics of Money Uses" in which he, in addition to Keynes and Schumpeter, mainly cites Schurtz (1971: 202).

economics as a part of his field of study and is inclined to treat it as such," adding that he has "no intention to impose your teachings on anyone as a scientific straitjacket."[12]

This dispute between Schurtz and Bücher, revealed from the archival correspondence, mirrors the well-known late nineteenth-century Bücher–Meyer controversy about the capitalist character of antiquity. Eduard Meyer's critique of Bücher came to be framed as a conceptual battle between "modernists" and "primitivists," the latter, represented by Bücher, insisting on a radical alterity that made any concepts derived from the study of modern capitalism inadequate for studying the ancient past or the noncapitalist other (Pearson 1957; Finley 1979; Reibig 2001). Like Schurtz, the young ancient historian Meyer attempted to create his own vision of "anthropology," an idea or term that had already moved away from being a "science of the evolution of man" to a "theory of general forms of human life and human development" (Tenbruck 1986: 245; see Hart 2000, 2017). This implied the radical proposition that contemporary and ancient societies should be situated in the same, but much expanded, conceptual universe. Schurtz even took a step beyond this conceptual symmetry that included enduring but transformed "archaic" societies by proposing to analyze "our" money and society through concepts that emerged from the comparative consideration of different types of money as well, an insight that later work on "primitive money" would neglect (Knight 1941; Dalton 1965; Melitz 1970; Tucci 1970; Firth 1972; Maurer 2018).[13]

The new economic anthropology of the first half of the twentieth century soon avoided the evolutionary thinking that had arisen in the previous century which helps to explain why Schurtz and the *Grundriss*—which even carries an evolutionistic term in its title—were so quickly forgotten. In his early unpublished drafts on the origin of money written in the 1920s, Schumpeter had, for instance, dismissed the comparative ethnology of money on methodological grounds, evoking the emergent anti-evolutionist consensus that contemporary "primitive societies" could not

---

12. Universitätsbibliothek Leipzig. Nachlass NL 181/Schn 213-216, Kasten Schl-V, Blatt 213–216. Letter from Heinrich Schurtz to Karl Bücher, November 13, 1899.

13. The epistemological principle that the "other" allows us to better understand ourselves remained central for some sections of German anthropology, in particular the circle around Fritz Kramer who influenced many current anthropology professors in Germany.

stand in for archaic ones, and cautioning that the sciences would soon lose the overview over the exponentially growing examples of types of money. This would then lead to endless debates about which societies had been using money "correctly or incorrectly" according to the latest theoretical fashion (1970: 15–18, 34; 1991: 522–25). Schumpeter's intuition was correct as two of the most cited works on "primitive money" illustrate. Both Paul Einzig, a prolific financial journalist who published his well-researched *Primitive Money* in 1949 (revised in 1966), and the Cambridge anthropologist Alison Quiggin who published her *Survey of Primitive Money* in 1949, for instance, are conceptually way more timid than Schurtz. Unlike the *Grundriss*, both books limit themselves to "primitive" or "preliterate" and "nonstate" types of money, and the authors use geographical regions as their ordering principle to fill their voluminous chapters with list-like compilations of different types of money.[14] By the middle of the twentieth century, anthropology had largely stopped crafting or even engaging with global histories, and had become fully weary of the intellectual search and concern for origins because of the Darwinian overtones of such questions. The influential economic anthropologist Melville Herskovits sealed the fate of Schurtz's *Grundriss* by concluding that, although not fluent in German (Pearson 2010), he was not concerned with "hypotheses as those of Schurtz" because they would be "too speculative to merit discussion" (1952: 237). It was the publication of David Graeber's *Debt: The First 5,000 Years* in 2011 that reopened an anthropological vantage point for a renewed engagement with the intriguing theoretical implications of the gripping, far-reaching, and popular question: where does money come from?

A Nonmodern Monetary Theory

Although Schurtz did not accept that money's origin is simply "lost in the mists of time" (Mirowski 1994: 315), his search yields contradictory answers, accepting, even embracing, the bewildering complexity of

---

14. The origin of this turn can already be located in the transfer of German anthropology to interwar anglophone academia, where most works on "primitive money" reuse, cite, or unpack Schurtz's examples and sources and often conduct fieldwork in the sites indicated by him without engaging with Schurtz's theoretical arrangement (Schmidt 1920: 119; 1921: 159; Thilenius 1921; Malinowski 1922; Thurnwald 1923, 1932: 262; Wieschhoff 1945, Lips 1949: 207; cf. Pearson 2000).

empirical reality. Schurtz did not seek an answer to the question whether money is a means of exchange emerging from barter, a measure of value grounded in political decrees, or the religious and philosophical practices of classical antiquity (Knapp 1905; Laum 1924; Schaps 2004; Seaford 2004), a system of accounting which Keynes called a "price list" that could be "recorded by word of mouth or by book entry on baked bricks" (1930: 3, 13), or part of a more generalized metrological symbolic counter (Codere 1968; Grierson 1978; Kula 1986; Seitz 2017) that emerged from debt, slavery, and violence (Aglietta and Orléan 1982; Hudson 2004; Graeber 2011). Schurtz acknowledges kernels of truth in almost all of these answers given over the course of the twentieth century while, at the same time, exposing the underlying questions as unresolvable economic antinomies that result from money's contradictory nature. For Schurtz, the difficulty of answering the questions of where money comes from and what its defining features are was not caused by insufficient empirical data. The accumulation of data can never be a direct route to theory, he notes, because "if mere collection was as straightforward and self-evident as some make it seem" then such material "would already have been abundantly brought together" in his time, and an adequate theory would have already been developed (p. 153).

Schurtz's solution was to display the moral and social tensions that emerged from the historical unfolding of money in different contexts, historical periods, and ethnographic areas, which convinced him of money's fundamentally contradictory nature corresponding to two opposing social "laws that set the course for the development of humanity as a whole"; on the one hand, the "the perpetual motion of money and purchasable commodities" that pushes individuals to separate themselves from their own society, adopt novelties and trade with others, and, on the other, the "forces" that "bind individuals to stable and durable valuables, to the home and hearth" (p. 172). The "best evidence," Schurtz suggests, for the assumption that "the emergence of two original forms of money was not mere chance" is the fact that "we still find these opposing powers at work today," shaping and transforming economic life (p. 173). This quasi-structuralist answer allowed Schurtz to circumvent the stark dichotomy between trying to pinpoint an origin in time or place, or to abandon the conceptual implications of the question of "origins" altogether. Instead, Schurtz's vision of money's generative double character that structures both international and local markets and political hierarchies, provides a conceptual starting point for understanding the creation of "new economies"—for example in an imperial and colonial context, after decolonization or when a new currency is introduced, such as the euro (Servet 1998; Peebles 2011; Pallaver 2022).

Sharing the more widespread nineteenth-century notion of an evolutionary link between money and inequality, Schurtz developed a detailed analysis of money as a creator of rank and standing, both within and between societies. He dedicates a tremendous amount of space in the *Grundriss* to illustrate the political and social consequences of the creation of monetary systems. He outlines how different types of money produce social differentiations, especially along class and gender lines, citing various examples of how only political authorities and social elites were allowed to receive and hold money which became more valuable as it aged in their hands, while, in other cases, women were only permitted to handle the less valuable small change of the retail trade. Sometimes, the same monetary object, he notes, is given a premium, discounted, or assessed differently depending on if it is a political authority, a commoner, a market woman, or a stranger handing it over (pp. 52, 72, 152). The simultaneous use of multiple types and categories of money within societies is thus an architectural principle in the generation and reproduction of inequality.[15]

This focus on social groups and social processes of differentiation exemplifies that Schurtz (1900b: 212) rejected the economistic conceptions of society as being "composed of individuals" and of individual transactions as "mere building blocks" of a "whole sum." This was not only a critique of methodological individualism, but also of the historical school. Schurtz defined the collective whole as not only including "the living but also the ancestors and future generations." He called this transgenerational frame a *Dauergesellschaft*, or an "enduring society," which does not allude to the typically German romantic idea of a suprahuman community or cultural soul, but rather to the great social tensions and cohesions produced by the hoarding and distribution of money through the cult of the dead and institutions of intergenerational transmission such as marriage and patrimony that contemporary

---

15. Schurtz also put great emphasis on the question of kinship and inheritance, as this represented the efforts to secure the financial security and thus social position of one's children (pp. 65–73). For more recent discussions on similar themes, see especially Colin Drumm's dissertation (2021), which exemplifies a rare level of original thinking on the history of money, and his courses on money, power, and value at the online-based Mimbres School for the Humanities.

economic history and theory largely overlooked (1900b: 212; see also Rospabé 2010).[16]

For Schurtz, who shared the "respect for the historical fact" and for broad and deep empirical foundations with the younger German historical school of his generation (Schumpeter 1954: 780), thinking about money's origins revealed an independent power steering the fate of human and social development. The unraveling of empirical contexts and historical contingencies also put him at odds with the ahistorical and theoretically contrived origin scenarios put forth by Menger and various British economists writing in the mid-nineteenth century, such as William Stanley Jevons and Walter Bagehot. In Bagehot ([1848] 1978: 243), for instance, who states that it is "misleading" to "speak of the state of barter as having ceased; in point of fact, gold is bartered for everything and everything is bartered for gold," we already find the curious neoclassical claim of money's "nonexistence" which denies money its multiplicity and autonomy in structuring the social relations within and between societies (Patnaik 2009; Aglietta 2018). It is hardly surprising that Schurtz rejected such instrumental perspectives in his significant article *Wertvernichtung durch den Totenkult* ("Value Destruction in the Cult of the Dead," 1898b) published just a few months after the *Grundriss*. The article, which could serve as a supplementary chapter to the *Grundriss*, starts with the remark that "utility theory" is "as clear as it is shallow and seeks to attribute all economically significant human actions primarily to the rational consideration of practical benefits, and which in its one-sided form could only arise in the fumes of the English factory districts abandoned by all muses and graces" (Schurtz 1898b: 41). Instead of falling into utilitarian thought, it is easy to imagine Schurtz siding with both Alain Caillé's *Mouvement Anti-Utilitariste dans les Sciences Sociales* as well as Andre Orléan's (2013: 52; 1992, 2014, 2023) project

---

16. The adherents of the "younger" historical school emphasized the social and reciprocal foundations of the economy. For Gustav Schmoller, one of the leading figures of the school, currencies also appeared in the form of "bride-price, fines, and taxes" that were paid in a "particularly coveted and popular good," which then simply became a "universal means of payment and exchange," both "for the market and other payments." The road to real "money," Schmoller says, however, "takes some nations thousands of years to develop" (Schmoller 1904: 65–67, see also Lotz 1894). Bücher ([1893] 1901: 62–65, 110) emphasized "gifts" and gift-giving as the fundamental element of the "original" "pre-economy."

of a "new foundation for economics" that understands the existence of "diverse forms of money" as a "response to the actors' frenetic demands" to get an answer to "the economic question par excellence … upon which all economic activity depends," namely "in which form is value to be found?" In both its modern and its "primitive" forms, which over the course of modernity were relegated to the status of collectible curiosities and superfluous ornaments or unrelated precursors with no political or scientific relevance, money thus not only matters (Guyer 1995), but galvanizes.

Note on Translation and Editing

The translation is based on the original German edition of Heinrich Schurtz's *Grundriss einer Entstehungsgeschichte des Geldes* published in 1898 by Emil Felber in Weimar. While maintaining the original text, we made some modifications to enhance readability. Although the original edition does not include a separate bibliography, we have added a complete list of references after the endnotes. We have also added a selection of illustrations between chapters 8 and 9. We have excluded the short original index. We have converted "d o u b l e d s p a c e d" words used by Schurtz for emphasis into *italics*. We omitted the original italicization of authors' surnames discussed in the text and have standardized Schurtz's inconsistent italicization of foreign terms. Schurtz numbered footnotes starting from 1 at every page; we restart them at each new chapter and have converted them into endnotes. The abbreviated book and journal titles in the original references have been extended for easier identification. In several cases where an author or text is only cited in the text, we have converted the reference into a new endnote. When Schurtz quotes authors without giving a reference, we located the reference and inserted a new endnote marked with square brackets. All editorial additions are clearly indicated within square brackets, while parentheses and abbreviations are retained as used by Schurtz himself. In cases where Schurtz translated references into German, we use the original English version or an authoritative English translation when available and mark it with "Orig.," or "En. transl."

Our editorial annotations have been added as footnotes, indicated by an asterisk, and if more than one footnote begins on a page, the sequence of symbols is *, †. In preparing the annotations, our guiding principle has been to offer contextual information and clarifications. We have focused on providing details about sources Schurtz cites, especially when they have been found to be inaccurately summarized by Schurtz or are of particular significance to current research. Additionally, we have included brief explanations to help readers understand the context of some of Schurtz's empirical examples, including explicit references to nowadays less well-known historical figures and controversies. It is important to note that these footnotes are not exhaustive and reflect our own expertise, particularly on African monetary systems.

Regarding outdated terms, we decided to use equivalents that are still understandable but also appropriate for the period when the *Grundriss* was published instead of modernized and not always equivalent terms (for example, "Caribs" instead of "Kalingo" for *Kariben*, or "Indochina" instead of "mainland Southeast Asia" for *Hinterindien*). However, we have chosen to consistently use "Sahel" in place of *Sudan* to avoid confusion with the modern states Sudan and South Sudan. In the nineteenth century, the geographic region known as "the Sudan" or *le Soudan* referred to the mostly Muslim belt of territories beneath the Sahara, extending from Senegal to the borders of Ethiopia. We have not marked the translations of place and ethnic names where the German version is a phonetic variation of a well-established English term (for instance, *Dschagga* is translated as "Chagga"). However, we modernized a few geographic and ethnic names to make it easier for the reader to identify the place or ethnic group referred to. To facilitate cross-references with the original sources we list these terms here: Abouré=*Kompas*; Azande=*Niam-Niam*; Dakpa=*N'Dakwas*; Dzing=*Badinga*; Ewondo=*Yaunde*; Fang=*Mpong*; Idah=*Atta*; Haya=*Wasiba*; Kalaallit of West Greenland=*Eskimos der grönländischen Westküste*; Kyrgyz=*Buruten*; Lemba=*Malepa*; Luwo=*Djur*; Marianas=*Ladronen*; Xhosa=*Kaffern*. An inevitable difficulty arose in the case of racist terms which we decided to replace. The term *Naturvölker* relies on the opposition between "cultural" or "civilized" versus "natural" or "uncivilized" people, and we have translated the term as "indigenous societies." The term *Eingeborene* has a colonial administrative tone to it, so we rendered it as "natives" which we also used for the German term *Indianer* that denotes various groups of indigenous people in the Americas (for example, we translated *Indianerstämme Guyanas* as "the native tribes of Guyana"). Regarding the use of common German racial categories of the period, we have used alternatives, such as "African," "Aboriginal Austrialians," and "Maroons of Suriname."

In terms of syntax, we maintained Schurtz's style, except in a few cases where we separated extremely long sentences. The German word for money can be highly combinatory or "cobbled" and it is unfortunate that composites, such as *Geldart, Geldstrafe, Geldsystem,* have to be translated as "type of money," "fine," and "monetary system." In most instances we aligned with the conventions of anthropology, monetary history, sociology, and comparative numismatics and especially relied on the authoritative German-to-English translations of George Simmel, Max Weber and Joseph Schumpeter. There were nevertheless a variety of terms which Schurtz coins or employs in specific ways, and we opted to not follow the established translations in these cases. We provide explanations as footnotes after the initial mention of some of these terms, such as "inside-money" and "outside-money" (*Binnengeld, Aussengeld*) and "sign-money" (*Zeichengeld*). Furthermore, we use hyphenations in some of Schurtz's compound nouns involving money. This approach helps retain the accent and subtle emphasis on the materiality of the first noun of the original German. Terms like *Eisengeld, Silbergeld,* and *Muschelgeld,* are thus translated as "iron-money," "silver-money," and "shell-money."

An Outline of the Origins of Money

CHAPTER I

Anthropology and Economics
The Natural Monetary System

If anthropology has the task to provide all related and already developed sciences with a broader and more solid foundation for their theories, then it must also review the doctrines of economics, either to better support them, reshape them based on deeper insights, or discard them altogether. This task is not always easy. Whoever resides on the top floors of a gleaming building is reluctant to inquire about the integrity of the base and the lower walls, and the anthropologist tapping at the foundations with a hammer is seen as a bothersome nuisance. It is far more rewarding to continue to add new towers and stories than to admit that the whole structure rests on shaky ground, or even to descend and, far from the noise and applause above, repair the faulty walls.

The history of money is one of the most instructive examples of the relationship between anthropology* and a closely related science. Insofar

---

*   We translate *Völkerkunde* consistently as "anthropology." Schurtz laid out his vision of anthropology most clearly in the posthumously published *Völkerkunde* (1903a: 1–4), where he divides the discipline into a "descriptive branch" called "ethnography," depicting "each nation impartially and comprehensively," and a "comparative anthropology or ethnology" which has to be developed from the former because "mere description is insufficient" as "humanity never remains the same as it is constantly changing, shifting, multiplying or decreasing." Schurtz saw anthropology as a kind of meta social science and considered economics, sociology, and

as this history is written by economists, following a good old custom, they almost exclusively rely on the records of ancient and modern civilized people which are considered unequivocally typical for humanity. On this alarmingly narrow basis, the most reckless theories then shoot up into the heavens, and men of gold and silver* preach their wisdom from dizzying heights to an astonished people. Amidst their noise, the request of anthropology to broaden the research base will certainly go unnoticed at first, but it will, finally, have to be heard when bewilderment can no longer be resolved in any other way, and truth instead of warring interests is once again allowed to have a say. Anthropology must also, for its own advantage, preoccupy itself with the questions of the origins and development of the monetary system, because although the concept of "money," as we currently use it, is a cultural achievement, its uncritical application to simpler contexts has caused all sorts of unfortunate misunderstandings, especially in travel accounts.

As the term "concept" has come up, it should be pointed out decisively that a work belonging to the field of anthropology can never involve the razor-sharp conceptual definitions that are commonly assumed to be the goal of all research in those sciences influenced by jurisprudence. Such definitions easily hinder insight into the course of development. Whether we want to use the term money to refer to the early beginnings of what we now call "money," or whether we give it some other name, is thoroughly irrelevant with respect to the actual problem concerning us as long as we remain aware of the fact that all rigid designations cannot do justice to the flow of development, and are thus nothing but superficial aids for anthropology. This remark may appear redundant for those familiar with anthropological thinking, but the number of those who expect salvation from the dissection of concepts instead of the impartial observation of the continuous flux of becoming and passing away is

---

political science to be branches of anthropology which had developed "independently" but without considering "the most developed and the least developed" societies in "an equally detailed manner."

* The metaphor of *Gold- und Silbermänner* alludes to the monetary theorists of the gold or the bimetallic standard. In the 1890s, the popular and academic consensus was that the value of money was based on the international price of gold, plus or minus the state's dues for minting (seigniorage) and the cost of manufacturing (brassage), while copper and, increasingly, silver coins were treated as a separate subcategory of "fiat tokens" (*Scheidemünzen*) (Lotz 1906).

unfortunately all too large. And so let it be said once again that the question here is not "What do we understand by money?" but a completely different one: "From which origins did money develop and which stages of this development can still be traced?" Only indigenous peoples can provide us with the answer to this question.

It cannot be claimed that anthropologists have already devoted special attention to this question. From a proper anthropological standpoint, only one person has addressed the problem, namely Richard Andree in a section of his *Ethnographic Parallels*, which has paved the way for many questions by applying the comparative method with rare diligence, and which therefore deserves forever to hold a praiseworthy position in the history of anthropology.[1] The first thing Andree had to establish was a simple and clear classification of the tremendous amount of material, and he did so by sorting the different monetary instruments into specific sets according to their *material* by subsuming them under the terms stone-money, shell-money, cloth-money, iron-money, salt-money, and so on. In doing so, a preliminary overview was achieved.

Shortly after, but independent of Andree, Franz Ilwof dealt with the problem in his text *Barter and Money Substitutes*.[2] His work represents an improvement over Andree, as it attempts to rely on ethnographic findings to improve economic doctrines. Unfortunately, the ethnographic part of the essay is the weakest, even though new concepts should arise from a sound ethnographic basis. Consequently, the impact of his otherwise commendable work has remained limited. Merely for the sake of completeness, we mention Oskar Lenz's essay *On Money among Primitive People*, which closely follows Andree, but offers nothing new apart from some noteworthy observations about African conditions.[3]

It is high time now to pursue the problem of the development of money, which has been noticeably neglected since then. What can be offered here is, of course, little more than a sketch, but it might still illustrate that the conceptual disputes of today have been present from the beginning. I do not intend to approach these questions here. However, a deeper understanding of the current state of things is impossible without possessing knowledge of the simpler, older forms. The goal of this treatise is, therefore, to offer a reliable foundation. Just as we cannot know the living conditions of a plant by contemplating its leaves and flowers while ignoring its roots, we cannot hope to find the real sources of the influences that shape and transform economic life up to the present day without the help of anthropology. At the very least, it will become apparent that the economists' truism about the consecutive stages of barter, money, and credit economies* does not remotely do justice to the real problems, and that alone is a step forward that inevitably will be followed by others over time.

Anthropology relies on laws applicable in many instances, and knowledge of these laws can even point us to answers to newly emerged questions. The first and best known of these laws teaches us that a new custom or institution never emerges out of nothing, but that beginnings and seeds are ever-present and have to operate secretly for long before more ideal forms emerge. It is therefore reasonable to assume that the concept of money has also undergone a long development. Moreover, ethnographic experience allows us to firmly reject the preconception that institutions arise from purposeful contemplations alone. We are familiar with cultural concepts such as religion, the state, justice, and so on, which nowadays appear unified but, on closer inspection, prove to be put together and artificially fused, and we know that in such cases, the concept often tends to be a confluence of very different sources, and that we can still observe these individual sources separately among indigenous peoples. What we now call "money" is also an illusory unity. Even a cursory observation reveals that money can serve as a measure of value or as a medium that stores the results of all kinds of work, like an electrical battery or energy accumulator does with various mechanical forces, while it, in the form of fines and taxes, performs purely social tasks, and is also used as a universally welcomed means of exchange that greatly facilitates commercial transactions from person to person, and from nation to nation.

If we search among indigenous peoples for traces of these various properties of money, we not only find them separate in completely recognizable form, but we are also made aware of how all the currents that became unified in the concept of money are tightly connected to the historical development of humanity itself. Parallel facts often make it easier to quickly understand a phenomenon than many words, and in our case,

---

*   The sequence "barter, money, and credit" corresponds to Bruno Hildebrand's (1864: 7) three stages of economic evolution, namely the "natural economy," the "money economy," and the "credit economy." Hildebrand, along with Wilhelm Roscher (1857: 210) and Karl Knies (1885: 5), one of the founding figures of the so-called "older" German Historical School of Economics, imagines the first stage as an agrarian society and the last stage as dominated by banknotes and central banks, and considered transitions between these stages as a form of utilitarian progress.

such a parallel can be seen in the historical development of *marriage*.*
The particular relation between a man and a woman that we now call
marriage has developed in quite different ways, depending on whether it
took shape within a tribe (endogamy) or as a result of hostile and later
friendly relations with other hordes and tribes (exogamy); only civilized
peoples have arrived at a more or less unified idea. The concept of money
has arisen in a similar way, originating from two distinct sources: What
functions as the foundation of wealth and measure of value for property
and serves social ends within a tribe is, in its origins, something entirely
different from the means of exchange that travels from tribe to tribe and
eventually transforms itself, as a universally welcomed commodity, into
a kind of currency. To acknowledge this difference from the very beginning, we ask to use, provisionally for want of better terms, "inside-money" for the first kinds of primitive monies, and "outside-money"[†] for the
second. Obviously, this classification initially seems to have nothing to
do with the purely material one used by Andree; however, as this enquiry
proceeds to show, there is no necessary contradiction between the two.

---

*   Schurtz's reference to kinship terminology suggests that his concepts of
"inside-" and "outside-money" were influenced by contemporary debates
about endogamous and exogamous marriage patterns. The study of kinship, probably anthropology's most important and influential subfield in
the second half of the nineteenth century, was dominated by the theories of Johann Jakob Bachofen and Lewis Henry Morgan who posited an
"original" matriarchal and primitive communism that displaced the "biblical" concept of an antediluvian fundamental family form. However, during
the 1890s, the problem of the universality of the incest taboo and the
social dimensions of exogamy were at the forefront of conceptual debates
in the field (see Tylor 1889; Westermarck 1891; Durkheim 1897).

†   We consistently translate the German terms *Binnengeld* and *Aussengeld* as
"inside-money" and "outside-money" instead of "internal" and "external"
money. The latter terms were already conventionally used to describe the
source of debts and the source of the money supply for national economies. Using them would give a false sense of a permanent and spatial
"externality" or "internality" which would make it difficult to grasp the
dialectic understanding of *Binnen-* and *Aussengeld*, which entails the possibility that inside-money becomes outside-money or even another society's inside-money. This Schurtzian opposition neither overlaps with the
well-established distinction between endogenous and exogenous money
in monetary economics nor with Gurley and Shaw's distinction of inside
and outside money (1960; see also Lagos 2010; Wray 2014) which are
both more concerned with the nature of credit creation.

CHAPTER 2

The Beginnings of Property
Measure of Value and Valuable Property
The Origin of Inside-Money

One cannot conceive of the beginnings and earliest seeds of money within a human community unless personal property has emerged alongside an original, all-encompassing communal ownership. Even today, here and there, this development has not progressed significantly, and within the family, the last form of consanguine solidarity in primitive societies, remnants of an ancient communism are still alive, and a sharp delineation of individual property is only partially realized. The study of the emergence of private property among indigenous peoples has been, unfortunately and undeservedly, neglected, and existing discussions on the subject mainly concern property rights in land;* these, however, develop much later and in entirely different ways than claims of ownership over movable goods or living beings. Moreover, one continually encounters the theoretical error that the individual is primarily and above all

---

* Schurtz certainly had Émile de Laveleye in mind whose influential *Primitive Property* (1878) was translated by Karl Bücher. In contrast to "older attempts by Laveleye or the more recent ones by Hildebrandt [and] Oppenheimer," Schurtz's article on the beginnings of land ownership emphasizes the diversity and complexity of the empirical situations and proposes to "let the facts speak for themselves" instead of committing to static models of the development of private property (1900c: 248).

attracted to *useful* things which he seeks to withdraw from common ownership.[1] The opposite is true: objects of practical use, and especially food, are the last to become indisputable property. In fact, the universally prevailing assumption is that everyone has a right to these things and those who accumulate them in excess should therefore share them with the needy of their tribe without receiving further thanks or compensation. Whenever members of civilized societies are transferred to simple and primitive conditions, such as the first settlers of the jungle or the prairie, a kind of communal property that encompasses all practical and useful things quickly emerges and only disappears once the option to buy food, tools, and the like arises nearby. Attitudes of this kind can be found among most indigenous peoples, and the ideals of the Galactophagi of antiquity, in which everything except their weaponry was common property,[2]* still have their parallels today. Drawing on a small sample from different parts of the world may suffice.

On the Tonga Islands, according to Mariner's testimony, everyone was allowed to enter any house at mealtime and partake in the meal, and nothing aroused the indignant astonishment of some Tongans taken to Sydney more than the fact that no one there invited them to a meal.[3] Among the Mongol tribes, all edible items were practically a common good, everyone shared what they had with the greatest generosity, while other possessions and livestock were only reluctantly given away.[4] According to Lichtenstein's report, anyone could participate in the chief's meals among the Xhosa, and wherever a cow was slaughtered, it was taken for granted that anyone who happened to be in the area could join the feast without a special invitation. Endemann reports of the Sotho in Transvaal: "This custom is often uncomfortable for the European. If

---

*   "Galactophagi" is an ethnonym originally used as an epithet by Greek writers and means "curd-eaters" as the people designated by it allegedly lived on cheese made from mare's milk. Known since Homer's *Iliad* (Hom. Il. 13.5) as the *Abii*, or the "the most righteous of men," they were regarded as "noble savages" in antiquity. It is, however, unclear whether they actually existed or were part of the mythical Hyperboreans who were believed to populate the edge of the earth. According to Strabo (7.3.7), the Greek geographer writing at the beginning of the Roman Empire, they were part of the "still present" nomadic Scythians living in the steppes above the Black Sea, and did not seek "money-getting but actually possess all things in common except sword and drinking-cup," and conducted trade by barter as they "know nothing about storing up food or about peddling merchandise either, except the exchange of wares for wares."

he has Sotho workers and they sit down to eat, it is their habit to allow anyone passing by to eat with them; they cannot comprehend that the employer does not readily want to permit this, because otherwise he would incur losses." Güssfeldt also praises the Loango Africans for their willingness to share their food with each other.[5] In the custom prevalent in the Orient, and even in Spain, of at least formally inviting onlookers to partake in a meal, a remnant of this communism is still alive.

One of the most alluring images is how the personality of an individual asserts itself, bit by bit, against the overpowering clan and tribal community, partly by achieving an internal autonomy of character and ideas, and partly by creating a zone of influence around itself and impressing its essence as a stamp on people as well as things in various ways. *Those objects that individuals affect and reshape with their own will are indeed the beginning of their personal property.* The shapes of tools and weapons, as invented by the human hand, reflect an individual's inner being, they are a part of his essence and therefore belong to him in a completely different way than a fruit plucked from a tree, or a hunted animal struck down by an arrow. When Röder says, "labour establishes between man and the objects which he has transformed a far closer connexion than mere appropriation," he fails to capture the basic feature of the phenomenon, because it is not bare physical labor which is decisive as it can also accompany simple appropriation, but rather the mental engagement with the object, which finds its outward expression only when form is transformed through physical labor.[6] How mystical imaginations forge an even tighter bond between humans and their works has been incisively pointed out by Karl Bücher. "The product of labour" he says, "is, as it were, a part of the person producing it. The man who transfers it to another alienates a part of his being and subjects himself to the evil powers."[7]

Fundamentally, the first thing that a person becomes aware of as personal property is his own body, and from this it follows that, at the earliest stage, everything meant to alter or adorn the body is also perceived as private property. Hair, artfully matted with clay, can certainly not be claimed from its owner by any fellow tribe member, but neither can the wooden comb, which has been carved out and stays nestled in the hair, be easily taken by someone else; anyone desiring it must either politely ask for it or decide to reciprocate with a counter-gift. Adornments thus become the earliest personal possessions, and this is true not only for ornaments on one's body: decorated tools and weapons, created by unique tastes and caprice, have property-bestowing powers as well. Ornaments can easily turn into proprietary marks, and since they often allude to mystical ideas, their owners simultaneously derive an intimate value from them, just as jewelry transforms easily into protective or magical amulets. If we also consider that quite a few ornaments serve as memories of individual heroic deeds in war or hunting, we have a multitude of converging motives that explain why the first rights of ownership extended to bodily adornments and to weapons and tools decorated by human hands.

In some places, there has been no progress beyond this stage of development. Martius says about the natives in Brazil: "With regards to private property, similar to our ancestors' view of a man's weaponry and a woman's dowry, men keep their weapons and ornaments, while women view their jewelry and garments, if they own any, as their own, those are merely adornments for them. All other things, hammocks, pottery, flour-making tools, and the like, are considered family property." This is also the case elsewhere, and women often know how to defend their rights with great determination: a woman from Teste Island (New Guinea) attacked her husband with a stick because he had secretly traded away her jewelry to the Europeans, and made him hand over the piece of hoop iron he had received in return.[8] It is particularly intriguing to observe how the property of women, generally established more slowly and later than that of men, first and often exclusively encompasses adornments, which, bypassing men, are passed down female inheritance lines, regardless of whether they are made of the most precious and desired materials that tempt the envy of male heirs. Among the Arabs of the Sahara, this custom is so common that many women possess considerable assets in the form of gold and silver jewelry.[9] The same custom is attested to on the Polynesian island of Nauru. According to Jung, the "items of worth brought in by the woman are her jewelry and other treasures. Upon her death, these are always inherited by the eldest daughter, and if there is no daughter in the family, these items are buried or sunk into the sea beyond the reef." Petherick reports similar things about the Dinka on the upper Nile.[10]

What individuals transform for themselves, what they, in other words, set aside from the common property by imprinting onto it a part of their being, initially holds a specific value for them alone, which entirely depends on the owners' whims and generally does not correspond to the object's function or utility. Yet, even this capricious appreciation largely stems from the influence of tribesmen who, while refraining from claiming these personal possessions, still co-determine their value through their judgments. When a young man crafts a piece of shell jewelry, he certainly does not aim to delight in it just by himself, but rather seeks to incite the envy of his fellows and the admiration of women, and, if he succeeds, the ornament gains a high value for him. However, this value can suddenly plummet to zero if someone else captivates everyone's attention through a more original design. This is similar to the way in which a child clings to a toy one moment and carelessly tosses it aside the next, and as we are actually dealing with the products of a playful artistic drive, this resemblance is noteworthy.

Especially in its early stages, private property is thus most strongly subjected to the judgment of fellow members of the tribe, and so naturally finds itself becoming an object of desire for those who highly esteem it. In this way transfers of property are animated. Through gift-giving, plunder, thievery, or exchange, desired possessions can pass from hand to hand, although this does not exactly lead to a well-regulated form of profit-oriented exchange. Initially more significant is another effect of general approval: one might refuse the idea of taking objects from their owner in whichever way, but the idea embodied in the ornament or instrument is not protected by a patent against copying, and so, as long as the necessary materials are available, anyone can recreate the much-desired object in a similar form—the human mimetic drive kicks in. From then on, the value of certain possessions is established by the more conservative inclinations of the whole tribe, rather than by the fluctuating whims of the individual. While some items appear in fleeting fashions only to disappear again, others become a stable, or at least only gradually changing, custom. The abundance of bodily adornments thus gradually disaggregates into two large groups: the first encompasses types of adornments that are individually or even collectively popular at a given moment but are subject to the varying judgments of taste; the second, on the other hand, includes the few things that escape the changes of fashion and, to some extent, become the fixed insignias of the tribe. This latter type forms the foundation of inside-money, as its long-lasting and uniform appreciation makes it suitable to act as a *measure of value*.

Once this foundation has been laid, the concept of *wealth* begins to develop. In completely primitive circumstances, an individual can neither acquire land nor will he profit from accumulating food supplies and other useful objects. In contrast, amassing ornamental objects has no boundaries, particularly among sedentary tribes who are not compelled to carry their property around. Due to these objects' material nature, the tendency to continuously amass them can barely be kept within reasonable limits. Everyone avoids senselessly hoarding food that cannot be entirely consumed and ultimately goes to waste. In contrast, adornments persist indefinitely, and the prospect of covering oneself with one piece today and another tomorrow opens unlimited and enticing prospects for the future. Nothing else is needed to activate the *hoarding drive*, whose irresistible power also manifests in innumerable other phenomena and plays a profoundly significant role in the development of money.[11]

Once some types of adornment are widely appreciated, the potential opens to purchase the goodwill and assistance of others through the gift-ing of such things. This will initially occur only occasionally and in an unsystematic manner, but the tribe's social conditions will soon lead to a livelier and more regular exchange. Almost everywhere, the custom of purchasing brides emerges as female children are viewed as the property of their parents and are then only given away in exchange for other private property; even more important is the emergence of *taxes*.

In primitive conditions, the chief, who often recedes into the background in times of peace, generally can claim only minimal or no revenues; at most he might receive a special piece of the hunting bounty, and general provision is made for his sustenance, but one cannot speak of taxes in the proper sense.[12] Such conditions can still be observed today, or have only been imperfectly eliminated. Chiefs in Liberia's hinterland can only levy taxes in the event of war,[13] whereas in northeastern Africa voluntary donations are often gathered only when the chief needs money.[14] Among Brazilian natives, chiefs receive neither tributes nor gifts but only a larger share of the war loot.[15] The conflict between power and justice occasionally leads to the unfortunate customs of the ruler carrying out raiding expeditions within his own territory to replenish his coffers[16] or keeping thieves in his entourage who steal on his behalf.[17] In Tahiti, the king's servants would ruthlessly plunder the people if taxes, the amount of which was not predetermined and which could be better described as gifts, were insufficient, and the king could simply confiscate trade goods exchanged with Europeans. In stark contrast, in the kingdom of the Luba lord Kalamba,* tax collection was not much more than some form of organized begging.[18]

Almost everywhere, the goal of bringing a portion of the possessions amassed by private individuals into the hands of chiefs is achieved indirectly, usually in the form of *monetary fines*, which in this sense are the

---

*   Kalamba Mukenge (b. Mukenge-A-Tunsele) was a "Kalamba" (great chief, "big man") of the Bena Kashiya clan of the Luba people in the valley of the central Lulua River on the middle Kasai, an affluent of the Congo river (Fabian 2000: 164–66; Ngalamulume 2011).

beginning or at least the trigger for actual taxation. As soon as considerable private ownership was established, it became possible to avoid physical punishment by surrendering assets, a path that met little resistance because of several factors. Firstly, a more precise gradation and weighing of penalties was now possible, which was inevitable anyhow for more civilized cultures; secondarily, the damaged party could be offered an actual compensation instead of a mere quenching of his thirst for revenge; and lastly, the chief, called upon as judge, was able to appropriate a part of the fine as a fee for his efforts or, if there was no injured party, could pocket the fine without further ado. This is how, in many cases, the first income streams of the chief develop, which often also remain his only ones.[19] It is quite natural that the entire judicial process therefore often seems to be geared towards extorting as much as possible from the disputing parties. At the same time the prestige of the adjudicating chief is promoted, the habit of keeping his good favor by regular gifting becomes common, and, mediated by this customary law, real taxation of the entire populace is gradually established. All generally and permanently appreciated possessions naturally present themselves as means of payment, which now in their new use truly deserve the label of "money." Where no external relations come into play, money is still principally used for the payment of fines, as Semper, for example, explicitly confirms for the peculiar inside-money of the Palau Islands,[20] where every kind of payment is still simply referred to as a "fine."[21] Even among more advanced societies, monetary fines serve as a regular source of income; a large part of the revenue of the Vandal kings in North Africa flowed from the fines that the majority of their subjects, staunchly Catholic, had to pay to their Arius-following rulers,* and indeed this exploitation of the Catholics became a royal prerogative.[22]

Fines, taxes, and frequent gifts render certain private possessions transactable, transforming them into a social power that shapes the whole inner life of the tribe. Deeply entrenched customs and practices succumb to this new power, and rigid forms become more flexible under its effect; not only can the criminal who violates laws and mores evade what would otherwise be inevitable annihilation, on some Polynesian

---

* Followers of a theological doctrine known as Arianism, proposed by Arius, a Christian presbyter from Alexandria in the early fourth century, that influenced some Germanic tribes, like the Vandals. One of the main propositions of Arianism was the belief that Jesus, though divine, was not equal to God.

islands, a frightened mother can use money to save the life of a superflu-ous child who, by ancient custom, was destined to die.[23] Power relations within the tribe begin to shift; apart from the chief, other characters step up whose services have to be purchased through payments, notably the priest or sorcerer who heals diseases, summons the rain, or foretells the future; the father of a beautiful daughter now only parts with that valua-ble possession in return for a corresponding compensation; and the more ancient communism fades away, the more numerous become the services and things that can only be had for money. It is primarily money that destroys communism; everyone is forced to raise money for unavoidable payments, and as not everyone will be able to produce their own mon-ey—which is made outright impossible anyhow with advancing devel-opments—individuals must more and more withdraw their labor and its fruits from common ownership and demand monetary compensation for services they provide to others. This creates a circulation of inside-money within the tribe, even though it cannot be used in outward transactions with other tribes.

We encounter typical examples of inside-money especially in Mela-nesia and Micronesia. The numerous varieties of Melanesian shell-mon-ey belong to this category, as do the peculiar types of money on the Carolines, which do not serve external trade but are exclusively used on certain islands. Kubary reports on their social significance: "The need to earn a living makes money indispensable to us, but the islanders have no need for money as all are self-sufficient. The arts and industry have not yet differentiated much among this people and are still possessed by the entire community, so luxury goods are unknown here. And yet, money plays a pivotal role in the life of the inhabitants. Conceived as an animal, man has enough here for sustenance, but if he wants to have a wife, found a family, be a member of a state, he must possess money. The existence of a community as a political state relies on the money owned by the heads of the families. The relations of exogamous marriage can only be maintained through a sustained exchange of goods or money. In reality, the seemingly carefree son of nature has far more worries than an industrious worker among us, who, once he has fulfilled his duties to the state, is his own master and only has to provide for his own family."[24]

In Melanesia admission into secret societies, which enhances one's social status, must, moreover, be bought with money,[25*] and it is quite

---

*   Schurtz is alluding to the "*Suqe* club" or graded male society on the Banks Islands in Vanuatu and variants of the *Dukduk* secret society on various

understandable that through such manifold coercive situations, which occasionally make obtaining money a necessity, a substantial dominance of the wealthy over the poor emerges, which, in places, is recklessly exploited. The poor must borrow and become dependent on their creditors. The idea that, just as for the rendering of any other service, compensation is to be paid for the lending of money suggests itself, and even among tribes whose internal monetary relations have developed relatively unaffected by external trade, specific interest payments must be paid by debtors. Practices of this kind are found on the Palau Islands,[26] as well as in the Bismarck Archipelago,[27] and on some of the Solomon Islands the unfortunate practice is present that a wealthy man can force others to borrow money from him, thereby bringing them under his sway.[28] In such cases, where the corrective effect of outside-money is missing, interest rates are often absurdly high. On the island of Nias, debt doubles annually, and it happens that members of an entire family become slaves for the initial debt of a single piece of brass wire.[29]

As money became more important and social standing increasingly depended on possessing greater wealth, it made less and less sense that the production of money took place within the tribe. As long as everyone was able to produce money in any desired quantity, the powerful position of wealthy men and chiefs could easily be undermined and the social structure of society upset. This was somehow bearable if the circulating medium was difficult to produce, like the *diwara* of the Bismarck Archipelago, the bulk of which originated in ancient times and has only insignificantly increased.[30] However, regarding many Melanesian shell monies we encounter a striking fact: in regions where the shells are found and manufactured into currency disks, this money is not used for transactions, but is instead exported as merchandise to neighboring areas and only put into circulation there. This phenomenon is well attested for on the Solomon Islands.[31] In Igbo areas along the Niger river, where cowrie shells are not accepted as payment, people engage in threading perforated cowries onto strings which are then exported to Bonny, where they circulate as money.[32] On the Caroline Islands, however, the prevailing currency is an ancient money of unknown origin that no one can replicate anymore.

---

islands of the Bismarck Archipelago (see also Schurtz 1902a: 334–38, 369–77). Dues were paid with *diwarra* or *diwara* on the Duke of York Islands, also called *tabu* or *tambu* by the Tolai of neighboring New Britain.

CHAPTER 3

Forms of Inside-Money

The defining traits of inside-money are its durability and the general appreciation it enjoys, which enable the accumulation of wealth. It does not need to be light in weight or generally useful. The first is unnecessary because the area where it circulates is limited, making its transport across long distances superfluous; the second is not necessary either, because its selection is frequently a matter of caprice and taste rather than practical reason. We can observe, therefore, grotesque excesses of inside-money, such as the curious stone-money of the Caroline Islands, which consists of hundredweight millstone-like pieces of aragonite that are brought over from the Palau Islands by way of daring oversea trips.[1] Finsch is probably correct in seeing them as colossal replicas of the small shell disks used as a circulating medium.[2] Despite having no practical use and rarely changing hands, these gigantic stones, especially the larger ones, are an embodiment of wealth and power; owning them confers a prestige that is unreservedly acknowledged by all.

When ancient communities of ownership* break down, all sorts of things that have real or imagined value can become "money" in a similar

---

*   Often translated as "community of goods" or "community of property," *Gütergemeinschaft* also refers to the sharing of material possessions by members of the early Church alluded to in the New Testament. It was a key term in the emerging secular socialism of the nineteenth century, made popular especially by Moses Hess (2004: 65) who defines it as the "communal ownership in all goods, internal as well as external, where the

way, insofar as power and prestige can be amassed and stored with and through them. In former times, before European trade directly encroached upon them, many African chiefs collected enormous amounts of ivory, without using it for any other purpose.[3] In Borneo, the Dayak regard antique Chinese porcelain pots, which are still sacred due to their relation to the cult of the dead, as the ultimate wealth.[4] In certain areas of Indochina and the Malay Archipelago, old bronze drums, possibly of Chinese origin,[5] step into this role, as also do, in other parts of the Archipelago, bronze cannons.[6]

All these partially or completely imaginary values,* which we can, in a sense, already call inside-money, are preceded by *living* monetary property, embodied in livestock and slaves. While the wealth invested in inside-money can easily lose its value as soon as a livelier economic life brings new ideas to a place and, as we will see below, remodels the nature of money decisively, the value of livestock and slaves, being fundamentally real, remains unshaken by such influences. More than anything, living beings are a directly interest-yielding and self-reproducing form of capital; the cattle's milk and the slaves' labor relieve the owner of the worries about his daily subsistence, and as long as there is sufficient grazing land and no outbreak of diseases, there are no limits to the multiplication of the livestock and thus the growth of wealth. Under certain conditions, the number of slaves can increase even more, as it does not necessarily have to be in proportion to the available arable land farmed by slaves; the use of large numbers of slaves in manufacturing and trade is quite common in less civilized countries. A chief from Nyangwe, along the upper Congo, opined to Cameron, in a naive but appropriate way, that it would be more prudent to deposit his trading profits in slaves than in ornament-money.[7] He explained that if he were to bring cowrie shells home, his wives would take them to adorn themselves, leaving him empty-handed; slaves, on the other hand, could be put to use immediately and would not lie idle, while the cowries would not yield any returns until he exchanged them for slaves.

---

treasures of society are open to all and nothing is tied to a person as exclusive property."

* Schurtz most often employs the term *Wert*, meaning "value," and the plural *Werte*, to describe something of worth, such as an asset, money, or other valued possessions. Given the nuanced nature of the term, depending on the context, we have sometimes translated it as "values," "assets," "valuables," "objects of value," or "symbols of value."

In the earliest periods of classical antiquity, we also find cattle and sheep serving as measures of value and wealth, as an inside-money in the proper sense, and they certainly also held some significance as a means of exchange, because they were widely appreciated. However, as should be clear from what has been laid out so far, it would be unjustified, based solely on this isolated fact, to place cattle-money at the beginning of the entire process. The cattle wealth of certain African tribes, like the Herero or the Dinka, developed even more starkly as inside-money, as they appear to be entirely inaccessible to trade; even recently, Emin Pasha felt obliged to resort to raids to secure necessary food supplies for his troops, as the natives were unwilling to part with their cattle at any price.[8] In contrast, the few available cattle among the Kru, which form an indispensable part of bride payments, constantly change owners and locations.[9]

While inside-money, due to its quality as a valuable property,* often appears in a static and unwieldy form, it is, as a measure of value, intimately related to the beginnings of measures and weights. It frequently catalyzes the creation of actual systems of measure and weight and likely contributes to the linguistic expansion of the numerical sequence. In present-day China, precious metals are almost always weighed, comparable to how gold circulated in unminted form in ancient Rome long after the introduction of silver currency.[10] On the other hand, the coins of civilized nations also supply certain tribes with a weight unit, such as in the well-known case of the Maria Theresa thaler which functions as the standard weight in Abyssinia.[11] A national coin that simultaneously represents a weight unit is the Thai and Burmese tical,[12] and the same holds for the shekel of the ancient Hebrews. Shell-money threaded on strings, on the other hand, necessitates the creation of a unit of length, a measure that some native Californians even tattoo onto their arm for permanent use.[13] More often, the arm itself is chosen as the scale, and it is very likely that the Californian measurement developed out of this imperfect one.[14] The method of measuring cloth used as money by the length of the forearm is still found, among other places, all over German East Africa. Even surface area units, whose origins overlap with the

---

*   We translated the complex term *Wertbesitz* as "valuable property" in most instances. It conveys the idea of "owned value" and relates to the concept of the hoard, yet we avoided "owned value" as it seemed too opaque. Conventional economic terms like "asset" or "store of value" appeared too modern. As its value is primarily contingent upon collective sentiments and dynamics, nor does *Wertbesitz* align with the idea of "personal possessions."

emerging division of land, are required where mats, furs, and blankets of specific sizes serve as measures of value.

Yet greater ingenuity becomes necessary when different measures of value coexist, and the complexities associated with multiple currencies begin to manifest themselves. Indeed, the persistent fluctuations in the value ratio of the two primary types of livestock-money, cattle and sheep, caused their replacement with metal currency in both Greece and Rome, initially a simple copper currency in Rome. However, because the most problematic fluctuations only occur once the money supply increases unevenly or decreases through external trade, we will postpone the discussion of these conditions for now.

If we look at how the development of inside-money takes shape under more or less normal conditions, a few simple principles reveal themselves: as the individual's independence grows in relation to the collective, so do claims to personal property, which he does not acquire through mere appropriation or through labor in the ordinary sense, but by transforming things according to his moods and tastes, that is, according to his deepest being, thereby associating these things with his personality. As a uniform appreciation for certain objects gradually establishes itself, these are eventually recognized as valuable property and universal measures of value. This recognition makes the individual's property more mobile; he can now use it more effectively to prevent imminent threats, to pay for a death sentence to be commuted, and to secure the goodwill and support of the powerful. As soon as certain people, particularly chiefs and priests, begin to pull valuable property towards themselves, social disparities develop and intensify,[15] while the possibility of breaking through social barriers by means of the new instrument of power also arises simultaneously. The more the ancient common property dissolves into private property, and the further the division of labor advances, the greater and more varied becomes the number of possible types of money, including those that no longer possess money's fundamental original peculiarities. Certain types of money serve more as valuable property, while others more as instruments of power or primarily as measures of value, thereby giving rise to all sorts of distinctions. Indeed, differently developed forms can exist side by side. *Inside-money, in its typical form, is therefore not yet a means of exchange analogous to that of contemporary civilizations, since the ability to circulate easily, thus its usability for trade, is not among its essential features. However, in essence and in practice, inside-money already closely resembles our money, or, to put it more precisely, it constitutes the primary root of our culture's monetary system.*

Sign-Money

Inside-money can perform its essential social functions even when it is too bulky, too precious, or too fragile to change hands frequently; but this immovability can, when taken to the extreme, prove to be cumbersome. In any case, the hoarding drive invariably brings huge amounts of money to a standstill and withdraws it from economic life, and this tendency, peculiar to and quite consistent with the nature of inside-money as an instrument of social power, often persists in the case of coined metal, resulting in an undesirable and nearly unresolvable chronic shortage of circulating coins. In South Asia, a significant percentage of circulating silver-money disappears annually, often because amounts of money that had been buried can no longer be located after the owner's death and are rediscovered only sporadically by chance; in Persia, a chronic shortage of small change is partially caused by similar reasons and partially because the Shah aims to accumulate as much metal currency in his treasury as possible.[1] Similarly, all cash ended up in the state treasury or was buried by its owners in Korea.[2] Even cowrie shells in Africa, despite their low value, have been buried and thereby withdrawn from circulation.[3]

Agreed upon valuables might become unsuitable for the smaller social tasks of everyday life. This shortcoming can be remedied in several ways, primarily by the emergence of smaller, less valuable types of money alongside the larger, more precious ones, which are then used for minor purposes, while the more unwieldy money is only mobilized on particularly significant occasions. The situation on the Caroline Islands offers a fascinating illustration of such a process, grounded in the principles of inside-money, which has been detailed extensively in Kubary's already mentioned work. The most valuable money on the island of Yap is the *gau*, a type of shell-money, which only changes its owner in the case of war and is kept as the highest treasure by the chiefs not because of its weight but because of its age, and because it was introduced in limited quantities from distant islands via a trade route that has long since vanished. It is followed in value by the already mentioned stone-money, originating from Palau, and available in pieces of varying sizes; a captain called O'Keefe, who brought numerous, unusually large blocks of Aragonite to Yap on his ship, amassed a fortune in this manner, while the value of the smaller stone-money of course declined significantly. The third type of money there and the actual small change are mother-of-pearl shells, which are strung on threads and considered the money of women. Larger pieces of mother-of-pearl shells imported from outside are deemed more valuable than the local ones and only chiefs are permitted to own them—an interesting example of how the nature of inside-money always accentuates social differences. All minor payments are settled with mother-of-pearl money, and it can be added to stone-money in the manner of small change;* for instance, a pig costs a small piece of stone-money and twenty mother-of-pearl shells.

The emergence of smaller types of money, suitable for circulation, is significantly driven and favored by external trade, as will be seen below. However, even within the tribe, there was the possibility of bringing about a more rapid turnover of otherwise stagnant wealth, at least to some degree, through the introduction of *sign-money*.†

Sign-money, seemingly epitomized in its most ideal form by our banknotes, is commonly considered an achievement of the most civilized societies. Yet, if we interpret the concept of sign-money not too

---

* We translated *Scheidemünze* as "small change" or "small coin." The term is difficult to translate as it refers to a kind of "fiat token coin," typically low-denomination coins whose nominal value is above their metal value and which were not easily convertible to gold coins or redeemable notes. *Scheidemünzen* were usually used for smaller purchases in internal markets and opposed to *Kurantmünzen*, whose nominal value corresponds to the precious metal value of the coin.

† We translated *Zeichengeld* as "sign-money" instead of "token-money." Schurtz conceptually redefined and broadened the geographic applicability of the term which usually only referred to European paper financial instruments in the nineteenth-century literature on economic history.

narrowly, this is totally incorrect. At its core, even inside-money in its simple ornamental form, is not much more than a recognized symbol of value that fulfills its purpose within a specific community but remains ineffective outside of it. Let us imagine that a tribe using shell-money is conquered and wiped out by another tribe that values cloths and pearls as measures of value: the shell-money treasures, so highly esteemed by its former owners, would likely not be noticed by the conquerors, much less be appreciated in the same way. A European would probably throw the precious money of the Palau Islands, which consists of pieces of old glass and pearls, onto a rubbish heap if it were handed over to him without further explanation; the Palau Islander of past times, who stood outside our cultural sphere, might have treated European coins in a similar manner or possibly kept them as curiosities. Insofar as the value of all inside-money is based upon arbitrary appreciations which are only accepted because they became solid and fixed over time, it is not at all inconceivable that even purely imagined values could fulfill the role of inside-money within specific communities.

To understand the nature and efficacy of sign-money, one must recall the gambling chips of Europe's civilized nations. A group of individuals, who trust each other's integrity and solvency, agree to forego cumbersome payments during a game and instead use tokens which are redeemed at the end of the game. In a society where a passion for gambling is particularly intense, tokens of this kind can even take the place of real coins; in Indochina, porcelain, lacquer, and clay tokens issued by Chinese gambling dens often serve as small change in local transactions, providing makeshift substitutes for scarce coins.[4]

Other kinds of sign-money have also been successful, such as the coin-like coupons issued by numerous South American horse-drawn bus companies, that resemble gutta-percha,[5] or our postage stamps, which were issued for a distinct purpose, but have come to serve as a popular means of payment. It is possible that certain prehistoric shards, which were discovered here and there in larger quantities and have often been considered money due to their uniform size,[6] might have actually been gambling chips that were temporarily used as coins.

It is obvious that the subjective value of sign-money depends on trust alone. If an entire tribe agrees to regard this or that object as a means of payment and if everyone is willing to accept it at its fixed value, it will circulate as a true and proper money. The term "agree" is chosen merely for the sake of brevity, as the process is typically less simple, although the result remains the same. If a chief or lord wields the necessary influence, he can arbitrarily create new means of payment to alleviate a shortage of small change. The history of Russia provides a very fine example. Instead of the impractical fur-money circulating throughout the empire, tsars of the earlier ages issued small, stamped pieces of the scalp of those animals whose furs were then stockpiled at the tsar's court and used for international trade alone. The attempt was extremely successful because confidence in the ruler was boundless, the objects of value represented by this sign-fur-money were in fact available, and trading with foreign countries, which would obviously not have scraps of leather foisted upon them, had little impact on the daily life of the people. When an enormous mass of furs had accumulated in the "Siberian Chancellery" in Moscow, the opening of trade with China in 1698 provided relief, and as furs flooded into China, so many Chinese products and commodities flowed back into Russia in return that Empress Anna, in the absence of cash, paid the salaries of her officials and officers with these commodities.[7] Perhaps inspired by this precedent, the Russian government later endeavored to withdraw all silver-money and replace it with copper sign-money twice, but both times this resulted in a catastrophic destabilization of Russian credit and commerce. Russia was no longer an isolated state that could rely on a pure inside-money of a symbolic kind; it was a part of Europe and influenced by Western European ideas about money. Sweden's attempt to alleviate its depleted finances by issuing sign-money failed in a similar way.[8] In England, it appears that leather sign-money survived well into the Middle Ages, and in Sicily, the Norman King William I attempted to withdraw all cash from circulation and replace it with leather coins in 1161, apparently not without success.*

The Russian leather-money is also noteworthy because it might offer advice on how to interpret older, enigmatic cases of leather sign-money, such as those of the Britons, Scandinavians, and others. If these types of leather sign-money did not also represent convenient substitutes for animal furs, they may have symbolized living livestock. Somewhat related is the practice of a Chinese emperor who, in return for gifts from his vassals, distributed small pieces of white deer hide instead of real money;

---

*   This historical episode seems apocryphal and first appears in a text from the sixteenth century. Contemporaries of King William "the Bad" did not mention his attempt to replace the *Sicilian taris* coins with leather currency, suggesting the story might be borrowed from an ancient myth about Dionysius I of Syracuse, often labeled a "tyrant" (Grierson et al. 1986: 127).

he kept a large number of these animals in his zoological garden.[9] The mysterious Carthaginian sign-money, made up of an unidentified fabric sewn into leather, on the other hand, might have had a different meaning and could have initially belonged to the types of "sacred" money to which we will return later.

As a very interesting transitional link, the cacao-money of the ancient Mexicans[10] makes the change from real to intrinsically valueless money palpable. Among the varieties of cacao, one had especially large kernels that produced the least appreciated cacao, which was only occasionally consumed. But interestingly it was precisely this variety that circulated as money while varieties of higher quality were considered commodities! A part of the value attributed to cacao-money was, therefore, already imaginary.

The simplest and most recognizable forms of sign-money generally arise from those types of money that have a practical purpose. Once the circulating monetary medium no longer meets its original purpose, it becomes a mere symbol of the actual fundamental value and thereby turns into sign-money. Fabrics seem most likely to undergo this transformation. The strips of cotton cloth circulating as money in the central Sahel are often so narrow that they cannot be reused in any useful way. In ancient Bohemia, pieces of cloth, impractical due to their loose weave, circulated as money,[11] and the small mats, which were in circulation in the lower Congo, and, bearing the government's stamp, even served as a general means of payment during the Portuguese era,[12] have been rightly labeled a form of paper-money by Klemm.[13*] The same is true for the mat-money in the northern New Hebrides, about which Codrington reports: "The mats are long and narrow, made for no other purpose than to represent value, and are in Aurora and Lepers' Island valued the more, the more ancient and black they are .... The mats are kept in little houses specially built for them, in which a fire is kept always burning to blacken them. Though these mats will buy anything of sufficient value to equal a mat, they are mostly used for buying the steps in the *Suqe* Club .... A

---

* The raffia mat-money used in the kingdoms of Loango and Congo was known as *macute* or *macoute*. It was frequently cited as an example of "primitive money" by Enlightenment political economists and philosophers such as Kant and Montesquieu. James Steuart (1767: 531), for instance, refers to it as "Angola money" and used it to illustrate his concept of the "money of account," though, in reality, the mat-money had varying denominations and fluctuating exchange rates.

rich man will keep fifty mats and more in his house, hung up and decaying, a proof of ancient wealth." Coote, who also describes the mat-money, has pictures of the above-mentioned smokehouses, and notes that a high-quality mat of this kind corresponds to the value of a full-grown boar along with its highly appreciated tusks.[14] Here we may have the most typical example of a primitive sign-money, which neither embodies a practical nor, as it is the case with adornments, a subjective value. Yet, it still performs all the tasks of a proper money, being a measure of value, a medium of exchange, and an embodiment of wealth.

In curious ways a kind of sign-money can even implant itself in relatively civilized circumstances, which emphasizes the already semi-blurred distinction between inside- and outside-money again more sharply. The full-value gold and silver coins from the South American republics, particularly from Peru, had been flowing out for a long time as a result of these republics' negative trade balance, and, in their place, inferior Bolivian silver coins unfit for foreign trade spread widely until they had almost become a mere inside-money.[15] This phenomenon is even more pronounced with the paper-money of states that are partially or fully bankrupt; such money always continues to circulate longest in the country's small retail transactions, which unavoidably require small change. This was observed, among other instances, after the large financial crash in Peru* where, in the absence of a better alternative, utterly devalued paper-money continued to circulate in petty market trades.[16] In difficult times, small-scale commerce even comes up with its own symbols of value that circulate within a limited area and adequately fulfill their intended function, as has recently been the case in Jerusalem where the *bons*† of Jewish butchers and bakers as well as the brass tokens from a guesthouse owner circulated as money.[17]

These types of sign-money rarely cause significant disruptions in a society's internal economic life; these tend to occur when a lord or chief introduces a sign-money clearly intending to replace circulating assets with his newly created money. The result is, of course, that all assets flow into the hands of the ruler, and if this process is further exacerbated by

---

*   The 1873 financial crash in Peru is often considered one of the nineteenth century's most severe episodes of hyperinflation and state bankruptcy.

†   The source, cited by Schurtz (Guthe 1882: 31), describes the *bons* or coupons as palm-sized paper slips bearing the Arabic numerals 10, 20, and 40 and the butcher's name in Hebrew. They were redeemable for meat, bread, and milk but "everyone gladly accepts them for cash at the souk."

the ruler making all his payments in sign-money, while demanding taxes to be paid in real types of money, then the most profound destabilization in the daily life of people is inevitable. As soon as real money is removed from economic life, international trade becomes extremely difficult and only possible in the form of barter; some remedy is introduced when the ruler claims a monopoly on foreign trade, thereby also drawing all the profits to himself. This approach consolidates the entire economic power of the people in the ruler's hands, certainly a very desirable situation for the ruler but only bearable for the people if they can meet their economic needs independently. Isolation from the outside world is both a precondition and an effect of primitive sign-money, which, by possessing this trait, proves that it is an extreme form of inside-money. On a grand scale, Kublai Khan, the ruler of the Mongolian empire, drove out metal-money with sign-money, specifically stamped pieces of paper, evidently following the Chinese example; Marco Polo's accounts indicate that the endeavor must have temporarily succeeded only because of the tremendous power and authority of the ruler, with the result of a vast accumulation of gold and silver in the Khan's residence.[18] Given the colossal size of the Mongolian empire, nearly all trade was internal trade and remained undisturbed by paper-money as long as its value was maintained by trust in the ruler's power. However, it appears that in the border areas engaging in foreign trade, this sign-money did not gain a foothold and was eventually completely withdrawn.

CHAPTER 5

Sacred Money

The argument thus far has sufficiently demonstrated that those objects which first differentiate themselves from others as property and subsequently as money do not possess a real and universally accepted inherent value, and that this value, if it is present, is a mere secondary aspect alongside a purely subjective valuation. The first and main cause of this subjective valuation, namely the transfer of someone's own essence into an object through artistic transformation in the broadest sense, has already been described. However, as the concept of money continues to develop, numerous other supplementary sources of value appreciation occur, leaving aside humanity's always active mimetic drive or herd instinct.

An object can be valued higher than others and eventually acquire the characteristics of a typical inside-money simply because it is rare and difficult, perhaps even dangerous, to obtain. For instance, the teeth of the sperm whale, which was rarely hunted successfully, served as a measure of value and a peace symbol in Fiji that chiefs used to send to each other;[1] they also circulate as money on the Gilbert Islands.[2]* Similarly, almost circularly curved boar tusks are highly valued and used as a means of payment in German New Guinea;[3] the red-feathered scalp

---

* Parkinson, a well-known German trader and ethnographer, whom Schurtz cites here, mentions the use of dolphin, not whale teeth. There is no direct English translation available, though a similar portrayal of the Gilbert Islands in Kiribati can be found in Parkinson's compiled work published in 1907 and recently translated (2010: 186).

of a woodpecker circulates among the Karuk, a Native American tribe in California;[4] and animal skulls, preserved as hunting trophies, are used among the Mishmi in Assam as both valuable property and money, facilitating trade with neighboring tribes.[5]

Occasionally, the entire money supply originates from an earlier time, as is the case with the currency of the Palau Islands,[6] or the age of individual pieces enhances their value, as we saw with the mat-money of the New Hebrides. While this shrouds the origin of money in mysterious darkness, it allows the imagination to play around with mythological fabrications, which in turn contribute to the extraordinary increase in the value of the circulating monetary instruments. The old shard-money of the Palau Islands, for instance, is believed to be of celestial origin,[7] produced by mythical birds and fish or found on the shores of mysterious islands; when exchanging particularly valued pieces, a premium must be paid to "appease the money's feelings," which is believed to possess a spirit.[8] Similarly, a mythical origin is attributed to the abalone shells of Northwest America.[9]

Yet, this is only one, comparatively infrequent, path by which money attains mystical attributes; another one leads directly back to money's simplest original form: *ornamentation*. Many objects worn as jewelry serve also as protective amulets, warding off all sorts of malevolent influences, especially the teeth, claws, and beaks of animals, strangely shaped roots and stones, mirrors, and the like. Other ornaments are supposed to have a calming effect on the ghostly beings that threaten humans because of their beautiful appearance or are believed to encapsulate a protective spirit within them.[10] Such ideas are often expressed in the decorative style of various objects. Shells, which stand out among primitive jewelry and money, are also used as amulets, especially in South Asia.[11] This valuation might stem from the resemblance of certain shells and snails to horns as the latter are popular objects used to defend oneself against malevolent influences. Even the best-known money shell, *Cypraea moneta*, appears to be used as a talisman, as a note by Isert suggests.[12] Lander observed a sorcerer in the Yoruba region who had draped himself with an immense mass of cowries, an estimated 20,000 pieces, probably not merely for personal adornment but driven by mystical motives.[13]

It is understandable that while such ornaments, to which different mystical beliefs are attached, do not lose their special meaning even when they find a more general use as a means of payment,[14] certain coins, like the well-known *Georgstaler*, can, conversely, transform into talismans.[15] In Mecca, the center of Islam, old Venetian gold coins featuring depictions of Christ and Mark the Evangelist serve as the most popular amulets for women,[16] and in Tibet, Indian rupees quickly became vernacular partly because the image of Queen Victoria was taken for that of the Dalai Lama, which conferred a special mystical value upon the coins.[17] Thereby, a new impetus for the accumulation of money emerged. However, we have to consider yet another cause for the emergence of "sacred" types of money, namely the direct or indirect relation of money to the dead or to the cult of the dead.

The extent to which concerns about conditions in the afterlife stimulate the acquisition of wealth must be briefly mentioned. On the lower Congo, large quantities of mat-money were formerly collected to enshroud the bodies of the deceased, turning the corpses of noblemen into shapeless bundles;[18] in the hinterland of Angola, European cotton fabrics are still acquired and hoarded for the same purpose.[19] Money that is placed into the graves of the deceased is lost for the living, as nobody wants to possess it, and even if it is accidentally unearthed, it is deemed to be of no value.[20] Even the money inherited by relatives is often treated with a certain wariness, because the claims of the dead, who are commonly imagined to be envious and vengeful, are not to be easily dismissed. The New Britain custom of distributing shell-money at festivals of the dead in honor of a relative is possibly based on this sentiment;[21] at least, as will be shown below (chapter 6), there is no shortage of similar customs suggesting that donating the deceased's property is preferable to keeping it for oneself. Given that all money that circulates for long has at some point in time been in the possession of those now deceased, notions of the uncanny and the magical easily attach themselves to it. Generally, inherited and precious items from earlier times easily acquire a certain sacredness and value far beyond the ordinary; one example is the Imperial Regalia of the German emperors without which no coronation was deemed truly valid and whose possession was therefore most actively strived for by contenders to the throne. Such valuables, which embody the dignity of the ruler, are also not unknown among indigenous peoples.

But the cult of the dead itself can even directly create new objects of value. The old Chinese porcelain vases, the possession of which is the ultimate aim of any Dayak, most likely owe their tremendous esteem to the fact that they were used to store the remains of the deceased and are now attributed with supernatural powers.[22] We are thus dealing with a kind of relic worship, also familiar to European civilizations. The remains of the dead themselves can also become valuable property and even a means of payment through this process. Whether Hernsheim's isolated statement that the remains of dead noblemen wrapped in mats circulate as money on Yap holds any truth may be left aside.[23] In any case, the skull cult, which directly evolves from ancestor veneration,[24] can easily lead to the appreciation of amassed skulls as valuable property that can also be transacted under certain circumstances. "The possession of heads," says Ling Roth about the northern Dayak, "gives them great consideration as warriors and men of wealth, the skulls being prized as the most valuable of goods."[25] According to an older report, human skulls did indeed serve as money among the Batak.[26] The fact that some of the notorious captains who long terrorized the South Seas massacred harmless natives to use their heads for the purchase of sandalwood may be mentioned as demonstrating a genuine business spirit.[27]

It is not always possible to discern the causes behind the mystical value attributed to some types of money, but its frequent presence seems undeniable. Old glass beads that are preserved in parts of West Africa as testimonies of a former trade are associated with numerous legends and superstitious beliefs.[28] The peculiar copper plates that are valued to the utmost on the northwest coast of America and passed down through generations, have a specific cult dedicated to them. Each individual shield has its own name and house and receives regular meals. No woman is allowed to enter the house. Almost every tribe has a legend about their copper plates' origin; some say someone received them when he visited the man on the moon, others that they come from a chief residing in the ocean and so on.[29] This cult is much less developed among the northern tribes.[30] Many Melanesian types of money are ambiguously intertwined with the concept of *tabu* or *tambu*, a concept that likely originates from the cult of the dead.[31] Shell-money is stored in "*tambu* houses," the large *diwara* rings of the New Britons are called *tambu alolei*, and in New Guinea, we find that the word *tautau* is used for money.[32] Sperm whale teeth are also called *tabua* in Fiji, and a "spirit of the whale tooth" is mentioned.[33] The Northwest American practice of using the corpses of slain slaves as bait when fishing for the Dentalium mollusks used as money likewise suggests some mystical idea.[34]*

---

*   Schurtz cites Aurel Krause (1885: 185) for evidence of this practice of using "the body of a slave especially killed" to serve as "bait." Krause himself refers to an account by a Russian naval officer named Davidof from Kodiak Island in Alaska which was originally published in Russian in 1810 and translated to German in 1818.

The above-mentioned copper plates also served as a kind of bell, and it is plausible that the mysterious sound they emit when struck significantly contributed to their perceived sacredness. For the same reason, Chinese bronze drums may still serve or have served as valuables and money in the Philippines, and elsewhere in Indonesia and Indochina.[35]

Among advanced peoples, money attains a degree of sacredness in a completely different way. Just as money was given to the spirits of the deceased, valuable things, precious metals, and eventually coined money were also sacrificed to the gods. It may be mentioned in passing that at times gods are deemed more conservative than humans. In Italy, for instance, the raw copper pieces that previously circulated as a means of payment were still presented as offerings long after the introduction of minted coins.[36] Enormous treasures thereby gradually accumulated in temples; some, like those at Delphi, eventually succumbed to the inevitable fate of being plundered or carted away by unscrupulous rulers or enemies of the state. Even though a portion of these treasures, in the form of precious equipment, remained as immovable property within the temple premises, the priesthood was nonetheless eager to lend their surplus to reliable individuals at an appropriate rate of interest, while fairs and markets held in the vicinity of these sacred sites further facilitated the circulation of the accumulated assets. "The gods were the first capitalists in Greece, their temples were the earliest banks," concludes Curtius, who has devoted an intelligent treatise to these issues.[37] Notably, the priests of Aphrodite Urania, whose temples stood in all trading ports, introduced monetary transactions and credit, and they were also the first to stamp metal pieces with the image of their goddess, thus giving rise to the beginnings of coinage. Priests of other deities also distributed minted coins early on as medals and mementos during competitions, and when the state finally regulated the monetary system, it was natural that the temples continued to serve as mints, and that an aura of the sacred remained intrinsic to all processes associated with minting. According to Curtius, "all Hellenic money was sacred, and the place of mintage holy ground." And, therefore, even during the time of Alexander the Great, no sovereigns were depicted on coins, only the images and symbols of the gods.*

---

* The beginning of "coinage" remains a complex topic but Herodotus already proposed the idea that coins were first minted in Lydia, Asia Minor, during the seventh century BCE. These "first" coins were made from electrum (an alloy of gold, silver, and copper), and usually contained the city's unique emblems such as the reclining lion of Miletos, but the Lydian

Stopping the degeneration.

What is true of Greece can justifiably be asserted for parts of the Orient as well, particularly for Phoenicia, which preceded Greece in matters of commerce and frequently served as its role model. It can be assumed that the money changers, whom Christ, as a defender of a higher worldview, drove out of the Temple in Jerusalem, had a certain historical right to be there: money, trade, and religion had a good relationship with one another in antiquity,[38] and a glimmer of sacredness even radiated from the dirty small coins that wandered from hand to hand in retail transactions or gathered on the money changer's table.

King Croesus (561–546 BCE) was the first to introduce separate gold and silver coins (Wallace 1987). Kroll's article (2008) on the use of weighed bullion clarifies the place of metals and other materials not in coin form in monetary history (see also Ridgeway 1892; Servet 1984).

Accumulation of Property by Individuals Countermeasures

Even in places without actual inside-money, all things considered self-reproducing or durable types of valuable property can obviously be acquired and accumulated by individuals in disproportionate quantities: this accumulation of property is precisely one of those seeds from which real money evolves. In Polynesia, where an inside-money circulating as a means of payment is almost nonexistent, there are still disparities in wealth, which manifest not only in the unequal distribution of land but also in the fact that the wealthy begin to invest their excess income or the surplus created by the labor force they command in specific things, particularly in enormous amounts of bark cloth (*tapa*)[1] or in mats which are even inherited from generation to generation and valued according to their age in Samoa.[2] This last aspect already shows the emergence of that imaginary valuation so characteristic of proper inside-money: true forms of money have a value that does not lie in their practical use, but is created and sanctified by provenance; they are, in a sense, the aristocracy of possessions. Compared to useful goods, these items confer a different kind of influence to those who own them in great quantities. They guarantee not just the possibility of a comfortable life, but real power and, in some circumstances, something akin to sacredness.[3] These instruments of power do not always accumulate in the hands of the leaders of the people, the chiefs and lords, or at least, for reasons to be discussed shortly, they do not remain with them permanently. This opens a path for others to gain dominance through the ownership of money, particularly for the priesthood in whose temples immense treasures often accumulate without reentering the transactions of daily life. This is not limited to civilized nations. The inhabitants of the small Polynesian island of Funafuti, for instance, bring their wealth, beautiful mats and mother-of-pearl fishing hooks, en masse as offerings to the temple, and all foreign valuables that somehow reach the island follow the same route.[4] Similarly, other members of the tribal community are also able to gain various forms of influence and undermine the previous social order by accumulating money.

Inside-money, in a narrower sense, differentiates itself from other real assets primarily because, at least in the realm of imagination, there is no barrier to its multiplication, allowing the hoarding drive to unfold its full force. Someone gripped by it no longer works to merely sustain his life and to make it comfortable, but to *acquire*.* In just this one word, the immense significance of this process for the development of humanity is expressed. The fact that the acquisitive sense does not remain confined to individuals but is inevitably transmitted to the entire social organism is ensured by the social transformation brought about by wealth: everyone is now compelled to join the competition for property or he will be pulled into the vortex created by one of the newly emerging centers of power and property, where he will need to work hard to be able to live at all. For the property owner, no temporal limit constrains his view on the perpetual increase of his wealth; the civilized man hopes that his accumulated riches will ease his children's existence and allow him to live on and enjoy life through them; the primitive man, in contrast, believes that he will have access to all the goods given to him in the grave, even in the afterlife. Thus, he too knows no bounds to acquisition.

---

* *Erwerben*, "to acquire," is rendered by Talcott Parsons as "profit-making" in his translations of Max Weber (1922: 48; 1947: 191). Parsons adds that he chose the term "profit-making" because "Weber is here using the term in a technical sense as the antithesis of *Haushalten* or the subsistence household economy. 'Profit-making' brings out this specific meaning much more clearly." Parsons thus translates *erwerben*, *Erwerbstätigkeit*, *Erwerbsmittel*, as "profit-making," "profit-making activity," and "means of profit." On the other hand, *Erwerbssinn*, *Erwerbstrieb*, *Erwebsstreben*, and *Erwerbsleben* have been translated in various editions of Weber's *Protestant Ethic* ([1905] 2001: xxi) as "acquisitive sense," "acquisitive instinct," "the pursuit of wealth," and "capitalist commerce."

It hardly needs saying that this new phase of social existence does not meet general approval. If the primordial purpose of the community and its members was to keep themselves in balance with surrounding nature, and if any labor that went beyond the absolutely necessary was voluntary, now the prospect of an endless, essentially enforced, activity and toil emerged, which was rooted in and incentivized by the inequality of anticipated rewards and completely shattered the old communism and irretrievably annihilated natural life's heavenly comforts. Naturally, this threatening process was not clearly recognized, it was only intuited, and, in full accordance with one of the most important anthropological laws, people semiconsciously made use of customs that originally served another purpose to counteract the menace. They thereby managed to control the excessive accumulation of wealth in many different ways, and it is quite instructive to take a look at these methods.

In a way, wealth itself inherently tends towards self-destruction, as it often leads to the degeneration of its owners. Many of those who seem to have acquired, alongside their wealth, the prospect of infinite pleasure, perish miserably in their ill-fated attempt to savor all the pleasures now within reach. This applies even more to the *descendants* of those driven by the desire for acquisition. The degeneration and "stupefaction" of noble lineages or wealthy merchant families, which is one of the most common phenomena in Europe, is found in exactly the same way in China, where the great fortunes of merchants often vanish into thin air within a brief period due to the carelessness and hedonism of their children or grandchildren.[5] The propensity for gambling, which is not unique to many members of civilized societies but also highly developed among, for example, the natives of North America and in numerous other primitive societies, contributes to the disintegration of wealth; however, several other factors also counteract the accumulation and, especially, the inheritance of money.

For once, remnants of the ancient communism remain alive enough for a long time to effectively block attempts to amass as many assets as possible in a single hand. And in places without an actual system of debt and interest, the powerful individual, into whose house the tributes of the people flow, has indeed little choice but to "represent" by way of his wealth: in other words, to allow the people to participate in his indulgences. His gain lies entirely on a moral level, for although the hoarded treasures provide him with a certain moral superiority, they only become fruitful when he generously distributes them to his friends and followers, winning their hearts and thereby establishing real power based on loyal devotion. This view was quite common among the old Germanic tribes: the ideal figure for those troops that turned Rome to dust was not the chief or king who brooded over his treasures like a dragon, but the generous army leader who held an open table, gave away treasures to his followers eagerly, and tied the fearless and stalwart fellows to himself with abundant gifts. Even in the Middle Ages, the most glorified quality of the lords, besides bravery in war, was *Milte*, an inexhaustible generosity, and poets like Walther von der Vogelweide never get tired of demanding and lauding it. Speaking with high praise of the Landgrave Hermann of Thuringia, he says:

In the Landgrave's service, loyally I stand.
I am always to be found beside the finest lord in the land.
Though other lords display their generosity
none as steadfastly: he was so and still is.

And the generosity of Leopold of Austria elates him:

One saw the young prince give,
as if he no longer wished to live.
Many marvels were performed with goodness then.*

The Native American tribes of the Missouri Valley held exactly the same views: generosity earned respect and power, and the grand gift-giving feasts, just as glorious deeds in war, were painted on the cloaks worn during ceremonial occasions.[6] The rulers of Tahiti also almost spent more than they earned; all profit was quickly distributed among their followers.[7] If mutual jealousy and rivalry come into play as well, the most fantastic squandering of possessions develops. Even the destitute Aboriginal Australians of Queensland like to distribute gifts to their peers to make a name for themselves.[8]

Generosity is practically an imperative when property consists of consumable substances prone to spoilage, but it wanes when durable

---

* Walther von der Vogelweide was one of the most renowned *Minnesänger*, medieval German poet-singers who performed romantic songs and comical praise poetry. There are no available English translations, so these have been translated into comprehensible English with a basic rhyme. To facilitate cross-referencing, we mention the first and last lines of the poems in the German original here: "*Ich bin des milten lantgraven ingesinde,*" and "*Dâ wart mit guote wunders vil begangen*" (Vogelweide 1864: 214, 169).

types of money embody wealth. The Tongan chief Finow had well understood this danger when he spoke disparagingly about coined money in a conversation with Mariner: it would lead to the piling up of wealth "instead of sharing it out, as a chief ought to do."[9] This is reminiscent of a scene in Goethe's satire "Gods, Heroes, and Wieland":

> Hercules: We had the bravest fellows among us.
> Wieland: What do you call a brave fellow?
> Hercules: One who shares what he has. And the richest is the bravest.[*]

"Sharing" can even become a duty. Such views are still, for instance, dominant among the civilized Kalaallit of West Greenland. "Even if he had a faculty for laying up riches," says Nansen, "which he very seldom has, his needier fellows would have the right to enforce a claim upon such of his possessions as were not necessary for himself. Thus we find in Greenland this unfortunate state of things: that the European immigrants, who are in reality supported by the natives, often become rich and live in abundance (at any rate, according to the Eskimo ideas), while the natives themselves are in want. The Greenlander has not even unrestricted rights over the game he himself secures. There have been fixed rules from time immemorial according to which it is divided, and there are only a few sorts of animals which he can keep pretty well to himself and to his family."[10]

The communist countermeasures against wealth generally do not endure, and their effect is uncertain. Certain kinds of property seem to favor greed directly, especially cattle farming, which can literally turn into a hoarding addiction. Bülow, for instance, claims that the remarkable greed of the Herero can be explained by their excessive appreciation and multiplication of livestock.[11]

Nevertheless, there are additional barriers that counteract the unlimited accumulation of movable property. A whole set of ideas and customs stemming from the cult of the dead leads to the constant

---

[*] Schurtz does not provide a footnote to this line from Goethe's famous comedic play *Götter, Helden und Wieland* written in 1773. The play transports the author Christoph Martin Wieland, who represents the established literary scene of the German Enlightenment, into the company of ancient gods. In the referenced scene, Hercules, a symbol of ancient virtues and values, discusses heroism and bravery with Wieland, focusing on the deployment of excess (Goethe 1868, 16:170).

destruction or rendering useless of valuable property, and thereby prevents hoarded wealth from being inherited and growing into a dangerous instrument of power. This later purpose is achieved somewhat accidentally and has nothing to do with the original rationale that ultimately relies on the belief that the deceased does not give up his rights of ownership but jealously guards over his property to ensure that no heir makes use of it. To avoid the wrath of the dead who roam around as ghosts, one places their belongings in the grave or on the funeral pyre, or leaves a hut with all its contents untouched to decay. Essentially, the intention is to put the accumulated property at the disposal of the dead, but as the property is actually eliminated, its threatening social impact is abolished as well. At times, the sole purpose of a person's profit-making and accumulating activity is to gather sufficient means for the journey into the afterlife and for life in the land of souls, and no one would consider withholding even the smallest thing from him after his death. As an example it may be mentioned that "King" Powhatan in Virginia had filled a treasure house with furs, copper, glass beads, and so on, but all these treasures were intended to be used solely for his burial.[12] In some parts of West Africa, the wealthy hoard enormous amounts of fabrics; after death, the corpse is wrapped in these until a shapeless bale emerges for which a special house must be built.[13] In the Yoruba region, after the death of a chief, one of his wives destroyed all of his valuable property and shell-money and then committed suicide;[14] along the Niger, in Idah, during Lander's visit, a great sacrilege took place when the new chief unearthed the shell-money treasures buried with his father (reportedly enough to fill seven to eight houses) and used them for himself; the indignation about the son's abnormal act was widespread.[15]

The actions of the chief of Idah may not have been guided by any deeper motives. Nevertheless, it is clear that although the destruction of hoarded money and valuable property may mitigate a social danger, it also, on one hand, often reduces national wealth in an undesired way and, on the other, diminishes the amount of circulating money to an inadequate level. Civilized states have therefore felt compelled to legally control this practice; a decree by Emperor Theodoric forbade his subjects to give money into the graves of the dead,[16] and a Japanese law from the year 646 ordered that "gold, silver, copper, and iron shall not be placed in the grave .... Pearls and gems shall not be put into the mouth; shirts made of pearl and armor made of precious stones shall not be put on the corpses. All this is done by foolish people."[17]

The destruction of property is not limited to gifts to the dead, whose last remnants are the well-known coins for the dead which are generally meant to pay the fare for the departed's passage.[18] Equally extraordinary are the destruction and squandering of valuable property, particularly livestock and food, during those grand festivals of the dead that evolved out of sacrifices and are, among some peoples, not only an effective obstacle to the accumulation of wealth but have turned into economic calamities. Even the parsimonious Herero slaughter large amounts of livestock without hesitation at the death of a chief,[19] and among the Balanta all the deceased person's livestock is immediately killed and consumed.[20] These festivals of the dead are most developed in the Malay Archipelago, where a family is completely ruined in the case of frequent deaths,[21] or where (as on the Kai Islands) a funeral is often postponed for a long time because the necessary and extraordinary means have not yet been raised.[22]

At times, the destruction of property is circumvented in a peculiar way, yet always without letting it fall into one hand alone, thereby effectively preventing the potentially dangerous accumulation of fluids and diverting them to individual nodes without causing harm to the social organism. This is achieved by having all members of the tribe, and not only the descendants, act as heirs, apparently under the assumption that the large number of participants confuses the dead person's vengeful feelings or intimidates him; ancient communist ideas are, of course, also effective here.

A transition to this idea is illustrated by the custom of the Bubi people on Fernando Pó who give the deceased his jewelry but distribute his shell-money and other belongings.[23] The property of a deceased Inuit is a common good.[24] The Motu near Port Moresby ceremonially adorn the dead with all his jewelry, but take these valuables away from him at the last moment and distribute them among those present.[25] Generally, the distribution of large gifts at festivals of the dead is a custom in many and diverse regions; in New Zealand, however, it has degenerated into a kind of legal plunder,* which gave rise to very strange effects in the past.[26]

---

* Raymond Firth (1929: 126, 394) described the Maori custom of *muru* as a "compensation for offences by the confiscation of property" through "a plunder-expedition which stripped the offender of all his goods." Firth notes that European observers often misunderstood *muru* "as the acme of lawlessness" and proposes that, in contrast, it was "regulated by a well-defined code of procedure, and was very useful as an instrument of social justice."

All these different countermeasures against wealth are often, as already mentioned, only semiconsciously applied. But at least in one location where inside-money is prevalent, namely on the *Caroline Islands*, several such measures are united and adhered to in a conscious way, because the little money that exists must constantly remain in circulation.[27] Here, the chiefs in whose hands money naturally accumulates are not only fined in the same way as everyone else at every suitable opportunity, but they must also disburse particularly large amounts which returns the money to the public. Within the community, the circulation of money is already sufficiently ensured through the numerous dues and penalties to be paid in cases of insults, purchases, diseases, and deaths, but, additionally, it is stipulated that no one is allowed to use the objects of practical use that he himself produces; instead, he must sell them and replace them with purchased ones. All prices are firmly determined by convention; in this way inside-money achieves the purpose of maintaining social equilibrium within the community quite well, in stark contrast to outside-money, whose unimpeded operation often leads to uneven wealth accumulation among individuals. At the same time, this example shows in what sense the typical inside-money is only a precursor to European currency money, without resembling it completely.

While the restrictions on wealth noted so far have developed from the actions of the owners or their heirs, the material obstacles that arise from the nature of primitive money itself must also be mentioned. First of all, the amount of available money is often not significant and its value not too great; it is thus not even possible to hoard it in dangerously large quantities. Furthermore, many types of primitive money do not last indefinitely, they are "treasures moth and rust destroy,"* such as the old mats in Melanesia and Samoa, all kinds of fabric-money, and base metals. Lastly, they are often too bulky and unwieldy, and of too little intrinsic value to be accumulated en masse; to make excess wealth impossible, Sparta famously retained its inconvenient iron-money, even when the other Greek states had long since moved to silver currency. Particularly the nomad, who constantly changes his whereabouts, cannot possibly carry heavy masses of money with him; his wealth are the herds grazing around his tent. This certainly does not improve his position: livestock diseases threaten his property, and the envy of warlike neighbors keep him in a state of constant unrest. After all, the robber is often the

---

*   The expression paraphrases Matthew 6:19. The original line in the Luther Bible is a bit longer, suggesting Schurtz is quoting from memory.

ultimate remedy against wealth, and it is not only Schiller's Karl Moor*
who believes he is fulfilling a higher mission, his robber philosophy is
quite familiar to many bandits in Italy or Spain.

---

*   Karl Moor, the central character in Friedrich Schiller's 1781 play "The
Robbers" (*Die Räuber*), is a young nobleman who becomes the leader of
a band of robbers after being wrongfully disinherited by his father. The
character is a typical "noble bandit" (Hobsbawm 1981: 43) characterized
by the initiation into outlawry not by crime "but as the victim of injustice"
who turns to banditry to "right wrongs" and redistribute wealth or "take
from the rich to give to the poor."

CHAPTER 7

The Influence of External Trade
Primitive Forms of Exchange
Outside-Money

As already mentioned, inside-money is the primary root of the monetary system in general, and if it develops normally, it can fulfill the greater part of those tasks the money of today's civilized nations is meant for. Yet, especially in its typical forms, which are always appropriate for the mentality of a specific tribe or society, it loses its value and purchasing power if it has to take over the tasks of external trade as well. Expansion of a people's horizon and of their commerce therefore must have a trans-formative impact on the conditions of their monetary system in mani-fold ways. Perhaps none of the forms of inside-money that we can still study today has remained entirely unaffected by external trade, but the impact has occurred in very different ways and with very different results.

We should first recall the already mentioned fact that even though inside-money frequently circulates as a real monetary instrument only within a tribe, it is often not produced by the tribe itself but imported as a commodity from a neighboring area. The difficulty of obtaining it, one of the most desirable characteristics of inside-money, is thereby to some extent guaranteed. Once a means of payment has been accepted by the tribe in question, it behaves entirely like a proper inside-money, serving both commerce and social tasks within the society, while it loses its significance for any trade outside of it. Each district in Abyssinia, for instance, possessed its own pearl-money, which had its own name, and was brought into the country through trade but circulated as money only within the district;[1] the agate beads circulating as means of payment in Darfur and Kordofan came from India. But especially pearls in their double meaning as jewelry and money are subject to the influences of fashion, which is stimulated by the abundant supply of the trade and changes in capricious ways. This causes rapid changes in pearl fashions and thus in the internal currency among numerous African tribes. Even in Tabora, where the pearls are hardly used as jewelry anymore and only serve as a means of payment, these capricious changes in taste are still at work.[2][*] Many voyages to Africa have failed partly because the pearls taken along proved to be worthless, either because they did not appeal to the taste of the natives or because a change in fashion had occurred since the last contact with European travelers. The unfashionable pearls can then at best be given away as gifts, but they cannot be used for buying and trading.

Not infrequently, traders will deliberately seek to promote the widespread introduction of inside-money and thereby temporarily achieve great profits; the consequence, of course, is usually a rapid devaluation of the money and the breakdown of the small social organism in whose veins suddenly too much blood circulates. The cowrie shell has probably been exported most frequently as a commodity that then circulates as money in certain districts, in this case generally without too many adverse effects, since the territory in which it was accepted tended to expand simultaneously. The vast quantities of cowries that are in circulation in West Africa all originate from the Maldives or East Africa and have been introduced in countless shiploads by European merchants. China must have obtained its cowrie shells, which formerly served as money there, via seaborne trade as well. It has already been mentioned how European captains enabled the inhabitants of the Caroline Islands of Yap to acquire enormous pieces of their favored stone-money. The dentalium-money of the Northwest American natives was completely devalued through the massive import of shells and now only serves as jewelry; the shell itself was only brought into the country after attempts to introduce

---

[*]   Schurtz cites an account by Hans Hermann Graf von Schweinitz (1894: 91), a German colonial officer in East Africa, who describes the "capricious" changes in types of "pearl money": "Here, fashion regulates financial conditions; for instance, when an excessive import threatens to cause a devaluation, suddenly a type of bead that is scarcely available becomes fashionable and thus valuable" (see also Pallaver 2009: 24).

porcelain imitations had failed.[3] Even the copper plates used as money in the same area were imitated, but the new pieces are not nearly as highly valued as the authentic old exemplars.[4]

Such imitations and counterfeits have often been attempted, though usually without success, as the fraud was quickly detected and the peculiar relations of inside-money to customs and superstitions prevented their adoption. European traders had the most luck with an imitation of the wampum-money of the North American natives,[5] which was initially very scarce and perhaps only became a universally used means of payment in some places as a result of the substantial supply from outside, although it then also gradually lost its value; wampum made from porcelain was at first rejected but gained acceptance over time.[6]

Yet, trade will always tend to create its own media for commercial transactions, which it usually does not take from the inside-monies but selects from among the trade goods. This is how new types of money develop which do not have to fulfill social tasks within the tribe but are just meant to facilitate the exchange of goods and enable clearly structured prices. The fact that this development does not proceed too quickly and in many cases has not progressed beyond the initial stages is explained by the emergence of trade relations in general, which we should now have a cursory look at.

Nearly everywhere where we find primitive tribes engaged in trade, we observe reciprocal gift-giving taking place as an important and indispensable practice. This is particularly noticeable in Africa, where European travelers definitely need to expect this custom. In newly explored areas, whose inhabitants have not yet been influenced by European or Arab business principles, trade recedes to the background altogether; the traveler sends his gift to the chief who in turn reciprocates with food and shelter, that is, if the natives are at all benevolent. *Such gifts are not considered part of a business deal but are seen as signs of friendship.* Here a cultural stratum reveals itself to us in which one cannot speak of trade in the strict sense; instead, only two types of encounters between neighboring tribes are conceivable: the warlike, where loot is violently sought, and the amicable, which is reinforced by the exchange of gifts. Conditions of this kind can still be observed today. Gisborne asserts of the Maori that they originally had no concept of trade. Rather, being at war was the normal state, while tribes related in friendship gave each other gifts; in addition, hospitality, in the broadest sense, was practiced. Micronesian trade has also been described as an exchange of gifts, and Sievers says of the Arhuacos: "They accustom themselves with difficulty to the system of buying and selling; with gifts, one achieves more than with money, although they gladly take the latter, but bury it or pass it on to their women in the form of necklaces."[7]

Remnants of this idea are to be found particularly in Africa, and a few examples may illustrate how trade in certain places has not yet become what we usually understand it to be. The beginnings of the Arab trade with the Wahuma states* described by Emin Pasha are very instructive: "It is the practice in Unyóro, as well as in Uganda, for every trader on his arrival to present about the half of his goods, especially powder, lead, shot, and guns, to the ruler, who in return places at his disposal a house and garden, and gifts of cattle and fruit, and finally, at his departure, makes him a present of ivory, the value of which usually amounts to five times that of the original present. Both parties make a good thing out of the transaction; the Arab, whoso capital brings him a return without any trouble to himself, and the king, who pays nothing for the ivory, since it is supplied by his faithful subjects."[8] The Arabs thus skillfully adapted to the prevailing ideas. According to the testimony of Leo Africanus, the merchants who arrived at the court of the king of Gaoga[†] practiced a very similar gift trade by handing over their goods to the king and receiving counter-gifts worth double or triple in value.[9] Likewise, in German Southwest Africa, the first merchants to appear in the country seem to have opened trade through gifts. "The golden age of Omaruru," Bülow says, "was the sixties and seventies. Back then, white hunters had lavishly gifted away guns and ammunition, clothes and alcohol, horses and food, to receive ostrich feathers and ivory in return that were brought in through the hunting activities of the natives. Now

---

*   The British explorer John Hanning Speke coined the term "Wahuma states" during his travels to Lake Victoria. The term implied an historical continuity between East African societies near the Great Lakes and the so-called "Hamites" whom the discredited and racist Hamitic hypothesis described as descendants of Ham, a son of Noah in the Bible. Hamites were thought to constitute the pastoralist ruling class of "lighter-skinned herders," such as the Bahima, Tutsi, and sometimes Oromo as well (Kiwanuka 1968).

†   The existence of the kingdom of "Gaoga" or Bulála is still debated. Those who claim that it existed believe that it was a non-Muslim kingdom between Lake Chad and Darfur founded by an African slave and related to the Kanem–Bornu empire (Fisher 1975). For a critical overview and evaluation of European sources for Africa before 1900, see Fage (1994) and Jones (1987).

the trade has declined and consists of the retail sale of food and clothing for oxen and sheep."[10] Generally, the custom of opening and also closing trade with gifts has been preserved as a remnant of the exchange of gifts, so that business deals, wherein pleasantries come to a halt even in Africa, are, as it were, framed by this older amicable custom. In former times, reciprocal gifting was a prelude to any barter trade along the Gabon,[11] and similar East African customs are reported in detail by Reichard.[12] At the Niger river delta, the opening of a commercial transaction by presenting gifts to the chief was termed "break the trade."* Again and again we find the custom that the less powerful or the stranger who has a distinct request, gifts first, and the other then reciprocates the gift as he sees fit; the gift is at first just a pure sign of peace and friendship, its material value of secondary importance.

While taxes arise from the voluntary gifts of subjects, trade duties and tariffs gradually emerge from the gifts of foreigners and travelers, to which we will return soon. These, too, are basically remnants of an older social innovation, which is adapted to entirely new purposes and can sometimes bring about the very opposite of the original custom. The old custom reoccurs in other remnants as well. For instance, in Kano, it was customary for the seller to return two percent of the paid purchase price to the buyer because such a gift would bring blessings,[13†] and the strange practice of always paying only half of the agreed price prevalent amongst the Yoruba is likely based on similar views.[14‡] The Luba frequently give

---

*   Schurtz uses the English expression "break the trade" in the original German publication without a specific bibliographic reference. The expression "breaking trade" was a pidgin English term for a trade custom in Bonny and seems to have been mentioned for the first time by Richard Jackson in 1826 (1934: 78, 83; see also Jones 1963: 94, 108–9).

†   In Schurtz's reference, Dixon Denham (1828: 284) calls it a "universal practice" and equates it to the "luck-penny": "the seller returns to the buyer a stated part of the price, by way of blessing, as they term it." Denham furthermore notes that these trade practices were facilitated by the cowrie: "I may here notice the great convenience of the cowrie, which no forgery can imitate; and which, by the dexterity of the natives in reckoning the largest sums, forms a ready medium of exchange in all transactions, from the lowest to the highest."

‡   This remark refers to customs observed by the British explorer Richard Lander in the Yoruba Muslim walled town of "Chaadoo." Lander (1832, 1: 136) also adds a detail suggesting that this custom was a form of bargaining between strangers: "after a buyer has agreed to pay a certain sum

something extra when completing a trade deal, called a *mukallo*.[15] The traffic in gifts has transformed into a form of social courtesy in Tibet and Mongolia, where certain silk scarves are exchanged frequently as greeting gifts.[16] On the other hand, guest gifts often become a heavy burden, and even offer a pretext for extortions that utterly destroy the beautiful essence of the old custom; Kyrgyz chiefs in Turkestan used to demand that caravans make a stop at each one of them and reciprocate their hospitality with disproportionate counter-gifts.[17] In Africa, trade is often completely paralyzed by the exorbitant gift demands made by the chiefs.

However, trade relations can, it seems, not only develop from the amicable traffic of gifts, but also from its opposite, war. That is, in principle, to be expected.

Just as the individual person in primitive conditions must be capable of solving a multitude of tasks from which the civilized person is spared by the division of labor, early human societies are organisms that must satisfy their essential needs self-sufficiently and have to stand their ground in the struggle for survival by adapting to natural conditions. These conditions, whether favorable or unfavorable, create differences that arouse envy and desire: one tribe has fish-rich waters at its disposal, another has an abundance of certain fruits, a third exploits salt deposits or salt springs. Typically, the initial thought is usually not to obtain a share of these special riches peacefully but to try to seize them through bloody fights. Tacitus reports about the battle between the Chatti and the Hermunduri* that erupted over the ownership of saline springs and ended with the victory of the latter; the sources of highly prized earth pigments in Northwestern America were often battled over in wild fights, and

---

for an article, he retracts his expressions, and affirms that he only promised to give about half the sum demanded. This has occasioned violent altercations between our people and the natives; but it is an established custom, from which there is no appeal."

*   The battle between the two Germanic tribes of the Chatti and the Hermunduri in 58 AD is known as the "Salt Battle" (*Salzschlacht*, Tacitus, Annals, 13.57.1). Schurtz often alludes to Tacitus's proto-ethnographic account of the "Germanic tribes." By the late nineteenth century, an increasing number of German medievalists and anthropologists made great efforts to revalorize "Germany's tribal origins" on the margins of ancient "civilization" (Kipper 2002: 272) and aimed to gain insight into the Germanic tribes bordering the Roman empire across the Rhine by finding "parallels" (Bruns 2009: 21) with the societies being colonized in the modern period.

the famous sacred pipestone quarries, once the common property of all surrounding native tribes, were ultimately violently seized by the Sioux.

Weak tribes facing the threat of being wiped out by stronger ones often attempt to buy mercy by surrendering a portion of their possessions, and from this one-time gift, a regular tribute can easily develop. If the more powerful tribe offers counter-gifts, the seeds of trade are present, albeit a form of trade always inclined to suddenly change back into its initial form. In some regions, development has not even advanced this far. Bock characterizes the conditions in the interior of Borneo, perhaps somewhat sweepingly, with these words: "Trade in its most embryonic state hardly existed, for no man would think of giving anything in exchange for an article that he coveted; sufficient for him that he was strong enough to gain it by force, by murder if need be, and to keep it by virtue of his reputation as a Head-Hunter."[18] Venyukov aptly portrays how robbery and other forms of exchange sometimes maintain a close relationship: "In the eyes of the Turkmens, a stranger is essentially a legitimate victim, and if he appears rich enough and defenseless, his fate is to be robbed .... In those cases where the Turkmens cannot rob a stranger, their aim is to extract as much money as possible from him in trade, to beg for as many gifts as possible, or finally to steal from him."[19] Robbery and violence appear as the more honorable acts, while buying and paying seem low and unworthy. Moltke's habit of paying for everything during the military campaign in Kurdistan provoked the disapproval and astonishment of his Turkish companions, for "whoever is able, takes without money."[20]

A form of trade that takes place without previously establishing friendly relations is the "silent trade," during which buyers and sellers do not interact closely or at least do not communicate with each other. It has been frequently described since ancient times and still occurs today. Whether this form develops directly out of warfare or is an independent method of initiating trade relations shall not be examined here: it is entirely possible that in some places, it is also a regression from more advanced conditions. More undeniable is the close connection between piracy and trade as it is typical of the ventures of aspiring seafaring nations, be they called Phoenicians, Portuguese, or English.

In all these beginnings, a need for a general medium of exchange and measure of value is not yet clearly present, and inside-money, if it exists at all, has nothing to do with the matter.

A look at the primitive native tribes of Guyana described to us vividly by Everard im Thurn teaches us how regular trade relations can even emerge in simple circumstances without money: "Each tribe has some manufacture peculiar to itself; and its members constantly visit the other tribes, often hostile, for the purpose of exchanging the products of their own labour for such as are produced only by the other tribes. These trading Indians are allowed to pass unmolested through the enemy's country.... Of the tribes on the coast, the Warraus make far the best canoes and supply these to the neighbouring tribes.... In the same way, far in the interior, the Wapianas build boats for all the tribes in that district. The Macusis have two special products which are in great demand amongst all the tribes. One is the ourali used for poisoning arrows and the darts of blow-pipes, the other is an abundance of cotton hammocks.... The Arecunas [Pemon] grow, spin, and distribute most of the cotton which is used by the Macusis and others for hammocks and other articles. The Arecunas also supply all blow-pipes: for these are made of the stems of a palm which, growing only in and beyond the Venezuelan boundary of their territory, are procured by the Arecunas, doubtless by exchange, from the Indians of the native district of that palm," etc.[21] The inviolability of the traders nicely points to the emergence of trade from the exchange of friendship gifts. Even the initial forms of intermediary trade are already present, for the exchanged goods are not exclusively used for one's own needs but are brokered again to other tribes. A quite lively trade is thereby carried out in the simplest manner, without the need for money in our sense.

Perhaps the conditions in Guyana have stalled at this stage for so long because inside-money never emerged among the local native tribes, likely due to their unique social development. In a sense, the products with which the various tribes trade may be referred to as the beginning of their money, but of a type of *outside-money*, the fundamental significance of which is as a means of exchange. A Macusi who crafts many cotton hammocks thereby indeed obtains money with the help of which he can buy all the products of neighboring tribes and, because of the middlemen, even those of more distant tribes. The character of commodities as a kind of money becomes even more pronounced in the actual intermediary trade: someone can, for example, amass a lot of salt, which he neither produced himself nor intends to use, yet it still has a value for him; if the commodity is durable, highly desired, and easily marketable, it will be gladly accepted in payment and will eventually be equated with inside-money, wherever the latter has already developed into a determining factor of social life. Thereby, the barrier that proper inside-money had established between individual tribes and nations collapses, the previously separate tasks of inside-money and out-side-money blend into one another, their capacities complementing each other. The result is what we recognize as the money of civilized nations, that indispensable tool of social life and trade. Occasionally this fusion can still be observed in its initial stages. On the Caroline Islands of Yap, there exists a well-defined inside-money that circulates only within the social community, whereas in the external trade with neighboring islands mostly bundles of turmeric are used, which are exchanged for loin belts, sails, twine, and jewelry made of coconut shells. As an intermediate form between inside- and outside-money, specific ornamental and other items can be used to purchase commodities in internal transactions, yet they are not able to fulfill the crucial social tasks of an actual inside-money. Sometimes, however, such a hybrid money [*Mischgeld*] is added to the original inside-money as a supplement during payments, foreshadowing further developments.

With the introduction of outside-money, the number of types of money increases by countless practical goods. However, the boundary between the concepts of commodity and money will always remain more or less blurry in the case of outside-money. Then again, certain types of inside-money that gain widespread acceptance can spread over vast areas and, in addition to their other qualities, acquire value as a medium of ex-change, thereby becoming a more ideal form of money than any of those that arise from pure barter could ever become; the concept becomes blurred when money is transformed into a mere ornament or vice versa. In contrast, inside-money that does not achieve a significance for trade will gradually perish. When considering questions of this kind, it must not be forgotten that reversions are possible, and simple forms of com-merce may resurface in the absence of a better means of exchange, even in places where developments had long gone beyond that. For example, in Paraguay, during the time of the Jesuit missions, the scarcity of cash caused the resurgence of organized barter. "Should a Spanish woman," writes Dobrizhoffer "need tallow candles, she sends along her black slave a basket with some cotton, tobacco, Paraguayan tea, sugar, and salt. The seller of the candles then selects whatever they like from it, but according to an established law of prices.... The prices of all natural productions are regulated by the magistrates, and are diligently learnt and observed both by the seller, and the purchaser."[22]

The second source of the concept of money can now be succinct-ly defined in the following manner: *Outside-money is a commodity that is universally welcomed, easily sold, can be stored for a long time due to its*

durability, and, as a consequence, is capable of serving as a medium of com-
mercial trade. As it transforms into a measure of value and a valuable prop-
erty, it becomes an ideal type of money; this usually happens through the in-
fluence of inside-money which in turn is soon displaced or transformed and its
effectiveness extended by outside-money. Combined, they constitute money as
it is understood by true civilizations.

The fusion of outside-money with inside-money, or the transformation of the former into the latter, often proceeds in a way that parallels
the emergence of inside-money. While the gifts to the powerful, and
subsequently fines and taxes, initiate the circulation of alienable private
property which is then finally transformed into a general means of payment, the voluntary and involuntary gifts of the traders, namely the market and customs duties, bring substantial amounts of certain trade goods
into a chief's possession, and thereby enable, like inside-money, the accumulation of wealth and the filling up of the treasuries of the powerful.

The fact that tariffs initially appear in the innocuous form of gifts
can still be confirmed in many cases; certain tariffs may, however, also be
regarded as moderations of the original practices of complete plundering
or even killing. The European merchants on the African coast at first
gave gifts to the chiefs for permission to trade with their subjects but
these voluntary offerings soon became customs (*coutumes*) and in effect
regulated tariffs, while only minor and variable supplements maintained
the pretense of voluntary gifting. Among the taxes that had to be paid
in the gum trade along the Senegambian coast, one emerged that carried
the classic name of the "obligatory gift,"[23]* a term which, in only two
words, illuminates the whole course of the development.

Alongside market duties and transit fees, we also find other taxes
that predominantly burden the merchants and are common among both

---

*   Given the importance of the idea of the "obligatory gift" or *present forcé*
which Schurtz translated from French into German as *erzwungenes*
Geschenk, it is important to note that the source for the term is René
Caillié, a French explorer in Saint Louis in the 1820s. The English translation of Caillié (1830: 134) uses the term "forced present" to describe the
taxes payable to a local middleman on the mouth of the Senegal River.
Along the West African coast in the seventeenth and eighteenth centuries, such *coutumes, kumi* or *comey* were a common kind of rent arranged
and instituted between Europeans and local political rulers and brokers.
While in effect these payments were tributes, Europeans insisted that they
were voluntary gifts, often calling them simply a "gift" or a "*dash*" (Law
2004: 107; Martino 2022: 83–84).

primitive tribes and civilized nations. These include bridge and ferry tolls, for which there is abundant evidence from Africa. For instance, Serpa Pinto observed the bridge tolls in Benguela's hinterland;[24] according to Eberstein, it is customary in the coastal region of Kilwa;[25] and, per Büttner, in Angola.[26] Close to Zaminiasso in the land of the Bambara, there was a bridge which was overseen by two guards who collected tolls from all foreigners while the locals were exempted.[27] Ferry tolls are mentioned even more frequently, multiple times by Cameron,[28] from Dahomey by Reade,[29] and so on. Additionally, other privileges must be paid for as well. Büttner, for instance, had to pay a toll for using a newly constructed road,[30] Lander found that road tolls were customary in Yorubaland,[31] and in the land of the Bari, Marno was asked to pay a fee for the shade of a tree under which he camped.[32] A payment for the permission to graze salt grass was noted by Passarge from Adamawa.[33]

It is self-evident that traders initially pay their dues with a portion of the commodities they carry with them, even more so because these commodities must already be partly considered a kind of money. However, occasionally, there are also demands for all tariffs to be paid in the form of a very specific commodity which forces the merchants to always carry some of this commodity, even if they do not intend to trade with it. In some places in East Africa, for example, the toll must be paid in the form of iron hooks, all of which come from Usukuma [along Lake Victoria];[34] even in medieval Germany ship tolls were required to be paid in specific goods, irrespective of what the cargo of a ship consisted of.[35] In the hinterland of Senegambia, tariffs must usually be paid in cowries despite the fact that other money substitutes exist and no stable currency yet dominates; certain toll stations on the lagoon of Whydah only accept rum as payment,[36] and so on. The desire to gradually separate the more suitable kinds from the overwhelming abundance of types of outside-money and to allow only a limited number to simultaneously serve as a measure of value and a means of exchange shows itself to be efficacious everywhere.

CHAPTER 8

The Fusion of Inside- and Outside-Money

Like nature, the mind does not make abrupt leaps but instead gradually adapts to new conditions and only learns to fully exploit the tools it has forged over time. Money is one such tool that is still occasionally employed with a degree of clumsiness, and it unmistakably bears the traces of its double origin, even though it has long since become something unified. While a main characteristic of civilized money is that it allows one to buy anything available for sale, this attribute is, actually, artificially conferred upon it or applies primarily to certain types of money, specifically to precious metals or, in countries operating under a pure gold standard, exclusively to gold. You cannot buy a house with a mountain of small copper coins, as no one is obligated or inclined to accept such an inconvenient mass of money; it is only through the ability to convert these small coins into precious metals that the unlimited purchasing power of money is established, at least within the confines of a given state.

This difficulty, which is one of the main causes of our endless currency controversies, is also not adequately overcome by less civilized societies. It is mainly outside-money that suffers from this difficulty, but inside-money is not exempted either for the simple reason that it often exists in such large and indivisible pieces that it can only be used to purchase very valuable things. As a result, its owners can easily find themselves in a position analogous to a man who has no loose change and only a thousand-mark note that no one can break. This often gives rise to a specific custom where certain objects can only be bought with particular types of money, making it entirely pointless to offer small change for them, for instance cowrie shells instead of cattle.

As mentioned above, it is the system of outside-money which struggles far more frequently with this difficulty as the notion of commodity is, more or less firmly, always linked to outside-money. The thought that they are not actually buying but bartering remains firmly entrenched in the minds of traders. Even where a regular currency has been introduced, people may find it difficult to become accustomed to the universal means of payment. In the days of Heinrich Barth, cowrie shells were accepted as a measure of value in Bornu, and Maria Theresa thaler were in circulation. Yet despite this, it was at times very difficult to purchase food in the Kukawa marketplace. "A small farmer," Barth writes, "will on no account take his payment in shells, and will rarely accept a [Maria Theresa] dollar: the person, therefore, who wishes to buy corn, if he has only dollars, must first exchange a dollar for shells, or rather buy shells; then with the shells he must buy a *kúlugu* or shirt; and, after a good deal of bartering, he may thus succeed in buying the corn. The fatigue to be undergone in the market is such that I have very often seen my servants return in a state of utmost exhaustion."[1]

Conditions are more favorable when specific commodities are brought into a simple and stable ratio with one another. An interesting primitive example of value measurement is when a certain measure or weight of one commodity is equated to the same measure or weight of another, essentially weighing one against the other. Burton notes that in his time, sea salt on the African coast was sold in exchange for an equivalent amount of holcus (grain), and, likewise, for an amount of holcus, the same amount of cowrie shells was dispensed.[2] If salt production yielded little, its price was simply doubled. The fact that valuable things were once "worth their weight in gold" among us is evidenced by this still commonly used saying; in West Africa, this practice can still be observed, especially with the rare aggry beads, which are often paid for in gold equal to or even double their weight.[3]

One frequently encounters the belief that certain valuable commodities can only be acquired with a means of payment whose significance somehow corresponds to them: it is not the quantity of money that is crucial, but the quality. In Africa, slaves, in particular, often cannot be purchased with the common means of exchange used to procure daily necessities. Instead, very specific and precious objects, such as ivory, firearms, or gunpowder, must form at least part of the purchase price. When purchasing ivory in Angola, gunpowder and firearms are also indispensable.[4] According to Lichtenstein, the Tswana did not sell cattle for tobacco but demanded iron or cloth in return, while their cloaks could only be exchanged for live cattle.[5] The sacred pots of the Dayaks can only be acquired with gold dust, agate stones, and slaves.[6] Spears among the Chagga are almost only exchanged for firearms, other goods are only reluctantly and exceptionally accepted.[7] A Black man who wanted to sell his knife to Büttner for fabrics was prevented from doing so by his fellow villagers.[8]

According to Nebout's testimony, the Dakpa along the upper Ubangi River also adhered to an unusual system of trade: they sold their manioc exclusively for a specific kind of fabric, but if one wanted any other food products, one had to offer cowries, pearls, lead, and other types of fabrics.[9] In West Africa, gold cannot be readily exchanged for just any commodity. In the region of Bambouk, for instance, one cannot receive gold in return for glassware, tobacco, cloves, or liquor; these items could only be bartered for food products. Gold was handed over exclusively in exchange for fabrics, salt, or amber.[10]

The emergence of such idiosyncrasies is unsurprising and tightly intertwined with the evolution of outside-money. When one tribe interacts with another, exchanging, for example, pots for arrows, the firm idea easily takes hold that arrows must always and everywhere be paid for with pots, and that other goods or types of money are unsuitable for this purpose. In Australia, a particular tribe exploits a greenstone quarry and accepts spears in exchange for the much-desired mineral; thus, greenstone can only be purchased with spears.[11] Another tribe trades its eels for roots, a third one swaps its shields for belts, and so someone who has caught many eels can indeed amass a large quantity of edible roots in return, but certainly not a shield. A delightful illustration of the emergence of such exchange values is found in Köler's account: sailors landing at the mouth of the Niger River typically take with them one of the abundant grey parrots found there, and since they customarily exchange these birds for one of their shirts with the locals, a steadfast tradition has developed that a red sailor's shirt must be paid for with a parrot.[12]

That inside-money can also develop in a similar manner has already been noted. Finsch describes three types of shell-money from New Ireland, each possessing a distinct purpose: "The first type (*kokonon luluai*) is used in everyday transactions and is most often used for peacemaking. The natives are known to carry strings of this shell-money, tied to their hair, to make small purchases or to ransom themselves in the event of an attack.... The second type (*kokonon*) is of higher value than the preceding one and is predominantly used to acquire women.... The third type is the most valuable; it is particularly used for the purchase of women, canoes, and so on, and is valid along the entire northwest coast."[13] According to Kubary, similar conditions prevail on the Palau Islands, where the various types of ancient pearl-money have been brought together into an intricate system: "Taro, oil, syrup and tobacco are paid for with the usual *mor or kaymó* and *matál o adolóbok*. But if you want to buy a sail, you have to give an *adolóbok* of the important type; if one is to pay the matrimonial contribution dictated by custom, one must give a money-piece corresponding to one's social rank, and so forth in numerous matters. Therefore, if someone has a payment to make, he must ask all his acquaintances and eventually secure a loan against collateral."[14] To change or convert a large piece of money is an intricate affair, sometimes nearly impossible.

The lack of a stable unit of value causes all sorts of attempts to somehow regulate the prices of the more valuable items with the help of the different types of money that coexist next to one another independently, usually in such a way that the purchase cannot be made with a single kind of money but that several must be present in certain proportions. Fischer, for instance, paid the Maasai 30–40 pieces of iron wire rings, 10 brass wire rings and 40–100 strings of beads for each ox, and 1½ loads of iron wire, 50 brass wire rings, 600 strands of beads and 14 war cloaks as an atonement for several Maasai who fell in battle.[15] The prices in the ivory and slave trade on the West African coast tend to be even more diverse. "On every tooth [tusk], if it be of any considerable size," says Wilson, "he must have so many muskets, kegs of powder, brass pans, copper rods, wash-basins, plates and gun-flints—the whole number not being less than thirty—and these must be reduplicated in proportion to the size of the tooth. If it should weigh as much as one hundred pounds, the seller would not expect less than ten of each of these articles. This is what is called the 'round trade.' It is carried on by a most tedious, and, to novices, a most annoying process."[16]

In this way, the concept of money becomes elusive again, as the countless means of exchange which captivate and confuse the Black Africans' desire prevent the emergence of a stable measure of value, while European types of money remain incomprehensible to the natives because of their own conventional value. In such circumstances purely imaginary measures of value emerge, which are a particularly developed feature of West Africa but occur elsewhere as well. Typically, a certain quantum of the most frequently traded commodity is used to set the unit, named arbitrarily, and then used as a measure for all values. The best known, the *kru*, which serves as a measure of value in Cameroon, originally corresponded to a specific amount of palm oil, and has recently been equated to twenty German imperial marks;[17] on the coast of Sierra Leone the *bar* ("iron bar") was introduced as a measure of value, and the *round* from Cape Mesurado to Cape Palmas.[18] In Bonny the *bar* was in use (called *intsche* or *atsche* by the natives)* and corresponded to, for instance, five heads of tobacco or a flint rifle;[19] in Angola, the *piece* (*peça*) or *long* was common.[20] At Ambrizete, the *musket* (*fusil*) is the exclusive measure of value for the ivory trade, while for other commodities, it is a piece of cotton fabric.[21] This odd method of calculating prices, which certainly requires an infinite patience during trade negotiations, is not entirely unappealing to the European merchant as he can reap significant profits by skillfully manipulating the price ranges, while never showing the Blacks the cards he is dealing with. A related phenomenon is observed amongst the Gilyak who imported the Chinese unit of value and calculate according to it without using the Chinese coins on which it is based.[22] The many different imaginary measures of value among civilized societies in part developed out of these simple beginnings.

---

*   We retained the Germanized spelling *intsche* or *atsche* from Schurtz and the original source, Hermann Köler (1848: 148), a German doctor and philologist who lived in Bonny in the 1840s. The exact meaning of the term is unclear but Köler refers to it as an "imaginary unit of value" equal to about a British shilling or a gallon of palm oil.

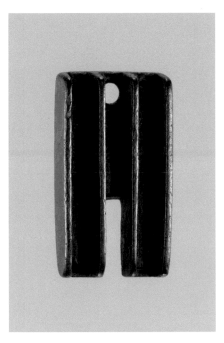

Figures 1 and 2. "Coins," Han dynasty, China, 206 BCE–220 CE (The Metropolitan Museum of Art, Gift of Edward B. Bruce, 24.13.20 and 24.13.17, CC0).

Figure 3. "Coin depicting two calves' heads," Lesbos, Greece, 550–440 BCE (The Art Institute of Chicago, Gift of William F. Dunham, 1920.2953, CC0; see p. 49).

Figure 4. "Ear spools," jewelry made of spondylus shell, Colima or Jalisco, Mexico, 200 BCE–200 CE (The Art Institute of Chicago, Maurice D. Galleher Endowment, 2001.152.4-5, CC0; see p. 112).

Figure 5. *Perlenkette,* "Bead necklace," France, Merovingian period, c. 600 (Staatliche Museen zu Berlin, Museum für Vor- und Frühgeschichte, Klaus Göken, Va 5737, CC BY-SA 4.0; see p. 126).

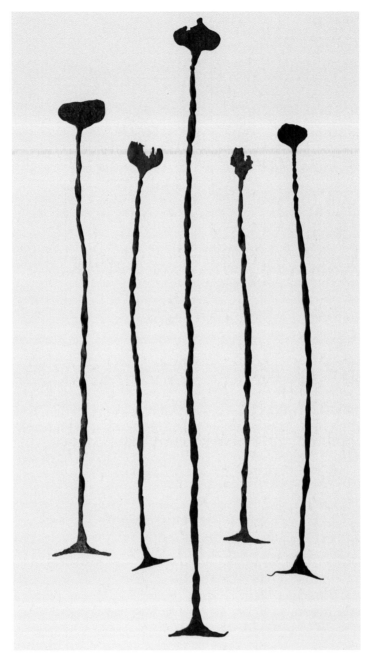

Figure 6. "Kissi iron currency," West Africa, 1863 (Collection of the Smithsonian National Museum of African American History and Culture, 2008.10.6.2, CC0; see p. 145).

Figure 7. "Measuring shell money," Tolowa, California, c. 1923 (Library of Congress, Edward S. Curtis, photographer, https://www.loc.gov/item/97507102/, CC0; see p. 49).

Figure 8. Treasure or pottery filled with *nzimbu* (*Olivancillaria nana*, from the island of Luanda), found during excavations carried out at the supposed site of the ancient city of "Congobela" near Kinshasa, c. 1950 (HP.1956.15.8158, collection RMCA Tervuren; photo H. Goldstein, s.d. © Sofam; see Dartevelle 1953: 154).

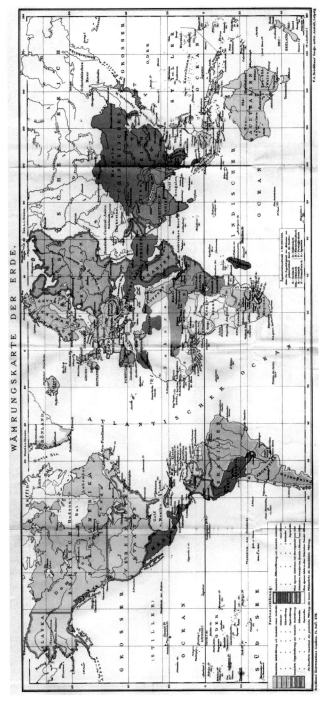

Figure 9. "Currency map of the world." This map illustrates the dominant ideas of different monetary standards globally in the 1890s. Areas in gold represent various types of gold standards, predominantly in Europe and the British Empire. Regions in blue indicate different kinds of silver standards, especially in Asia. Within countries, variable color outlines signify bi-metallism or a discrepancy between the legal standard and the actual currency in use. Areas left blank represent regions without their own money, or without the circulation of foreign coins" (Brockhaus 1897: 1013).

Figure 10. Raffia "Status cloth," Kasai, Congo, c. 1850 (Cooper Hewitt, Smithsonian Design Museum, 18411465, CC0; see p. 135).

Figure 11. Yap stone money, Caroline Islands (Courtesy of the Penn Museum, Gift of Dr. William H. Furness, P1744; see pp. 47, 52).

Figure 12. "Basket." Quiggin (1949: 47) ascribes this to the Bambala, Congo, and says they were used for carrying *nzimbu* shell money (Department of Anthropology, Smithsonian Institution, E169131; see p. 116).

Figure 13. "Copper ingots," Luba, Congo, 1200s–1600s (National Museum of African Art, Smithsonian Institution, Gift of Tom Joyce, 2002-10-3, CC0; see p. 131).

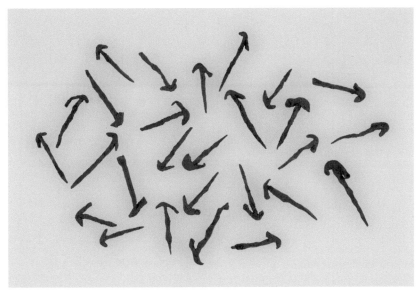

Figure 14. "Iron currency," shaped like a miniature arrow, Akwa, Nigeria (Copyright Pitt Rivers Museum, University of Oxford, 2017.74.4; see p. 148).

Figure 15. "Paper money," printed by Hall & Sellers, Philadelphia, 1776 (New York Public Library, EM4262-730, CC0; see p. 52).

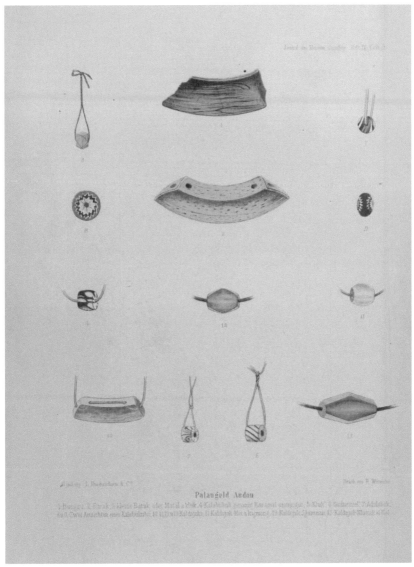

Figure 16. *Palaugeld*, "Money from Palau," Micronesia, c. 1873 (Kubary 1873: Table 2; see pp. 53, 60, 157).

Figure 17. "Iron spade blade currency," Zande or Bongo, Central Africa, c. 1850s (Copyright Pitt Rivers Museum, University of Oxford, 1898.61.2; see p. 148).

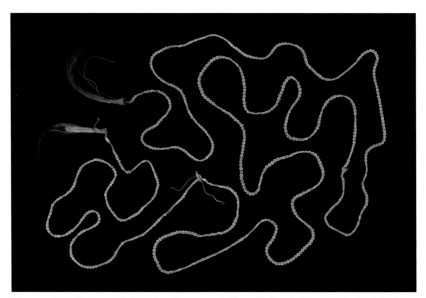

Figure 18. "String of shell bead money," New Ireland, Bismarck Archipelago (Copyright Pitt Rivers Museum, University of Oxford, 1900.9.1; see p. 89).

Figure 19. Maria Theresa thaler, Günzburg Mint, Austria, 1780 (Wikimedia Commons, CC0; see p. 129).

Figure 20. Maria Theresa thaler "Cross Pendant," Ethiopia (Courtesy of The Spurlock Museum, University of Illinois at Urbana-Champaign, 2012.03.0699; see p. 127).

Figure 21. "Tlingit copper," Haida Gwaii, British Columbia (Courtesy of the Penn Museum, 29-31-1; see p. 62).

CHAPTER 9

Overview of Primitive Money
Ornament-Money in General
Shell-Money

Several varieties of primitive money have already been mentioned. To truly grasp their development, it is essential to provide a systematic overview, which undoubtedly presents its own challenges, especially when striving for a clear understanding of the conditions. The phylogenetic classification into inside-money, outside-money, and sign-money, and so on, does not directly offer an overview of the entire subject matter, because in many cases it is still impossible to trace the development of individual monetary instruments and to assign them a definite position within this framework. Alternatively, a simple classification based solely on the external attributes of the means of payment is too superficial, as it conceals the internal relations and leads to a flawed understanding. The term "iron-money," for example, encompasses not only crude metal bars but also hoes, shovels, spearheads, and even ornamental iron beads—things that have only their material in common. Nevertheless, for many types of money emerging from trade, a classification based on material is quite appropriate, and for others, it is at least preferable for the time being.

It is thus probably best to strike a middle ground.[1] We can, first of all, sort out the historically well-defined group of types of ornament-money, which, with very few exceptions, either are a type of inside-money or have emerged from one. If this broad category is to be divided further, then it is only proper to do so by material differences, resulting in subcategories such as shell-money, pearl-money, metal-money, and so forth. Apart from ornament-money, the second broad category encompasses all *useful* items (hence it might aptly be termed *use-money*), which could further be divided into foodstuffs, luxuries, various utensils and tools, and even includes livestock- and slave-money. Its internal opposition to the first category is based upon the fact that it predominantly developed out of outside-money. Between these two main categories, we find *fabric-money*, which is sometimes primarily considered as an adornment and sometimes more as a useful commodity, and, consequently, is more or less subject to the changing influences of fashion and sentiments, influences that have a striking effect on jewelry and, partly, on the money derived from it. With this in mind, we can attempt to provide a very brief overview of primitive types of money.

As we turn our attention to ornament-money and, more specifically, to its most important variety, *shell-money*, another differentiation becomes essential. Shells used as ornaments and money either remain unprocessed (except perhaps for simple perforations for the purpose of stringing) or are transformed into disks or other arbitrarily shaped pieces through more or less tedious forms of work. The difference between these subcategories is not very clear, but undeniably significant.

The most famous and most widely distributed among all minimally or completely unprocessed shells is the *cowrie shell*, which is actually a type of sea snail, *Cypraea moneta*. The fact that it managed to conquer such an extensive territory is even more remarkable considering that it originally could only be harvested in a single location in the Indian Ocean, near the Maldives from where it could be exported to the remotest regions, because that location was near an ancient maritime trade route. In more recent times (according to Al-Masudi, not later than the tenth century), a shell closely related to the cowrie, *Cypraea annulus*, began to be extensively traded in large quantities from the East African coast, and circulated especially in West Africa, valued on par with *Cypraea moneta*. Cowries were also reportedly exported from Bima Island near Sulawesi in the East Indian Archipelago[2] and, according to Antonio de Morga's accounts, from the Philippines from where they appear to have been sent primarily to Indochina.[3] Details regarding cowrie extraction in the Maldives can be found in the older writings of Arab scholars, later complemented in desirable ways by François Pyrard. Branches or coconut leaves were thrown into the water for the snails to attach themselves to, and harvesting was done twice a month; the cowries were packaged in baskets of twelve thousand and predominantly exported to Bengal where they were exchanged for rice. In the time of Ibn Battuta, they were sent in bulk to Yemen and from there probably to the Sahel. Within the Maldives, the shells circulated as small change, while more significant payments were conducted with silver. It is very remarkable that the cowrie never served as money on the neighboring Malabar coast and in Ceylon.[4] There is no doubt that the export of cowries from the Maldives has been in full swing since ancient times, involving, apart from the islands' inhabitants, Arab traders from early on and likely also the Chinese. Later, the Portuguese seized this lucrative trade, transporting the shells not only to Siam and Bengal but also to the West African coast. The Dutch soon followed suit, replicating their success. Most recently, German merchants also extracted substantial profits from this trade, especially when they introduced the cheaper East African shells en masse to the West African coast, until the inevitable devaluation occurred and ended the business.

There is already a small body of literature about the cowrie. Volz's "History of Shell-Money"[5] deals almost exclusively with it, Andree and Ilwof dedicate a part of their essays to it, and Hertz has recently dealt with the topic quite extensively.[6] At this point, it may suffice to provide a brief overview of its past and its current distribution which do not entirely coincide; over time, the cowrie has lost vast provinces of its domain but in return has conquered new ones. It is very odd how the shell's appreciation as money, on the one hand, and as an ornament, on the other, relate to each other. While the cowrie is no longer used as a means of payment in some regions, it persists as an adornment. Elsewhere it was introduced as a popular ornament before it was thought to be used as money, and in yet other areas, it is practically only used as money and is not at all popular as an ornament.

It may be mentioned in passing that the cowrie circulates as money in two forms, namely in the form of individual pieces counted or measured by volume, and as strung together on threads. The first form appears to be more common and is currently found, for instance, in Bengal, Siam, the Hausa states, and several parts of West Africa, where colonial trading posts, as in Porto Novo, employ native women as shell counters. The second one was once common in China but also appears quite frequently in Africa. Stringing a specific number of cowries together somewhat corresponds to the minting of our metal-money, also in the sense that a sum akin to "seigniorage" is often deducted for this stringing process. In Dahomey, for example, cowries generally circulate unstrung, with only the king making payments using cowrie strings prepared by his wives; a single string is supposed to contain 2,000 cowries, but in reality, it contains only 1,500, with the difference being the labor cost for stringing. According to more recent information, groups of 30–35 shells are sewn into palm leaves but are valued as if they were 40.[7] Similarly, as one moves inland, the increasing price of the shells is reflected in the reduced number on each string: in the interior of Dahomey, according to Duncan, a string contains only 33 cowries instead of the usual 40, and a "head" only 47 strings instead of 50.[8] The individual sources are not in agreement with each other, as they originate from very different time periods, but they might still help to clarify similar facts elsewhere, such as in Timbuktu, where, according to Lenz, cowries are counted in a way such that 5 sets of 16 (5 × 16) are considered equivalent to 100.[9]

Regarding the area of the distribution of cowries, they have been in circulation as money in Bengal since at least the first century of our era and are still occasionally used for this purpose.[10] The claim that exports from the Maldives to South Asia began in the seventeenth century must actually refer to the renewal of the trade.[11] Today, large quantities of cowries still circulate in the interior areas of Indochina, especially in Siam,[12] but in the East Indies, they have been retained only in the Philippines.[13] The shell-money, however, has bit by bit lost an enormous area of distribution in Asia and Europe, but it is difficult to define the precise boundaries of this area since cowries likely also spread to countries where they were never used as money but only as mere ornaments and trade items. It is certain that they served as small change in Arabia and the same can probably be assumed for Persia. In contrast, archeological finds in the Caucasus and Eastern Turkestan[14] as well as the even more striking finds from prehistoric graves in Northern Europe, including Northern Germany, England, Scandinavia, and Livonia,[15] do not allow us to conclude that cowries were used as money. At least, one can estimate how highly the cowrie was valued as an ornament by noting that it traveled from the Indian Ocean to the Baltic Sea (likely as a means of exchange in the amber trade). The existence of a cowrie currency is definitely attested for in China and Japan, although it is more than likely that *Cypraea moneta* initially only established itself alongside other shells from the China Seas and either displaced or mixed with these in economic life. Apparently, strings of shells, already mentioned in the *Shijing*, and turtle shells were the earliest Chinese money; the character *pei* (shell) is used to form compound words that signify wealth and the like.[16]* China's history is replete with monetary experiments, and amid the frequent changes in currency, cowries seemed to be demonetized at one moment and reintroduced at another, although they actually continued to circulate unimpeded until they finally had to give way to silver and strung copper coins, which were probably imitations of the strings of shells. In the south, the cowrie persisted the longest. Marco Polo mentions them several times when describing his travels through Assam and southwestern China, noting that the shells originated from India.[17] The province of Yunnan paid a tribute of 5,769 strings of shells as late as 1578 but over the course of the same century, and after massive amounts of American silver had flowed into the country, the cowrie currency was officially disposed of here too.[18] In Tibet, silver had begun to displace cowrie shells from the twelfth century.[19]

The enormous reduction of the area of circulation of the cowrie shell was largely balanced out by its expansion into Africa. Since Hertz and Andree have dealt with the African circumstances in detail, a few notes and additions are sufficient here. It is certainly striking that, although the cowrie originates from the East and even though some of the shell-money is produced in East Africa, its dissemination currently almost exclusively proceeds from the West Coast. By the way, we have to make a sharp distinction here between the use of the cowrie as jewelry, observable in almost all regions of Africa, and its use as small change: what spreads from the East Coast to the interior seems to serve almost exclusively as jewelry, while the cowrie currency marches towards the interior from the West Coast. In Timbuktu, Leo Africanus had already found the cowrie used as a coin (in the early sixteenth century)[20] and it was mentioned even earlier in Arabic reports.[21] It appears that there was once a substantial dissemination of cowries from East and perhaps North Africa,[22] which gradually declined and was replaced by the one from West Africa; the East African cowries also have been mostly redirected to the West Coast recently, although some, at least a few decades ago, still

---

*   The *Shijing* or *Shih-ching*—sometimes translated as the *Classic of Poetry* or the *Book of Odes*—is the oldest collection of Chinese poetry, made up of poems from the eleventh to the seventh centuries BCE. It contains various references to cowries as ornaments. The Mandarin word *bèi*, 貝, means both "shellfish" or "cowrie." As the obsolete radical character for "currency," it is still found in many characters related to money, such as "to make a profit" and "to buy" (see also Yung-Ti 2012; Yang 2018).

found their way to Unyamwezi and further inland.[23] In Denham's time [1820s], the eastern boundary of the cowrie territory lay just beyond the city of Katagum; but the strong influx via West Africa allowed the ruler of Bornu in 1840, and later the one of Bagirmi, to introduce the cowrie currency in their states, thereby establishing a stable measure of value.[24] The King of Bornu opted for this regulation only after he had made an unsuccessful attempt to mint coins in Europe at his expense. Further to the east, cowries are highly prized as jewelry but are only exceptionally used as money.[25] The fact that pearls and cowrie shells are considered essential components of the bride-price among the Luwo in the upper Nile region might be viewed as a step towards their transformation into money.[26]

The amount of relief brought about by the introduction of the thaler and cowrie currency to the Sahel's perplexing money market, with its numerous and unsuitable types of use-money, is illustrated by Nachtigal's remark: "The process of counting involved in exchanging the [Maria Theresa] dollar for its equivalent in cowries is indeed a tedious and time-consuming business …. Against this toil and unavoidable inaccuracy, there is the advantage of being able to obtain all articles offered for sale in Kuka and its surroundings in exchange for dollars and their cowrie fractions, and of having in the cowries extraordinarily small fractional units of currency, whereas to the markets of the neighbouring countries strips of cotton, glass beads, paper, aromatic wood and other articles of small value have to be brought without always being sure that it will be possible, and if so, through what transitional stages, to get in exchange the goods that are wanted. The cotton strips, which are still current alongside the cowries and which to this day at any distance from the capital are the most important medium of exchange, vary considerably in quality, and therefore in value. When I was in Kuka, the average value of one cotton strip was four *rotl*, or about twelve pfennig, so that in very small retail transactions it was necessary, since the cotton strips could not be further subdivided, to substitute for them single pieces of paper, a few glass beads and the like. With the division of the dollar into 4,000 cowries, on the other hand, the minimum unit of value is about one tenth of a pfennig, so that the poor can purchase in the smallest quantities anything that can be subdivided."[27]

Along the West Coast, the substantial import of cowries severely depressed their value, as most of the imported shells remained in the coastal regions; in contrast, there was a noticeable scarcity of this small change in the Hausa states even in recent times.[28] On the coast some relief is brought by the fact that large quantities of cowries are often buried during times of war and are not recovered.[29] Forgeries using a small indigenous sea snail are known to occur.[30]

From the Sahel, the cowries also penetrated the Congo basin, and are extraordinarily widespread in the area from the equator up to where the Aruwimi River joins the Congo as well as along the Congo's tributaries.[31] To the east, a territory without cowries separates the distribution area of the Congo basin from the East African one. Among the Dzing along the Sankuru River, the shell serves as a coin,[32] while the Tupende primarily use it for ornamentation.[33] In the areas around Equator Station, it is a proper means of payment,[34] likewise along the middle Ubangi River.[35] Frequently, large quantities of cowries are placed into the graves of the deceased.[36]

There are conflicting reports about their presence in the Great Lakes region. The cowrie apparently spread from Unyamwezi to the Wahuma states and has occasionally been used as money but predominantly as jewelry. According to Grant, it circulated as money in Bunyoro and was frequently buried by owners, much like metal-money elsewhere. During Emin Pasha's time, the true domain of the cowrie currency was Uganda where it was introduced and systematically developed under the influence of the Arabs. Cowries were strung together by the hundred, and ten such strings formed a bundle. The shell also circulates along the German coast of Lake Victoria; chiefs pay cowries as tribute to the German stations.[37] In East Africa, cowries were occasionally used for practical purposes: their lime was extracted to use for the chewing of tobacco. A similar practice of burning them to produce lime was observed in parts of the western Sahel.[38]

In general, a single cowrie shell has a very low value which, at least in Africa, fluctuates considerably depending on the distance from the coast and the volume of imports. In the coastal parts of Togo in 1894, a pfennig was equivalent to 40 cowries, while in Keta, it equaled only 10 cowries. In Porto-Novo, 20,000 cowries equal 5 francs, implying that 1 pfennig equals 50 cowries.[39] During Barth's time [1850s] in Kano, a Maria Theresa thaler had a value of 2,500 to 3,000 cowries, and of 5,000 in the 1880s, while its value fluctuated between 4,000 and 6,000 in Bornu. In the Kukawa market, an egg could be purchased for 8 cowries, and a chicken for 32–160 cowries.[40] In Bosman's time (1700), however, a prostitute's wage on the Gold Coast was a mere 3 cowries, which was considered very little even back then, and can only be explained as an old customary price, but it still proves that the amount of circulating shell-money must have been relatively insignificant.[41] For comparison we might add that, according to Scherzer, 1,000 cowries were valued at 35 pfennig in Calcutta, and at 30–35 pfennig in Siam; around 30 cowries therefore make a pfennig, showing that the cowrie price on the West African coast has been pushed lower than the one in India due to the tremendous influx of Maldivian and especially East African shells. One might assume that the individual cowrie represents such an insignificant value that a division into even smaller change would not be necessary. Yet, there is at least one such case to mention: in the city of Idah along the Niger, groundnuts were used as the smallest coinage, with 4–5 groundnuts for one shell.[42]

The cowrie still dominates an extensive area today, as this brief overview has shown. But even in the areas it had to retreat from, it still exerted a certain influence, especially in China, where the strung "cash" seems to be an imitation of strings of shells.[43] Among the Shan in Burma, shell-shaped pieces of silver are in circulation, as was apparently once common in China as well.[44] Gold replicas of cowries were identified by Volz on an Ethiopian necklace, and Klemm believes that the earliest Etruscan metal coins owe their unique shape to the fact that the cowrie shell was used as a model. Occasionally, the name of the shell still reflects a memory of its old value, as in the case of the Maroons of Surinam, where it is called *papa moni* (father of money).[45]

The *mother-of-pearl* shells that still circulate on the Caroline Islands of Yap are another type of shell-money that has not been processed at all or only minimally; the shells are polished on the outer side and pierced at the edges to be strung onto strings. Mother-of-pearl shells also temporarily served as money in ancient China.[46]

The *dentalium* shells, which apart from being strung on threads were not further processed, served as a means of payment for Northwest Americans for a long time, until their value was pushed down to zero because Europeans imported them en masse. They used to be considered as adornments as well but after their devaluation they are now viewed exclusively as such.[47]

Though the ornamental character of mollusk shells is the foundation of their monetary value, it is intriguing that, by far, not all beautiful shells, which are perfectly suited and often used for ornamentation, transform into money. This is the case not only for unprocessed shells and snails; the effort of manufacturing those types of money that need to be produced by hard work often also seems to be a more important reason for their appreciation than the resulting outcome. The simple gray or white *diwara* strings of the New Britons, for instance, are not particularly attractive, at least to European eyes.

The most famous type of processed shell-money is the *wampum* of the North American natives, manufactured from *Venus mercenaria* and occasionally other shells. Depending on the part of the shell from which it was crafted, there was a more valuable red (blackish) version and a cheaper white variety. Small, polished pearls were arrayed onto strings. Wampum is especially peculiar because it not only served as jewelry and money but also, when embroidered onto belts in specific patterns, as a mnemonic device for messengers and orators, even as a chronicle of individual tribes. Furthermore, it was used as a talisman[48] and as a symbol of war or peace.[49]

Apart from wampum, other types of American shell-money are mentioned, like those of certain Californian tribes;[50] strings of shells were also commonly used as money in Venezuela[51] and ancient Yucatan.[52]

The shell-money varieties of Melanesia and Micronesia form a group on their own, about which Finsch has so far provided the most comprehensive reports without, as a lot of new sources indicate, exhausting the object of investigation. The *diwara*, primarily found in Blanche Bay on New Pomerania, is made from *Nassa callosa* and consists of small disks threaded onto strings; a less popular shell-money known as *apellä* circulates alongside it, and there also exists a "fake *diwara*" which is used only as a toy for children. On New Mecklenburg, a shell currency similar to *diwara*, called *kokonon*, is common in three varieties, while other types are present on the island's southwest coast.[53] In southwest New Guinea, the *tautau* circulates, likely crafted from either *Cassidula* or *Cypraea*, pierced twice and threaded on strings; it is absent on the eastern tip, and instead we find strings of red and white shell disks and arm rings made from *Conus*. *Tridacna* arm rings are, by the way, also found on the Solomon Islands. The *sanem* used in Finschhafen closely resemble the *tautau* but seem to be made from a different shell type; along the Huon Gulf, strung shell disks circulated as valuable money. It should be added to Finsch's information that shell monies of various types from the Solomon Islands have recently come into ethnographic collections. Here too, we are dealing with strings of shell disks of which one can distinguish a red and a white variety; the former is worth ten times the latter on Ysabel Island. While these strings circulate as genuine money, they also serve as adornments, and at times the wives of chiefs, covered in all the shell-money of their husbands, display themselves to an astonished community.[54] On the Fiji Islands, certain strings of shell are valued as precious assets and heirlooms, though not exactly as proper money. In Micronesia, the old shell-money found on Yap is very similar to that which formerly circulated in the Marianas.[55] Strings made of shell and coconut disks were used as adornments and money (*tekaroro*) on the Gilbert Islands and sporadically also on the New Hebrides.[56] Moreover, in the East Indian Archipelago up to Borneo, strings of *Nassa* disks appear as ornaments and likely also circulated as money originally.[57]

Africa possesses a few other types of shell-money besides the cowrie. On Fernando Po, there is one produced from *Conus papilionaceus*, whose individual pieces closely resemble the shape and circumference of larger silver coins,[58] and in Angola (south of the Kwanza River) and Benguela, we observe a type of money threaded on strings that comes from the hinterlands of Benguela and is made from the shells of land snails (*Achatina monetaria* and *balteata*); its strings are known as *quirandas de Dongo*.[59]

CHAPTER 10

Other Types of Ornament-Money

In comparison to shell-money, other forms of ornament-money are insignificant, except perhaps for *glass beads*, which, despite their European origin, have been adopted by many primitive societies and were transformed into a proper inside-money. The bead-money of the Palau Islands is older and its origins remain unclear; apparently it was also widespread on Yap in the past and only reached the Palau Islands from there, although it originally came from one of the East Asian civilizations according to Kubary.[1] The cases of ancient bead-money in Africa remain mysterious and unmistakably point to ancient forms of trade. Especially numerous are the so-called "aggry beads" found on the coast of Guinea. Duncan mentions old beads in Togo that were worth their weight in gold, and, according to Isert, similar beads existed on the Gold Coast. In Katunga, north of Yoruba, they were sold in markets and had a very high price according to Lander.[2] While the old beads are more to be considered a valuable property in these cases, they used to circulate as money along the Kru coast, with each piece worth a Spanish dollar. The Kru claimed that the beads were unearthed by their ancestors in the bush, and they were very skilled in distinguishing genuine beads from European imitations which were, unsurprisingly, also present.[3] The idea that these beads grow in the soil is widespread on the West African coast, apparently because beads are often found when digging up the land and were possibly buried during ancient funerals and the like. Many superstitious beliefs surround these old ornamental objects and enhance

117

their value. They are worn as amulets and one gives children the powder of crushed beads to eat so that they grow faster, for example.

A second region in Africa with old bead ornaments is the southeast, a gold area like the West Coast, where most of the aggry beads are found in the districts rich in gold. That the gold trade brought these beads to Africa is thus extremely probable. Merensky recounts: "When we first visited the Basutho of the Northern Transvaal in the year 1860, the natives soon drew our attention to a particular kind of pearl or coral, which was valued highly and worn almost exclusively by ruling chiefs and their wives, in particular a yellow and a black kind was in high esteem and often served as atonement money or as tribute money, through which the vice-chief won the favour or protection of the high chief. Never and nowhere could one buy these beads, indeed we were told that a man of low rank, if he possessed such beads, carefully kept them from the eyes of the intrusive, because he would otherwise have to fear that he could arouse the greed of the chiefs and would thus not be sure of his life anymore. All too soon we were asked if we perhaps knew a place in the world, where one could buy these gems, seeing that in South Africa one had apparently looked in vain for them among all the traders up to now. According to legend these beads originated from the land of Bonyae (situated to the east of Sofala, the old fable-rich Monomotapa). It is rumoured that in times gone by they were dug out of the earth there, but the hole, which was created through the excavations, had apparently collapsed later, therefore they are now so scarce."[4] Endeman also mentions a type of bead of unknown origin, valued to the utmost by the Sotho in Transvaal.[5]

The presence of peculiar ancient beads, found not only in Africa but also in almost every part of the world, proves the significance that certain types of beads must have had for global trade in the past. Whether all these beads stem from a single source, perhaps from Egypt as Andree assumes, or whether most of them, as Tischler tries to show, are of Venetian origin, remains an open question.[6] They, in any case, represent one of the most important and curious traces of an ancient international trade, a type of "index fossil" of the globe's economic history.*

---

* Schurtz's phrasing—*eine Art 'Leitfossil' der Wirtschaftsgeschichte des Erdballs*—makes use of two unique concepts. While geologists use an "index" or "guide fossil" as a proxy to identify geologic periods or faunal stages in the earth's strata, the phrase *Wirtschaftsgeschichte des Erdballs*, "global economic history" or the "globe's economic history" illustrates that Schurtz's vision

Lately, beads, which can be strung and worn in the same way as many forms of shell-money, have begun to displace and substitute the latter in some places, like on the Gilbert Islands according to Finsch, while blue beads are replacing the old feather-money on the Santa Cruz Islands.[7] In Africa, bead-money continues to spread, and the efforts of natives to establish a regular currency by favoring certain varieties are evident everywhere, although this is made more difficult by the mass introduction of new and seductive designs. Morgen found glass beads in the hinterland of Cameroon which were the preferred money of women managing the small trade with the caravans.[8] An attempt by King Suuna of Uganda to sow glass beads unfortunately did not yield the anticipated result;[9] however, one should not judge the king too harshly for this fallacy because the belief that beads are plant-based products and either grow in the soil, like the aforementioned aggry beads, or are harvested like fruits, is widely held in Africa. Lichtenstein, for example, could not convince the Xhosa that it was not true that beads were cultivated and harvested like grains among distant tribes, while Petherick was often blamed that his beads were "unripe" and did not yet have the right color.[10]

Beads made of clay and stone are also crafted by indigenous people and widely used as ornaments but rarely as money. The *magatamas* ("curved gemstones") of the prehistoric Japanese, which resemble the ornaments of the Ainu, may have been a type of money. From the present word for money among the Seminole, Clay Maccaulay infers that they once used stone beads as a means of payment.[11] Stone beads in the largest format include the millstone-like and perforated aragonite blocks of the people of Yap, which, despite their bulkiness, are nothing more than exaggerated ornamental items; they correspond to the stone-money of the New Hebrides, made of rings of limestone or feldspar. Coote also mentions stone-money from the Solomon Islands, a type of ring made from a kind of marble (?)* that circulates as a coin but is also worn as a talisman on the chest.[12]

---

for economic history went beyond the then more common cultural histories (*Kulturgeschichte*) of "civilization" or "world history" (*Weltgeschichte*), as it includes both prehistoric and ethnographic sources. Not until later in the twentieth century did a more systematic *Wirtschaftsgeschichte der Welt* or *Geschichte der Weltwirtschaft* emerge in Germany, which tended to use the term *Welt*, "world," rather than *Erdball* or *Erde*, "globe" or "earth."

* Schurtz probably added a question mark after marble, "*Marmor* (?)" because Coote (1883: 146) writes that the "coin" "seems to be a ring of

Gemstones and *semi-precious stones* are, of course, not to be omitted from the types of money, although they are more suitable to be used as valuables than as an actual circulating medium because of their extreme rarity. Jadeite served as valuable money in ancient China, while agate is still used for this purpose in Borneo. Agate beads imported from India also circulated in Kordofan and Darfur. Lenz found beads made from precious quartz varieties (agate, jasper, etc.) in Ujiji, used as a kind of money. Lastly, amazonite (nephrite) is worth mentioning, which among the Carïbs seems to have fulfilled most of the functions of money. It was, for example, used to purchase slaves and circulated in sculpted forms resembling fish and the like.[13]

Teeth are a popular ornament and consequently have become proper money here and there. This includes the rare circularly curved boar tusks that, along with dog teeth, function as money on the coast of Kaiser-Wilhelmsland.[14] Dog teeth also circulate on the Solomon Islands of Florida and Ysabel, dolphin teeth on San Cristobal and Malaita, and boar tusks on the Banks Islands.[15] Sperm whale teeth appear as money in Fiji and the Gilbert Islands,[16] and elk teeth among North American natives.[17]

Tortoiseshell is certainly only appreciated for the fact that it is an excellent material for crafting ornamental objects, as the use of turtle shells for divination in ancient China alone could hardly have resulted in their inclusion among the measures of value in the Celestial Empire. In any case, it is, alongside shell strings, mentioned as one of the earliest forms of money in China. Tortoiseshell-money, threaded onto strings, previously circulated on the Marianas; it was allowed to be produced only at a single location, and at the same time it served as a commemorative token which further increased its value.[18]

Feathers from certain birds may have been used as money in the past more frequently than can be established at present; the extraordinary appreciation of some feathers in Polynesia and amongst the ancient civilizations of Central America seems to suggest this. A genuine feather-money still circulates on the Melanesian island of Santa Cruz, consisting of the small red feathers that can be found under the wings of a parrot species. Smaller feathers are glued onto larger ones and the latter are then tied together in such a way that only the red remains visible,

---

marble." However, as Coote then also calls it a *bakiha*, we know that he meant the notable fossil giant clam shell (*Tridacna gigas*) carved into a doughnut-shape ring (Richards 2010: 99).

creating larger continuous pieces whose length determines their value. During festivities, the feather-money is unfolded and used to adorn the dancing area. It seems that it is no longer being produced, because Coote only found older pieces whose scarlet color was quite faded on the surface. A similar type of feather-money circulates on the Banks Islands, and the red fur from beneath the ears of flying foxes was used in the same way on the Loyalty Islands.[19] The red feathered scalp of a woodpecker, which served the Karuk in California as money alongside shell strings, also belongs to this category. According to Harnier, the Bari on the Upper Nile also have a type of feather-money, the only example of its kind from Africa.[20]

In agreement with older Chinese sources, Marco Polo mentions *corals* as the money of Tibetans.[21] Among the many money substitutes in the western Sahel, genuine corals appear as well; unfortunately, the term "coral" is indiscriminately used for both glass beads and actual corals in early reports, which makes it difficult to establish the facts.*

Amber is also popular as money in the Sahel, but in this case, many errors arise from the vague use of the word *ambre* in French sources and in the compilations drawing from them, because real ambergris appears as a valued money substitute in the same area as well, partly because of its fragrance and partly because it is (like camphor) a sought-after healing substance. Amber undeniably circulated as money in Bambouk, where it was exchanged against the gold produced there; in Bornu, one could formerly use it to purchase goods in the local market.[22]

Even cosmetic products circulated as currency, such as antimony powder, which is very popular in the central Sahel, and some time ago red ochre in Usambara.[23]

Ornamental forms of money were probably more varied and numerous in the past than they are today, given that a large part of humanity has since adopted the monetary systems of European or Asian civilizations. Especially ornament-money, the most genuine form of inside-money,

---

* The circulation of corals in Tibet is well established and linked to the history of and devotional practices of Buddhism. Yet, coral-money is a neglected topic of historical research even though it was, along with silver, exported from Europe to Africa and to Asia for many centuries. This neglect is partly caused by an overlap with the growing research on glass beads, because of the confusion between coral beads, glass beads, and "pearls" in historical sources (Vogel 2012; for Africa, see Ogundiran 2009: 377; Pallaver 2016; Green 2019: 152–55).

easily perishes when a lively external trade emerges, and what we can observe today might therefore just be remnants of previously more common phenomena. Unfortunately, prehistoric finds offer little insight into the problem of the monetary system because it is rarely possible to find out whether various ancient ornaments simultaneously served as money or not. In the case of the seashells that reached deep into the interior of prehistoric Europe, however, it is quite plausible.

CHAPTER II

Metal as Ornament and Money

While most varieties of ornament-money gradually lose their significance, one of them, *metal-money*, asserts its ground all the more and finally pushes its competitors out of the field. This development is not easily traced, as many types of metal-money belong to the category of use-money while others stand ambiguously between ornament- and use-money; however, if one keeps in mind the double origin of the monetary system, the main characteristics of this development can be determined with certainty.

The English-American theory of utilitarianism, which tries to attribute all pleasure derived from ownership to the practical use of property and truly embodies the cultural perspective of the Anglo-Saxon race, can only understand metals as exceptional resources in the struggle for existence, as convenient materials used to make tools, weapons, and machines. The fact that some less useful metals are particularly valued seems to be caused by their scarcity alone. But when we look at prehistoric remains or at the conditions in the African interior, it turns out that primitive societies make it very difficult for us to decide on whether they value metals more for their utility or because the most brilliant and durable ornaments can be produced from them. The amount of metal shaped into ornaments almost always far outweighs the amount transformed into practical tools. Turning our attention to civilized nations, we find that the inclination towards metallic adornments and pompous ceremonial artifacts has not decreased but that they have just become more selective with regard to the material, so that one no longer wants to wear jewelry made from iron or copper but instead from more beautiful, rarer, and therefore more precious, noble metals. The assumption that metal-money initially established itself due to its ornamental properties, and therefore is a true and proper inside-money, is thus certainly justified. It is worth recalling how often money made of either noble or base metals appears in the form of large and small rings which can serve as adornment for arms or fingers and can be strung together or sewn onto garments just as easily. Among the Germanic people of the North, precious metals seem to have circulated almost exclusively in ring form for a long time, and one produced smaller pieces by breaking these rings, as evidenced by the honorific title "Ring-breaker," which was given to generous rulers. Rings of gold and silver were also substituted for minted money in ancient Egypt. In gold-rich regions of West Africa, such as Bambouk, mined gold is, even today, immediately shaped by smiths into rings and other ornaments and is brought into circulation only in this form.[1] In Timbuktu, too, gold circulated in the form of rings and other women's jewelry but the weight of gold served as the measure of value.[2] The Funj in the Upper Nile region still used gold rings instead of coins in the first half of the nineteenth century.[3]

Where metals are rare, those that are not precious are used for adornment as well. Towards the end of the Bronze Age, even iron appears to have first established itself as an ornamental metal among European societies, and the vast amounts of brass and copper wire imported into Africa also are not designed for practical use but are almost exclusively fashioned into ornaments. However, before this, they circulated in many parts of Africa as real money: brass wire especially along the middle Congo and in East Africa, brass rings among the Lemba in Transvaal and elsewhere,[4] and small iron chains, wrought by local blacksmiths, among the Maasai.[5]

Regarding the noble metals, there can be no doubt that their suitability for jewelry and ornamental instruments forms the basis of their value, to which their rarity is added as a complementary factor. When one does not consciously keep this in mind, especially when considering the money of European civilizations, it is all too easy to lose the ground under one's feet and drift into theories that are attractive for their simplicity but lack a sound foundation. Metal-money made from noble metals is not a pure sign-money; it is at the same time a valuable commodity, the value of which depends on supply and demand. In its mature form, it therefore in itself embodies the fusion of inside-money with outside-money, of the sign of value and valuable property with the means of exchange. The nations that use precious metals as money, moreover, form a closed group *within* which, at least temporarily, a conventional agreement about the value of their money has to be reached, while realizing that the minted money is valued as a mere commodity and ornament *outside* of the group. Since a large part of humanity has not at all or has only incompletely adopted the European monetary system, this fact is of the greatest significance. East Asia and India have consistently absorbed large amounts of silver which has kept the price of silver relatively high despite its substantial levels of production. Other regions, like the eastern Sahel, in the past also drew in considerable amounts of silver.[6]

This uneven attraction to precious metals is directly caused by the initial and most immediate form of appreciation of them, which is the *aesthetic* one. Fundamentally, it remains a matter of personal or popular taste whether one prefers to use silver or gold for ornamentation, and if gold triumphs in the European monetary system, it owes its victory not so much to its greater scarcity but to the prevalent sense of taste. In remote areas almost uninfluenced by the currents of European culture, the appreciation of these precious metals may be reversed, and indeed gold may even be totally refused while only silver is accepted in trade and crafted into jewelry. Elsewhere, a conventional taste favoring silver does not permit such a rapid and thorough devaluation of silver as is possible in the civilized European states, and as a result, these regions retain the ability to absorb silver in greater quantities than gold. As we are not talking about small corners of the globe here but about densely populated and vast territories, such as East Asia and India, the repercussions for the European monetary market are quite remarkable. Karl von Scherzer has resolutely pointed this out. "Since both metals," he says, "aside from serving as coinage, are primarily used for luxury purposes, changing fashions may have a decisive influence on the fluctuating purchasing power between the two monetary representatives; an influence to which little attention is paid in the heated debates about the currency question. In the earliest periods of their use, silver was more sought after and more popular (though not priced higher) than gold, and in England, a law existed until the Stuart Restoration stating that no one should be obligated to accept gold as legal tender in amounts less than 20 pounds sterling. In our time, East Asia and Africa also display a greater preference for the inferior metal."[7]

A few examples can show that even today a pronounced preference for silver frequently exists even though the appreciation of gold has increased in some regions. In China, for example, it seems that gold was hardly in circulation in earlier times, as local Chinese merchants did not accept gold at all during the period when the Spanish took over the Philippines but only silver, while at present gold does possess purchasing power in China.[8] In South Asia, for centuries and until today, silver has been valued slightly higher than it is in Europe.[9] Hecquard claims that the Fulbe in Fouta Djallon (West Africa) prefer silver over gold,[10] and even in Morocco, gold is often rejected and only silver currency is accepted.[11]

This corresponds to the Germanic border tribes' preference for Roman silver coins about which Tacitus reports.[12] Such cases might partly be explained by the fact that the risk of being deceived by counterfeit coins is greater and more serious with gold than silver; but the inclination to use silver specifically for ornaments is undeniably a decisive factor. Within the entire realm of Islam, gold jewelry very much retreats, it must always be removed during prayer, and pious believers, therefore, do not wear it at all.[13] The effect of this preference on the price of precious metals is remarkable. However, there are still local differences; for instance, gold jewelry is virtually absent in the western Sahel despite the latter's proximity to the gold countries of the West Coast, whereas it is common in Wadai.[14]

With the aid of a few examples, it can also be demonstrated that the coined money of Europe is always initially perceived as, or converted into, jewelry by primitive societies, which causes a greater or lesser portion of circulating money to consistently flow out of Europe, depriving it of its original purpose. In the hinterland of Togo, newly introduced German silver-money has frequently been accepted as payment but after that it does not circulate further and is instead used to make silver jewelry; even the nickel-money vanished from circulation for similar reasons.[15] Lander observed that European silver coins were used as jewelry in Nupe, and in East Africa the silver-money of the German East Africa Company is occasionally accepted as payment but soon reworked into jewelry or buried, and it has only really circulated on the coast; likewise, European silver coins are often transformed into jewelry along the lower Congo River.[16*] In Java, significant amounts of Dutch silver-money are

---

*   Part of the Borgu Emirate, Nupe was the farthest navigable point on the Niger River reached by an expedition of the British navy in the 1820s. The report about this expedition (Lander 1832, 2:77) describes the overvaluation of the European coins: "We brought a quantity of new shillings with

annually reworked into jewelry and ornaments, while for crafting gold articles, they prefer the reddish English gold coins over the pale yellow Dutch ones.[17] The same holds true for large areas of the Dutch colonial possessions; the Papuans at the Berau Gulf, for instance, also accept Dutch coins willingly and make jewelry out of them.[18] Even in Persia, a part of metal-money disappears from commerce because it is reworked into ornaments, and, as a result, Russian coins pour into the country as a substitute.[19] In Tibet, Indian rupees seem to have been initially introduced and worn only as jewelry, until they came to be favored over the frequently forged Chinese silver and were allowed to circulate as actual coins.[20] And in Yemen, Maria Theresa thalers are not only the most important national currency but also a popular ornament.[21]

It hardly needs to be noted that coins were often, and here and there still are, used as jewelry in Europe. The delight derived from adorning oneself often aligns with the desire to wear one's valuable possessions on the body to constantly keep a close eye on one's wealth. The Indian women of the poorer classes do not bear the burden of being overloaded with silver jewelry out of sheer vanity but also out of prudence; similarly Moorish merchants, according to Maltzan, always wear a large portion of their capital in the form of valuable jewelry.[22] Such unproductive investment of capital is typical of all countries whose populations live in uncertain political circumstances, and of the Orient above all: "The condition of all wealth is that it can be moved quickly," says Moltke along similar lines and very aptly, while pointing to the Oriental preference for jewelry.[23] In medieval Europe as well, a tendency prevailed to store up all fortunes in the form of jewelry and pompous ceremonial artifacts which could be melted down as needed, but this was only true as long as the art of goldsmiths was less developed and the value of the object's form was not taken into account.[24] The tragic conflict between this old habit and the demands of an emerging art, which saw its painstakingly crafted masterpieces mercilessly melted down in times of war, was romanticized poetically by Chamisso.*

---

us from England, which are vastly admired by all classes of people here, on account of their shining property; and whilst the Spanish dollar sells for fifteen hundred cowries only, one of these little pieces is purchased willingly at a thousand. Each of these coins is attached to a ring, and worn on the finger of a lady as an ornament."

*   Schurtz does not provide a concrete reference but most probably refers to the poem *Ein Kölner Meister zu Ende des XIV. Jahrhunderts* ("A Master

When minted money disappears from circulation in this way, the most troubling difficulties arise for commerce and for the life of the people in general. Spain, which was virtually flooded with precious metals after the discovery of America, still experienced a severe shortage in the supply of coins, because a large portion of these metals immediately flowed abroad due to the unfavorable trade balance, while another portion was processed and hoarded in the homes of the wealthy as well as in churches and monasteries.[25]* In response, Philip III issued an edict in 1600 that not only prohibited the export of metal-money but also ordered that all gold and silver artifacts within the country be surrendered and minted into coins; when this failed to achieve the desired effect, an equally fruitless attempt was made to alleviate the situation by introducing a debased sign-money.[26]

The fact that European coins find it relatively difficult to gain acceptance as a regular means of payment in primitive societies is closely related to the inclination to use precious metals for ornamental purposes and to regard the form in which these circulate in commerce as unimportant. Weighing indeed allows for more than just a precise determination of value; in some ways this method is even preferable to our own, which allows worn coins to circulate at par alongside newly minted ones. Above all, weighing does not permanently fix the value ratios between the different monetary metals and thus better preserves money's inherent quality as a medium of exchange as well as its transactability, and thereby prevents too painful feelings about shifts in relative value. This also explains why even civilized nations have sometimes only hesitantly decided to adopt money coined from precious metals, or even avoided it

---

from Cologne at the End of the 14th Century") by the German romantic Adelbert von Chamisso (1882: 376). The poem narrates the story of how a master craftsman, celebrated for his skill and artistry, is asked by a prince to craft a unique gold table meant to immortalize the craftsman's legacy. However, upon its completion, a dispute with another prince strains the prince financially, leading him to melt down the table to sell the gold. This devastates the craftsman, who retreats to the mountains, shunning worldly distractions.

* The drainage of silver from Spain often served as a cautionary tale in mercantilist thought. For early modern political economy, and the later German neomercantilists of the nineteenth century (Schefold 1996; Helleiner 2021), the focus on gold and silver was essential and strategic as it aimed to keep one's respective nation wealthy or wealthier in the face of foreign traders and vendors of luxury.

altogether. In ancient Rome, only silver was minted in notable amounts, while gold, despite being the primary means of payment, circulated in uncoined pieces and was weighed like any other commodity during transactions. To this day, China has only small change made from base metal and no official gold and silver coins. If the system of weighing, unlike the assurance provided by the stamp of a reputable government, did not have the disadvantage of only being able to determine the quantity, but not the quality of the metal, it might have asserted itself even more tenaciously.

If no value is attached to the minting of coins but only to the quantity of metal, then the individual coins usually prove to be too large so that small quantities cannot be weighed with sufficient accuracy, and there is a general resort to break them into small and irregular pieces. This gives rise to *hacksilver*, the primary means of payment in many regions of the world, including previously in Eastern Europe and even in Germany, wherever Slavs resided within its borders.[27] Large amounts of hacksilver also circulate in China alongside silver bars and Mexican dollars, reaching westward to the borders with Russia.[28] It was also previously found in South Asia.[29] Meanwhile, Madagascar stands out as a completely independent small region with hacksilver.[30]

Once primitive societies recognize the merits of a particular minted coin, however, they cling to it with an iron-like insistence, since trust is based on the design of the coin that is, by convention, considered to be the only valid one. Perhaps the most peculiar example is the Maria Theresa thaler. Shortly after the coin's first appearance, some pieces reached the Orient and the eastern Sahel, initially just as an adornment and possibly because the bust portrait of the opulently built empress appealed to oriental tastes.[31]* Gradually, the thaler spread to Abyssinia, the eastern and central Sahel, the East African coast beyond Zanzibar, and Western Arabia. The coin's intricate details are well known and always considered during transactions. New coins with the old design are still minted en masse, especially in Vienna, and exported to Africa, but they often have to be artificially aged to be successfully handed over to the locals.[32] To make smaller denominations, the thaler is cut into regularly

---

* The common notion that it was the "bust" of the empress on the coin that made it popular is already found in the cited source of Samuel Baker (1868: 196), who writes of eastern Sudan: "the effigy of the empress, with a very low dress and a profusion of bust, is, I believe, the charm that suits the Arab taste."

divided pieces, which, unlike hacksilver, are obviously not weighed.[33] The importation of thalers has recently been banned in Zanzibar and along the East African coast, and with the coin now largely demonetized, it is often only accepted at its pure silver value.

Other silver coins have also conquered a vast territory of circulation, notably the Mexican silver dollar and the Spanish thaler which is directly related to the large silver production of these countries. Recently, the Indian rupee has been making inroads on various fronts, including into East Africa and Tibet, where it is popular because Chinese merchants are known to deceive in the most shameless way when weighing silver.[34*] The rupee is also frequently divided into pieces.

In primitive societies, gold primarily circulates in regions where it is abundantly available and typically appears in the form of dust and grains, panned from the sands of rivers and streams and weighed during transactions. Here and there, gold has remained a mere commodity[35] but as a rule it swiftly and decisively joins the ranks of monetary instruments. When it does so, it often maintains a certain prestige and is typically not used to purchase large quantities of low-quality goods but only exchanged for particularly beautiful or precious things.[36] Gold dust has apparently been a common form of money on the Gold Coast and in Ashanti since ancient times, with gold scales and weights displaying particularly interesting designs.[37†] Gold dust also circulates in Indonesia, China, and formerly in ancient Mexico as well. The so-called fetish gold of the Gold Coast, however, was cast into specific figures that most probably used to possess some mystical significance, thereby enhancing

---

*   The source cited by Schurtz refers to the use of rigged scales and adulterations: "they prefer Indian rupees to this species of money in bulk; because the Chinese merchants constantly cheat them by having two different scales, which always tell in their own favour, and also by preparing a very bad alloy; not unnaturally, therefore [they] prefer actual coins, the weight and value of which they understand" (Bonvalot 1892: 108).

†   *Vier Jahre in Asante* ("Four Years in Ashantee") was published in the 1870s by two Basel missionaries. Schurtz refers to the second appendix which was not included in the English translation (Ramseyer and Kühne 1875; Jones 1991). The appendix provides a comprehensive account of gold units and denominations ranging from the equivalent of 1 pence to 8 pounds sterling. It also describes the intricate bronze weights and how buyers and sellers used their personal gold scales in the market. Notably, transactions involving the purchase of everyday items like fruits and vegetables included the use of gold as well (see also Pietz 2022: 17–21).

their value through their form. This did not prevent this particular gold from being heavily adulterated or from being broken into pieces for smaller payments.[38]

With regards to primitive contexts, *copper* must categorically be placed among the ornamental metals despite the fact that it is always also used for practical objects, which gives it a somewhat ambivalent status, and although the tremendous production of copper in civilized nations has extremely devalued it. The ancient Roman copper currency, even as it transitioned from weight-based to coined money, could not be sustained in the long run; the more the value of copper plummeted, the larger and larger the quantities became that were necessary to make payments, and it became less and less convenient to use the metal as a medium of exchange. In contrast, both indigenous and imported copper in various forms is still widely used as money in Africa; especially remarkable are the cross-shaped copper pieces from Katanga, which circulate as money in a large part of the southern Congo basin and are known as *handa*, weighing between two to three pounds,[39] as well as the copper rods which circulate around Stanley Pool according to Lenz, or the copper rings along the middle Congo, which European traders unsuccessfully tried to substitute with imported copper-plated iron rings.[40] Among the Azande, copper rings of various sizes crafted from rods circulated as small change.[41] Because it was apparently too devalued, the iron-money which was common in Bonny on the West Coast has recently been replaced by a similarly shaped copper-money sourced from England, while the copper currency in Bornu was driven out by the silver thaler and cowries.[42] The copper plates of the Northwest Americans have already been cited in a different context above. Knife-shaped copper-money is said to still exist in the Beijing area.[43]

What can be said of copper applies broadly, with the obvious exception of iron, to the other base metals that were or still are sporadically used as money in commerce, such as tin, which circulated in ring form in Darfur, in the form of plates in ancient Mexico, or was minted into coins in Java and some small areas of South Asia.[44] Small sheets of zinc circulate in Cambodia[45] as do lead coins in the shape of stars or flowers in Siam[46] and zinc coins in China. Generally, the different base metals and their alloys have been extensively used to produce small coins in China and Indochina; in primitive societies, these coins then, however, only serve as ornaments.[47]

As an addendum to and inversion of the transformation of European coins into ornaments, it should be noted that the coins of civilized nations are often imitated by uncivilized tribes, perhaps because something mysterious and important is seen in them and the reason for their appreciation is not well understood. There are many such barbarian coins from classical antiquity; they were particularly common among the Germanic tribes, serving as mere ornaments and maybe also as amulets.[48] In recent times, South African natives have made crude replicas of English coins. As these do not actually circulate as money but are "stored away," they are rather like valuable curiosities which chiefs occasionally give to their followers as gifts.[19] Here, too, it is remarkable how metal-money, in primitive societies, has the tendency to revert to its ornamental origins.

CHAPTER 12

Clothes and Fabric-Money

While it is already uncertain whether monies crafted from base metals should belong to the concept of ornament-money or to that of use-money, this uncertainty might be even more justified with respect to clothes and fabric-money. Clothes have been made to serve very different purposes over time,[1]* most of which do not facilitate the transformation of fabrics into means of payment, but two specific purposes legitimately stand out in this regard: as clothes conceal the body and shield it from the elements, they are extremely useful and their utility determines their value; but as they provide the body, as it were, with a new surface the sight of which can either be pleasing or unappealing, and as adornments that once belonged directly to the body must now be represented on and through clothes, they become ornamental and subject to an appreciation of a totally different kind. Considering the immense significance of adornment in primitive societies, we can assume that the ornamental traits of clothes always play a more or less significant role when they are used as money. However, since the simplest kind of clothing-money, fur-money, has most clearly been developed among the tribes of the cold

---

*   In his habilitation thesis *Grundzüge einer Philosophie der Tracht* ("Elements of a Philosophy of Traditional Clothing," 1891a), Schurtz develops a theory of the origin of shame and describes the connections between clothing, ornamentation, status, and gender. He shows how clothes are related to stages of individual life cycles as well as world religions and offers an overview of the international trade in textiles with a focus on Africa.

zone, the appreciation of its practical value undoubtedly is of utmost importance in that case.

The practice of using the skins of highly valued fur-bearing animals as a means of payment surged wherever European trade began to exploit fur-rich regions. In many instances, the emergence of fur-money might indeed be attributed to this trade alone. This could be particularly true for Siberia where the natives had to pay tributes partly in furs[2] but also among the North American natives where a proper fur-money likely came into being only through the fur trade as well, although rudimentary forms might have existed before. While northern tribes used beaver pelts as their unit of value, southern tribes used those of raccoons;[3] and the Missouri tribes tanned buffalo hides which were used as a measure of value and a means of exchange at least in their encounters with traders.[4] The Northwest Americans, among whom the concept of money was more developed than among other tribes, considered sea otter pelts as a unit of value and the foundation of wealth, while the same can be said of reindeer hides among the Tlingit.[5]

Fur-money in its typical form once existed in Northern European societies, for instance in Scandinavia and among the Russians who, as already mentioned, put, instead of large and unwieldy furs, a sign-money into circulation that was made from small, stamped pieces of fur. On the Faroe Islands, sheepskin functioned as a kind of imaginary unit of value that was used for calculating, although the skins themselves did not circulate physically.[6]

Where the influence of European culture on indigenous people intensifies, the old fur clothing often disappears in colder areas and gives way to woolen blankets which are then not only used for bartering but also hoarded in great quantities by the natives as their most valuable property. In Northwest America, woolen blankets introduced by the Hudson Bay Company have displaced fur-money; there are four varieties which are marked by points, with one of them acting as the unit of value used for calculation.[7]* Similar conditions are found among many Native American tribes in the United States.

---

* The "points" Schurtz refers to were lines woven on the side of woolen blankets to identify the size of a blanket, ranging from one-point (smallest and least valuable) to four-point (most valuable). According to Dawson (1880: 135), a "two-and-a-half point blanket," valued at approximately $1.50 in 1878, served as a standard unit of value, the *blanket*, in the Hudson Bay Company's territory in British Columbia and elsewhere.

Nearly as primitive a clothing material as fur, bark only rarely appears as a type of money despite its broad distribution. Although *tapa* takes on many of the tasks of a typical inside-money in Polynesia, as it is accumulated as valuable property as well as used for tribute and the payment of fines, it cannot be called money in the proper sense.[8] Stuhlmann reports that small pieces of bark cloth once circulated as money in Uganda.[9] As Uganda is an area where garments made from bark cloth prevailed originally and as it is possible to combine individual pieces into larger ones, this might in fact be a case of pure use-money. On the other hand, bark is so cheap that these small pieces might better be considered sign-money. Cloths woven out of palm fibers, which used to circulate along the Loango coast and the lower Congo and were initially thought of as a type of use-money, also gradually became sign-money before disappearing from commerce altogether.[10]

In regions where an actual textile industry developed and where fabrics are produced in large quantities, such as in ancient Mexico, the foundation for the emergence of fabric-money is laid. Among the oldest types of money in China are small pieces of linen and silk fabric of specific size, although later on neither are any longer mentioned as means of payment; cotton fabrics are still used as money only in Tibet and the most saleable are those that are stamped, that is, in a sense, minted by the Chinese customs administration.[11]* In ancient Japan, fabrics appear alongside grain as regular tax payments, as in ancient Mexico, and gifts of textiles are also mentioned as payments for poets; compulsory labor services could be canceled out by paying dues in cloth and rice.[12] Whether these initial conditions led to true fabric-money remains an open question. At present, the most evident use of fabric-money occurs in the Sahel, mainly using a domestically produced cotton cloth alongside which cotton yarn occasionally makes an appearance. In Bornu, where originally a copper currency dominated, strips of cotton of a specific size were introduced as money, until cowrie shells were accepted as small

---

* "Tibet" refers to the Tibetan Plateau in the work of Bonvalot (1889, 2: 46), who traveled through the region: "At Osch [Osh, Kyrgyzstan] we shall also purchase cotton stuffs made at Kashgar and bearing the Chinese customs' stamp, which is said to be the best medium of exchange. In default of cloth, the people of the Hindu-Kush, the Pamir, and the Wakhan, will also accept the silver bars called *iamba*, bearing the Chinese stamp."

change;[13] red-dyed strips of cotton were once in circulation as money in Fezzan as well.[14]*

Along the West African coast, even Europeans often used the local fabrics as a means of exchange and a measure of value because they were cheaper and more popular than European textiles. The natives in this region indeed display a resolute inclination to consistently hold onto those familiar fabrics, the value of which they are clearly aware; thereby endowing them with one of the main traits of an ideal money: a stable market value. The Moors in northern Senegambia accept, for instance, only the dark blue Indian calicoes (*pieces de Guinée*) as payment for their gum and can distinguish it from all imitations by its smell.[15] In the central and western Sahel, we come across the peculiarity that it is often not just pieces of fabric of a certain size that circulate but rather finished garments, especially the shirt-like *toben*, which is the national dress of the Islamic population there.[†] Among the Missouri tribes in America, pants are one of the measures of value as are war cloaks among the Maasai and boots in Tibet.

In earlier times, European woven fabrics occasionally served as money within the countries they originated from, such as, for instance, linen pieces on Rügen and woolen and other textiles in Scandinavia; the easily divisible cloth-money became a popular form of small change alongside livestock-money throughout the Nordic countries, with the ell length of a standard cloth becoming a kind of monetary unit to which other types of cloth, livestock, and pieces of unminted metal stood in a stable value ratio. However, European fabrics gained their significance as measures of value only when they were introduced to less civilized tribes through trade, especially among African indigenous peoples. Cotton fabrics are

---

*   This reference (Stüwe 1836: 113) points to fabric money in Fezzan, southwestern Libya, specifically during the period of the Abbasid Caliphate and cites an account from 1067 indicating that strips of cloth temporarily replaced coins due to a shortage of the latter.

†   Schurtz does not offer a reference here, but when he discusses shirts (*toben*) as money in his article on "Clothing as Money" (1890a: 889, 911) he cites Barth (1857, 3:75) and Nachtigal (1889: 11). Barth mentions that he was able to "buy everything" with "white Bornu shirts" in the Kanem-Bornu empire, while Nachtigal adds that tributes paid to the Bornu empire sometimes included "dark blue *Indigotoben*." Several English and German sources of the period also use the term "tobes" or *Toben* to refer to the kaftan-like black cloths produced in the Muslim Yoruba kingdom of Nupe, Nigeria.

the medium of exchange that is least likely to be rejected, probably because the concepts of use-money and ornament-money are most intimately combined and mutually reinforce each other in this case. As soon as the ornamental element starts to dominate their appreciation, capricious shifts in fashion emerge, which only gradually transform into the more durable form of custom—obviously even more slowly the more plentiful and manifold the foreign fabrics flowing into a country are. As already noted, we everywhere observe the ambition to separate out certain fabrics as stable measures of value and to withdraw them from the variable judgment of taste, thereby creating a proper fabric-money. In Unyamwezi, for example, many kinds of fabrics are traded, but only the type known as "Bombay" circulates as money.[16]

Clothes are also able to express a person's rank and importance. This aspect seems to have contributed to the idea in oriental societies that the possession of many garments symbolizes power and wealth, and when rulers, along these lines, hoarded vast reserves of garments and gifted them to their followers, they gave clothes a new value and used them as a kind of money. Old Armenian sources refer to the administrator of the magician's robes as well as to the administrator of the clothes of Segestàn as court officials;[17]* the Bible speaks of the "keeper of the wardrobe" and in the Book of Job, we find the phrase: "Though he (the atheist) heaps up silver like dust and clothes like piles of clay, what he lays up the righteous will wear, and the innocent will divide his silver."[18]

---

* Segestàn or Seïstân was a province of the Parthian Empire in Persia, near the Helmand River. Friedrich Spiegel (1878: 636) cites a fifth-century Armenian historian called Faustus the Byzantine for the idea that "closely related to the administration of the treasury are also the administrators of clothes, of which the Armenians name two: the chief of the Magerk clothes (Faustus 4, 47) and the chief of the clothes of Segestàn."

CHAPTER 13

Use-Money
Food and Stimulants

The entire evolution of inside-money shows that objects of purely practical use will only be embraced as inside-money as an exception, least
of all those that satisfy the most immediate needs of human existence:
food. It can, however, be posited that the broad category of use-money also includes some types of food, because food will either partially
or completely drop out of common ownership following the development of the concept of property, after which edible items can be used
as outside-money as much as any other commodity. The number would
be even greater if food was not perishable and if many types of food
were not so ill-suited for small-scale hand-to-hand transactions, not to
mention the inevitable contamination caused by this, which children
and indigenous people quite guilelessly overlook. In any case and like
all types of use-money, food has an intrinsic value which, under certain circumstances, prompts members of civilized nations to invest their
wealth in consumable things or other commodities instead of holding
onto the devalued sign-money of a bankrupt state. This happened in
Sweden during the introduction of their notorious sign-money, as well
as in France during the time of the swindler [John] Law, and again during the French Revolution when assignats became wastepaper.[1] Mr. von

Grimm whose agent did not receive the news in time got nothing but a Brussels lace collar for several hundred thousand francs in assignats, as noted by Goethe.*

In his unusual treatise, "The Closed Commercial State," Fichte recommends the introduction of a pure sign-money for his self-sufficient ideal state but proposes *grain* as the measure of value.[2] He could have referred to the fact that grain has indeed often been used in this way, as well as in the form of an actual transactable currency such as in Denmark and elsewhere in Northern Europe in former times. The remuneration of certain officials, especially the clergy, often still consists of grain and other food which is only gradually replaced by money; in China, a large portion of taxes are collected in the form of rice, which in turn is paid out to officials as part of their salary (about half of it during the previous century).[3]

Livestock and grain were the most important monetary instruments of the Javanese in older times;[4] maize kernels circulated as small change in Mexico;[5] durra [sorghum], measured by hand or in containers, was used as money in Suakin and other parts of the eastern Sahel, with port fees also levied in durra.[6] In eastern Indonesia, sago replaces grain and also serves as a means of payment, formerly, for example, in the Moluccas[7] and currently still in the Gulf of Papua.[8†]

Among tree fruits, dates have to be mentioned, which are occasionally used as small change in Persia and Somaliland,[9] and walnuts which often have to serve as small change in Tibet.[10] Food of animal origin

---

*   Schurtz most likely refers to Goethe's autobiographical diary from 1801 (1868, 23:79), specifically to an entry mentioning the author and art critic Friedrich Melchior, Baron von Grimm, who grieved about his financial loss. Goethe adds that, before the complete devaluation of the assignats, people had converted them to tangible goods, such as rice or candles. The history of French paper-currency experiments is discussed extensively in the literature, in particular the assignats backed by land during the French Revolution and the numerous early eighteenth-century financial projects of John Law, including the fractional reserve private bank, *Banque Générale*, and the shares issued by the Mississippi Company that led to a financial bubble which bankrupted the *Banque* (Schumpeter 1954: 281–83; Kindleberger 1984: 96–100).

†   Edelfelt, a manager of Burns Philp Trading Station Motu Motu in the 1880s and Schurtz's source on the Gulf of Papua, describes how Motu people used sago to pay for goods, particularly for cooking utensils, from foreign traders on ships.

generally spoils even more easily than plant products but some have been temporarily established as a monetary instrument, such as stockfish in Iceland where it formed a measure of value alongside an ell of fabric,[11] cheese in Lapland, and, among other things, chicken eggs.[12]

Nonessential foods or *stimulants* are used as money far more frequently than basic foodstuffs. Just like fabric-money, the types of money that arise in this way are not pure use-money, which explains the immense preference for them. Just as hoarded ornaments seem to trigger endless visions of joy, so too do abundantly available stimulants which are not supposed to satisfy mere needs and whose possession therefore, more easily than the possession of other things, awakens a sense of wealth and freedom. A well-stocked wine cellar has a different effect on the imagination than one that is ten times larger but full of potatoes and turnips. This is why money made from stimulants maintains its relevance with much tenacity or revives itself time and again. The term *Trinkgeld* ["tip," literally "drink-money"] which has been reduced to signify nothing more than a semi-voluntary payment for services already suggests that it was originally supposed to replace the gift of an actual drink and that it was still assumed that the recipient would soon convert the money into some kind of liquor. Lately it can be observed everywhere that cigars, which are sufficiently durable, easily transportable, and almost always welcome stimulants, are being given out in place of *Trinkgeld*. Tobacco is also the most favored type of small change in many societies that have come under European influence, such as sticks of tobacco in Australia and the South Sea, where they are only refused on the Admiralty Islands.[13] Schweinfurth's illustrations show African tobacco-money,[14] bricks of tobacco circulate as money on Nias,[15] and tobacco leaves in the hinterland of Liberia.[16] The fact that tobacco sometimes substituted for the scarce small change in the early United States, and was even legal tender in Virginia, is detailed by Ilwof.[17]

Another monetary instrument is, unfortunately, liquor which, primarily introduced by Europeans, represents more than a mere trade good particularly in West Africa. Alongside cotton fabrics, it serves as the general means of payment along the Loango coast. According to Falkenstein, an egg costs a full glass of rum in the dry season and half a glass in the rainy season; a goat is priced at 4–6 pieces of cloth and 2–3 bottles of rum (750 ml each).[18] This phenomenon has, by the way, a parallel in East Asia: the Japanese supply the Ainu on Ezo with large amounts of rice wine and use it for all minor payments to the natives, who are not allowed to be in possession of metal-money. The Ainu therefore give the rice wine the ironic name "official milk."[19]

The even more destructive opium seems to circulate as money on Hainan.[20] Far more widespread is the harmless tea brick which is produced in China and serves both as a stimulant and as money in Tibet and Mongolia; for the latter purpose, it is sometimes divided into smaller pieces.[21] At the time when the Jesuit missions were flourishing, Paraguay tea was a substitute for money in Paraguay and also used to pay taxes.[22] It has already been noted that cocoa beans were a popular small change among the Central Americans in pre-Columbian times, and it has to be mentioned that betel nuts in the East Indies and kola nuts in the Sahel replace money occasionally. It is symptomatic that the kola nut remains the most popular gift even in areas where it does not have an actual money value, suggesting that it most probably developed out of a gratuity [*Trinkgeld*] to form a proper small change.

Spices seem rarely to be used as money and can mostly be found in the central Sahel where Nachtigal observed that red pepper, kimba, onions, and garlic served as small change; Stewart mentions bitter almonds as the smallest denomination in the western Sahel.[23]* Only one spice forms a splendid exception: *salt*. The need for salt among people whose main diet consists of vegetables, especially among the Blacks of Africa, is so great that it has given rise to migrations and wars, and people attempt, in many different ways, to make common salt or a substitute for it from the ashes of certain plants and even from cattle dung.[24] Salt is therefore an extremely popular commodity all over Africa but it only serves as money in the proper sense in specific regions, notably in Abyssinia where it is commercialized in whetstone-like pieces; it is wrapped with a strip of bark that, so to speak, represents its minting. During his stay in Abyssinia, Álvares found this salt-money already serving as the national currency, which, unsurprisingly, gained a higher value the further one moved away from the place of production.[25] This is a trait that salt-money shares with all outside-money that is sourced from a specific region and can therefore only dominate a certain area surrounding its place of production beyond which the transport costs excessively inflate the price of the substance or competition from other points of production makes

---

*   Gustav Nachtigal (1971, 4:38–39) refers to the area around Lake Fitri in Chad, where the means of exchange were "red Sudan pepper, kimba, salt, cowrie shells and beads, [and] onions and garlic are also used." *Kimba* is also known as "Senegal," "Ethiopian pepper," or "Grains of Selim."

itself felt. Where a block of salt is highly valued, the phrase "he eats salt" has become common and expresses the idea that "he is wealthy or lives off his money."[26] Salt blocks are also a popular money in the western Sahel and the Sahara. In Samatiguila, a slave could be purchased for thirty pieces.[27] Salt is also the preferred means of exchange in southern Wadai.[28] Whetstone-like salt pieces woven in reed, similar to those in Abyssinia, are used as money by the Kisama in Angola, while Lenz mentions salt as a measure of value among the Fang.[29]

Marco Polo gave a detailed report about a type of salt-money that circulated alongside uncoined gold in southwestern China: "They have salt which they boil and set in a mould flat below and round above, and every piece from the mould weighs about half a pound. Now, 80 moulds of this salt are worth one *saggio* of fine gold, which is a weight so called. … On the money so made the Prince's mark is printed; and no one is allowed to make it except the royal officers. And merchants take this currency and go to those tribes that dwell among the mountains of those parts in the wildest and most unfrequented quarters; and there they get a *saggio* of gold for 60, or 50, or 40 pieces of this salt money, in proportion as the natives are more barbarous and more remote from towns and civilized folk."[30] Petrus Martyr reports about salt-money circulating around the Caribbean Sea during the age of exploration.[31*]

---

* Peter Martyr d'Anghiera was an Italian chronicler in the service of Spain whose *De orbe novo* ("On the New World") published in 1530 describes the earliest contacts during this early colonial period.

CHAPTER 14

Iron-Money

The mass production of iron by the civilized nations of Europe has depressed the value of the most useful of all metals extremely, so that the thought of using it as money must seem almost grotesque to us. However, in many indigenous societies, it is still rare and precious enough to be used for this purpose and is indeed a very widespread and popular money. Primitive iron-money appears in the most varied forms, which can, however, easily be classified into two major groups: The first group includes differently shaped pieces of iron, such as bars, rods, and the like, which embody only the metal value and whose shape somewhat substitutes for a minting process; to the second group belong the iron tools that serve a practical purpose and circulate as money at the same time, so that the blacksmith's work increases the metal value. Since these tools can easily be recast into other shapes, they prove to be a very suitable medium of circulation, preferable to the actual bars. Despite their high estimation, both groups of iron-money are to be categorized as use-money even if the concept becomes ambiguous at times. The few examples of iron ornament-money that can still be observed today do not, of course, belong here.

Although Africa is the main region of iron-money today, it also frequently circulated in Europe during antiquity. The ancient Greek ὀβολός [obolos] was originally an iron rod or maybe a spearhead, in any case a distinctly shaped iron-money, which was displaced by silver-money early on. It was only retained in the conservative Sparta, striving to close itself from the outside, but it declined into a type of sign-money and regressed from an originally widely used means of payment into a typical inside-money whose use value was completely destroyed by a specific treatment of the iron.[1] Furthermore, it soon changed form and received the more convenient disk shape of other coins. Among the Britons, Caesar found iron and copper rods as money.[2]

On Asian soil, iron-money in the form of elongated flat rods is still found today in Cambodia. In the past, the Chinese government also issued iron-money because there was a lack of copper but it was replaced by the easier to handle paper-money.[3] These iron coins, which, by the way, are still found in Tibet today, are best assigned to the group of sign-money.[4] Iron coins, likely inspired by the Chinese case, also circulated in ancient Japan.

Africa's extraordinary wealth in iron ore might be the main reason why the iron industry has spread throughout almost all of Africa, while so many other seeds of civilization either withered away or only developed in a stunted form in this barren region. However, ore resources are not evenly distributed, so the rewarding task of spreading the indispensable metal to all places falls to trade, which ultimately elevates iron to the rank of outside-money and even of money in the full sense of the word. Yet, we should consider the fact that in various regions many blacksmiths have to pay their taxes in the form of iron tools. This practice serves as a starting point for the development of inside-money.[5] It is not possible here to cite, let alone to critically examine, the countless references to African iron-money but it is also not necessary because we do not aim to provide a very detailed picture of its geographical distribution. The most important and best corroborated cases shall be highlighted, making use of the abovementioned division into two groups.

Burckhardt reports that raw pieces of iron circulated as money in Kordofan, while, according to Rüppell's information, a government-issued iron-money circulated which had a shape more or less similar to a small anchor.[6]* Iron rods were the most important measures of value in

---

*   Rüppell (1829: 139) refers to El-Obeid in the state of North Kordofan founded by the pashas of Ottoman Egypt in 1821. Prior to this, the region was under the rule of a Melik who had established his residence there. Both the Melik and the subsequent Ottoman administration issued the currency in question. The three-inch miniature hooks, referred to as *Haschasch*, were used for smaller transactions in the area (see also Schurtz 1900a: 133–39).

Senegambia, where the term *bar* expressed the quantity of any commodity the value of which corresponded to that of an iron rod: twenty rolls of tobacco leaves were referred to as "a *bar* of tobacco," and a gallon of spirits, likewise, as a "*bar* of rum."[7] Here, in a very interesting way, one of those originally real, then imaginary, measures of value developed, as already mentioned above (p. 91): the *bar*, like the similar *bar* in Sierra Leone, gradually lost its original meaning and European merchants finally equated it with the value of two shillings. Another type of iron-money was used on the Gold Coast, "a sort of large iron pin with a semicircle at the end," which circulated as small change around 1600.[8]* The shape probably had no practical purpose, just like the horseshoe-shaped form of the iron-money formerly used in Bonny. The Fang have elongated, blade-shaped iron pieces that circulate in bundles of eight to ten pieces.[9] Besides these there are also various similar types of iron-money in the Gabon region, such as bell-shaped iron pieces bundled in fours (*biki*) or snail-shaped pieces (*miaha*) tied up in the same way,[10] as well as iron bars and arrowhead-like iron pieces bound together of which the Bremen Museum possesses a sample; Lenz probably refers to this type of iron-money when he speaks of thin rods about six inches in length, which are tagged at the top with a kind of flag and combined in bundles of ten to twenty pieces. The Ewondo in the hinterland of Cameroon use small iron rods, flattened at both ends, as money, but mainly for the purchase of wives.[11]† Especially large iron bars circulate along the lower Congo.

---

*   The earliest European observation of the "iron needle money" or "pin-money" can be found in Pieter de Marees's travel account from 1602. Marees (1987: 65) describes the use of "little Pins, about the length of a finger, with a Crescent made of iron at the top with which they pay each other small sums, as a substitute for coins or money" around Accra.

†   The types of iron money discussed in this section are all variations of the same type, and characteristic for the so-called Beti-Bulu-Fang group. John Leighton Wilson (1856: 304–305), an American Presbyterian missionary credited with the first ethnographic account of the Fang, observes that iron is "the real currency of the country, by which the price of every other article is regulated." This currency is known as *éki* or *ekuele* (pl. *biki, bikie, bikwele*) with the root *ki* meaning "strength, virility, power" (Balandier 1970: 157; see Guyer 2012 for illustrations). The late Jane Guyer (2013) remembered that her short article on the *bikie* from 1984 was the first article she "ever wrote on 'money'" and "changed the course of my career," as well as reshaped, we may add, the landscape of economic anthropology.

The curious iron spades of the Bongo mark a transition from the first to the second group. Although their shape suggests an originally practical purpose, it no longer quite fits this purpose (particularly the *loggoh kullutty* depicted by Schweinfurth and Andree with an anchor-like extension). They are thus almost exclusively used as money and hoarded in large quantities by the wealthy.[12] Comparable things must have occurred in the case of the shovel-shaped iron-money that, according to Álvares, circulated in Angot (Abyssinia) and was, despite its shape, only used as a means of payment.[13] The most essential tool of African agriculture, the hoe, has become a means of payment in many areas, alongside which many other types of money circulated. We find it as money among the Bari,[14] as tribute payments from the subjugated tribes to the Makololo in South Africa,[15] and as a toll collected in Ugogo. The hoes (*jembe*) made southwest of Lake Victoria of which about 150,000 pieces appear on the market in Tabora annually are, as Sigl writes, "carried by all caravans as the best trade object for procuring food throughout Ugogo and even close to the coast."[16] However, the major area of circulation for the iron hoe is the upper Congo, especially the area around Stanley Falls and the Lualaba River up to Lake Albert.[17] Shovels which have not yet been alienated from their practical purpose circulate in the hinterland of Delagoa Bay, to where they were previously exported en masse from Europe;[18] iron shovels also once circulated as money in Calabar on the West Coast.[19]

Iron in the form of weapons is too important to not also become a means of trade. According to Nachtigal's testimony, the throwing knife was the only money that the idolatrous tribes of Bagirmi accepted when trading grain;[20] iron spears (*assegais*) were originally the preferred money of the Xhosa tribes of South Africa, but spearheads also serve as a measure of value in some places in Northeast Africa.[21] The Haya on the southwest shore of Lake Victoria use spearheads and iron hoes for their external and cowries for their internal trade,[22] which, by the way, is a very good example of how inside- and outside-money can exist side by side without affecting each other. Spearheads also circulate among the Luwo on the upper Nile, and, at the upper Congo near Stanley Falls, Lenz found massive bundles of 1½–2-foot-long iron spearheads, which represented a specific value and circulated as money.[23]

Iron weapons as money can also be found in Indonesia. On Roti Island, knives circulate as a means of payment,[24] and on the Nassau Islands near Sumatra, the iron axe serves as a measure of value, which, like the knife, is also a tool of peaceful activity.[25]

European imports occasionally give rise to new forms of iron-money which, however, usually do not become permanent arrangements. While the desire for hoop iron has subsided among the societies of the South Seas, initially everything could be bought with it and all commercial transactions could be settled with hoop iron and nails on, for example, the Marianas.[26] It may have also been a good time to be a trader in Kamchatka when the natives still placed pieces of iron on poles in front of their homes as symbols of great wealth.[27] Needles and nails seem to have often been used as loose change, the latter particularly in more recent times along the Upper Benue River and elsewhere in Africa.[28]

Other Types of Use-Money

The development of use-money from barter and trade inevitably implies that the boundaries between money and commodity are never clear-cut and that transformations and regressions are not uncommon; a commodity can, for example, temporarily serve as real money only to hand over this role to another material without disappearing from commercial transactions. All reports on use-money should, therefore, be treated with a certain caution although it is not always possible to provide a critical frame for these reports. As stated several times before, it is anyhow not the purpose of our brief treatise to compartmentalize things into sharply delineated categories. Sharp boundaries between individual phenomena, as already mentioned, do not exist in the realm of anthropology, and it is irrelevant under which concept we discuss an object once we have clarity about its position in the sequence of the overall development. With these reservations in mind, we may list a few things that come close to or truly correspond to the term "use-money."

Among the objects that humans first separate from communal ownership as their personal property, besides ornaments, are *weapons*, and it is undoubtedly the labor used in their production—creating a new, in a certain sense, artistic form—which drives and explains this process. One should, furthermore, not forget the particularly close relationship humans have with their weapons. But the group of weapon-money could not develop in the same exemplary way as ornament-money did, above all because weapons are objects of practical use and therefore too exposed to the interventions of communism, and because they are, more or less, difficult to handle. This latter trait explains why weapons mainly appear as valuable property and, therefore, as a medium to pay fines or tributes with but rarely as the small change of commerce, which, in any case, is often managed by women who are generally unfamiliar with weapons. For the ancient Germanic people, weapons, particularly body armor, were the most important property; surrendering the latter could avert corporal punishment or enable the acquisition of women and slaves, but they would not be used as objects of everyday trade; the same applies to Homer's Greeks. The Mongols also held such ideas during their bellicose period when they conquered half of the world, their weapons and livestock being their wealth. The legal codes of the Kalmyks from that era frequently have chiefs imposing fines of one hundred armors, one hundred camels, and one thousand horses for severe misdeeds.[1]

In contrast, small and widely used weapons might at times circulate as small change, especially arrows and arrowheads. On the Banks Islands, delicately shaped wooden arrows once circulated instead of the currently common pearls and, at least as an initial form of weapon-money, one can note that the Aka pygmies of Central Africa purchase brides from their parents for a certain number of arrows.[2] Stone arrowheads, which Manchuria used to pay as part of its tribute in former times, might have often played the role of money in prehistoric times but have now been displaced by other weapons to an extent that such uses can no longer be observed. Instead, where European imports make their mark, gunpowder, bullets, and rifles readily join the ranks of primitive monetary instruments, in Borneo even, as already mentioned in another context, in the form of bronze cannons.

It is hardly worth listing all the other European trinkets that fashion has here and there elevated to a popular means of payment. It may be mentioned that in Bonny, empty glass bottles circulated as a generally accepted currency with which one could purchase food and works of art in the market.[3] Similarly, small glass mirrors, razors, flint stones, and the like, are very common.

Valued medicinal products also occasionally appear as a circulating money. Krapf found blue vitriol, which was very popular among the natives, circulating as a kind of coin in Usambara.[4] Camphor, which is also attributed with magical powers, seems to be used as money in parts of the central Sahel, and ambergris appears as one of the means of payment in Senegambia and the upper Niger region.[5]

Beeswax cakes served as money in various uncivilized tribes in Indonesia, as did benzoin cakes;[6] beeswax-money was also in use among the native tribes along the Amazon. And, finally, European writing paper should be mentioned, which manages to function as a real money in the central Sahel, because it is not imported in great amounts and is frequently used in the Islamic parts of the region.[7]

It is reminiscent of the already discussed custom of the Dayaks who store and invest their wealth in ancient Chinese porcelain vases considered to be sacred that the Lemba in the Transvaal use clay pots as a kind of outside-money.[8] While the large vases of the Dayaks do not properly circulate as currency, Chinese porcelain bowls fulfill the functions of a true money in southern Mindanao for not only are they used for the purchase of brides and are hung up as signs of wealth in huts but they also take the place of coins in transactions.[9]

We have already discussed the two types of use-money that are most important, livestock- and slave-money, and pointed out that they cannot simply be placed in the same category as the others. Here it may also be noted that, apart from herd animals and meat animals, other animals can also be used as a kind of money, for example, domesticated forest birds among the indigenous people of Guyana, or chickens that are not eaten and therefore have a purely conventional value among Brazilian tribes.[10]

Separating ornament- from use-money enables the establishment of at least some order within the chaos of primitive types of money, although one must always bear in mind that squeezing things into prefabricated templates contradicts the very essence of anthropological phenomena. Such general schemes, therefore, always remain crude and do not reveal the delicate roots of the whole development, and, for this reason, would have to be completely rejected if it was not necessary to gain a preliminary overview.

The opinion that anthropology should merely collect and accumulate material for decades to come, and that the intellectual apprehension of the collected material should carefully be avoided is not acceptable at all: if mere collection was as straightforward and self-evident as some make it seem, then the material, which allegedly still provides an insufficient basis for further research, would already have been abundantly brought together.

In reality, it is the theoretical analysis that helps us to recognize the problems and points us to the ways in which they can be solved. It poses those questions that the pure empiricist does not answer because he is not even aware of them. The attempt presented here, as little as it has managed to exhaust the subject, might in this sense at least help to clarify what the problems are.

CHAPTER 16

Monetary Systems and Value Ratios

An overview summarizing the types of money used by primitive societies, in the way it has been given here, sheds light upon quite a number of
facts, but it can, on the other hand, easily lead to the false conclusion that
the number of measures of value is extraordinarily large everywhere and
their relation poorly defined. Alongside this overview, a detailed description of all the monetary systems that different societies and tribes developed from ornament- and use-money, should be provided for the sake of
completeness. However, this task would be difficult to accomplish even
in a comprehensive work, not to mention the scarcity and unreliability of
the current literature on these issues.

The emergence of specific internal monetary systems is always supported by the inclination to transform outside-money into inside-money, and to employ money not to facilitate external trade, as one might
assume according to common theories, but rather to obstruct it. Along
these lines, for instance, a ban on the mining and panning of gold existed in Korea, because this universally desired precious metal promoted
and stimulated trade with foreign countries in an unwanted way, ultimately culminating in complete isolation from the outside world.[1] Japan
adhered to similar principles for a long time. The fact that in previous
centuries every small state strove to have its own monetary system and
its own special combination of the weight and fineness of coins, and
that even today a single monetary union cannot be achieved, can also be
traced back to the desire to create an invisible commercial border around

the country and to prevent objects of value from flowing back and forth too quickly. This principle also guided Russia's past favoring of barter over monetary transactions at its borders, attempting to keep precious metals within the country.[2]

It thus occurs that the means of exchange for external trade join the ranks of inside-money and find their place within the different systems, while, elsewhere, inside-money, on its own, generates a range of measures that serve to evaluate both smaller and larger quantities of goods. Primitive types of money suffer much more than precious metals from the difficulty that not every type of money is suitable for all purposes; while one can use one type to express the smallest values, it cannot be used for large payments due to the low value of the material; conversely, the precious types are unsuitable for small-scale transactions. Here and there, monetary systems develop in regular and logical ways, but in most cases a kind of struggle takes place between the measures of value originating from different sources, which ultimately ends in a settlement. Estimation of value is carried out in very different and often curious ways; a few examples of primitive monetary systems may explain what has just been said.

Two of the most intricate systems, implemented with great ingenuity, are the already mentioned ones from the Caroline Islands of Yap and the Palau Islands, both of which Kubary describes in detail. There, the sets of money are composed of very different elements that have been brought into relation with one another but, at least on the Palau Islands, their sheer number and the artificially increased difficulties of estimation caused the emergence of a simple measure of value, namely a basket of taro, i.e., a specific quantity of the main type of food. Among the types of money on Yap, there is, first of all, an old shell-money (*gau*), whose few available strings do not enter into circulation; as the strings are decorated with sperm whale teeth at both ends, these teeth have also attained a certain value without developing into real money. The second type of money consists of round aragonite stone disks perforated in the middle the value of which is calculated according to the diameter in hand spans but which has declined sharply since the import of numerous pieces by Europeans. The simple estimation by hand spans and the existence of large and small pieces enabled a fairly accurate determination of value, while the unwieldiness of this stone-money prevents its general use in small transactions. Mother-of-pearl shells strung on threads circulate as small change in the proper sense; during payments, commodities of various kinds, that is, outside-money, are often added to the proper monies. The system of the Palau Islands is far more intricate. Here money is composed of old pearls and fragments of glass and baked earth. As their number and diversity are so extraordinarily large and only few completely identical pieces exist, it is almost impossible to give a clear overview. Kubary divides the various types which each have their own names into three main groups according to the quality of the material, which are, in turn, broken down into subgroups. As already mentioned, none of these monies is the actual measure of value, a role taken over by the basket of taro or, more accurately, by the total of 10 baskets. "The natives," writes Kubary, "have a very precise system, a scale, whose starting point is a piece of money regardless of its quality, as long as it can pay for 10 baskets of taro." The unit of 10 baskets of taro, each having to contain about 60 smaller or 30–40 large roots, is called *mor a kaymó* (goes for ten) from where the following scale results which, admittedly, does not give a very clear picture due to Kubary's somewhat unclear phrasing:

1. *Mor a kaymó* = 10 baskets of taro
2. *Honiákl* is almost the double of 1
   If of full value, the piece is called *matál adolóbok* (so 2 × 1)
3. *Adolóbok* equals the sum of the two previous ones (so 3 × 1)
4. *Matál a kluk* is again higher by one *mor a kaymó* (so 4 × 1)
5. *Kluk* equals the sum of *matál a kluk* and *adolóbok* (so 7 × 1)
6. *Eket a kelkúl* is a piece valued at more than one but less than two *kluks*
7. *Kalebúkul* is worth up to 5 *kluks*

As one can see, the value measurement using the unit of ten baskets of taro is systematically applied only at the lower levels, and Kubary's terminology, which apparently corresponds to the ideas of the natives, allows us to realize that one does not multiply the unit but that higher values are achieved by the simple addition of lower ones.[3] This style of calculation might be further clarified by looking at a value system from another area of the world which illustrates even better how an existing unit of value is not used continuously but only serves as the starting point of a strange system of addition. Among the natives of the Missouri region, the knife was the smallest unit of calculation at the time that Kurz resided in their land, and the system based on it was the following:[4]

2 knives	= 1 pair of leggings
2 knives and 1 pair of leggings	= 1 blanket
2 knives, 1 pair of leggings, and 1 blanket	= 1 rifle
the preceding ones and 1 gun	= 1 horse
the preceding ones and 1 horse	= 1 leather tent
the preceding ones and 1 leather tent	= 1 woman

Currency is relatively uniform in that part of New Britain where the shell-money called *diwara* circulates.[5] The money, threaded on strings, is measured in arm lengths; the measure from the tip of the index finger to the elbow is called *a turoaië*, from the fingertip to the shoulder *a wiloai*, and a man's full arm span is *a pokorno* or *param* (derived from the English word "fathom"). A pig cost 6–9 fathoms in 1881, the fine for murdering an ordinary man was 50 fathoms, and 20 pieces of tobacco could be exchanged for 1 fathom. The natives typically do not like it when Europeans acquire *diwara* and thereby reduce the amount of available inside-money, and, as a result, a kind of outside-money has developed from the barter trade, especially in the form of tobacco.

The conditions on the Solomon Islands, where very interesting forms of inside-money exist alongside each other, are not as well documented. Codrington only mentions that a dog tooth corresponds in value to 5 porpoise teeth on the Florida Islands, while on San Cristobal it only takes 1–2 of the latter to compensate the former.[6] The feather-money from the Santa Cruz Islands is stored in pieces about 15 feet long, with shorter lengths serving as small change. Shell-money from the Florida Islands is also divided into strings with specific lengths, 6 strings are called a *rongo*, 10 *rongos* an *isa*, and it seems that red and white shell-money are used interchangeably without making a distinction. It is different on Ysabel according to Coote[7] who offers the following table:

10 coconuts	= 1 string of white shell money or 1 piece of tobacco
10 strings of white shell money	= 1 string of red shell money or 1 dog tooth
10 strings of red shell money	= 1 *isa* or 50 porpoise teeth
10 *isas*	= 1 good-quality wife

1 marble ring (*bakiha*)	= 1 head (among the headhunters) or 1 very good pig, or a medium young man*

This table, the individual valuables of which have been detailed earlier, shows in a very interesting way how the most popular indigenous use value, the coconut, and the piece of tobacco that had penetrated the area as outside-money, have been placed into a very simple relation with the inside-money of the smallest value without meticulously estimating labor time or manufacturing time. Rather, the decisive factor was the ease of calculation using ten fingers. After all, even the civilized man strives to use rounded-off values and prefers the simplicity of calculation at the expense of precision, as shown by the recent disappearance of copper-money in the larger cities of northern Germany. Besides that, Coote's list is not entirely clear; in particular he does not explain the term *isa*. It probably denotes, as on the Florida Islands, a larger number of strings of white shell-money, in this case, probably 100 pieces. The large money, *bakiha*, does not seem to be put into a definite relation with the money used as small change.

This separation between large and small measures of value also occurs elsewhere. Mollien[8] provides a small table of values from Bundu in the western Sahel, which also indicates two groups:

1 slave	= 1 double-barreled gun and 2 horns of gunpowder
	= 5 oxen
	= 100 pieces of cloth

---

*   For translating the terms we relied on Coote's (1883: 146) original English terms, including "porpoise" and "good-quality wife." The literature on "South Sea 'money'" (Malinowski 1921: 15) is extensive and we encourage readers to explore it. It is interesting to note that Schurtz's discussion of Melanesian money influenced German psychology in the 1920s. While Max Wertheimer (1925: 125–28, 107), one of the founders of Gestalt psychology, elaborates on Melanesian systems of calculation and calls Schurtz's *Grundriss* particularly "instructive," Géza Róheim (1923), the founder of psychoanalytic anthropology, takes Schurtz's ideas on the links between money and the cult of the dead as a point of departure in his *Heiliges Geld in Melanesien* ("Sacred Money in Melanesia").

1 string of glass beads	= 1 calabash of water
	= 1 measure of milk
	= 1 bundle of hay
2 strings of glass beads	= 1 measure of millet
	= 10 eggs

If the slave appears as a fixed value here, this, obviously, only applies to normally developed slaves of youthful age and male gender. Generally, the slave is not well suited as a measure of value as the differences not only of outward appearance, gender, and age but also of origin, educability, and so on, result in the most varied gradations; this partly explains the emergence of imaginary measures of value that can be observed in the West African areas of the former slave trade, as discussed already on page 91.

A well-developed small monetary system is found among the Bali in the hinterland of Cameroon. Here, the monetary unit is the *brass*, a brass wire hoop that is 1 yard long when extended, and the ratio of this large coin to small bead-money and the main foodstuffs was as follows in 1893:

1 *brass*	= 1 handful of small beads
	= 20 large beads
	= 1 chicken
	= 2 bundles of plantain
	= 10 eggs

In nearby Nguti, on the other hand, there is a cloth and tobacco currency; in 1893, an egg cost 1 tobacco leaf, a chicken 4–5 leaves, a goat 3 fathoms of cloth. Among the Banyang, 1 tobacco leaf was equivalent to the value of 3 eggs, 8 corn cobs, 1 large yam, or 1 bowl of groundnuts; a goat cost 5–6 fathoms, a pig 4–5 fathoms of cotton cloth.[9*]

No other world region apart from China, whose monetary history, as far as it can be assessed by non-Sinologists, entails the most remarkable

---

[*]   Prices fluctuated from year to year and varied widely by area during the rubber boom and the German colonization of Cameroon in the 1890s. Cloth money was used to acquire larger items such as ivory. The exchange ratio was very lucrative: a pair of ivory tusks sold in Hamburg could land a

experiments and changes, could provide such excellent information about the attempts to create stable value ratios in a large and economically very diversely developed region. Hopefully, a qualified person will soon devote himself to this fascinating material!

trader a net profit of 2000 marks, roughly the annual salary of an educated German civil servant. Cloth and porcelain buttons, which could be used to buy food, were used to pay carriers and local soldiers. In Europe three yards of cloth ("*Faden Zeug*") cost about 70 pfennig (Nkwi 1989: 19–21; Oestermann 2022: 22).

CHAPTER 17

Anthropogeographical Considerations
Ethnographic Zones

It will always be futile to attempt to detach sociological and economic problems from the environment in which they emerged, and to toy with concepts as with building blocks or a deck of cards. Like the sturdy trees of the forest, facts of economic life are rooted firmly in Mother Earth, and anyone who severs them from their native land with a sharp axe only carries away a part of the whole organism and fails to understand the vital forces that have created and sustained it, forces that will also, as with all living things, ultimately abandon it and leave it to its demise. Those seeking to investigate the history of money thus cannot entirely avoid the anthropogeographical problems that result from this history; they may examine them more cursorily than the pure sociological ones, the exploration of which is their primary aim, but they have to be clearly aware of how the major disputes of comparative anthropology affect their inquiries.

The most important of these disputes, which repeats itself in every single manifestation of human culture, will always be whether a cultural institution has grown in situ or whether it has been transferred from other regions through migration and contact between societies. For a time, it seemed as if an opposition between schools of thought was forming out of this most basic of questions, so that one group of researchers would always and everywhere advocate for independent origins and another—since one-sidedness gives rise to one-sidedness—argue the case for borrowing with equal fanaticism. This artificial opposition had to collapse under its own absurdity in the long run; facts of borrowing can be observed so abundantly everywhere that it was impossible to completely overlook them, and the proponents of the theory of borrowing had in turn to concede that every cultural innovation has come into being independently at least once somewhere, and that similar needs lead to similar practices without a model being present every time. The only correct method is therefore to examine each individual case without prejudice and to fruitfully combine the purely sociological method of investigation with the anthropogeographical one.

In our case, the question how the origins of the different types of primitive money relate to each other must be raised. It is of course not possible to examine each of the countless forms but at least the more important ones deserve our intensive focus, for we can assume that some benefit will result from this for sociological thinking as well. The best way to gain a preliminary overview is to follow the suggestion I made elsewhere and to form ethnographic zones,[1*] that is, to put areas in which similar forms occur together in groups: from this foundation, it is then possible to investigate the causes of their homogeneity without any preconception influencing the course of the investigation.

Of particular importance among the forms of primitive monetary instruments are the diverse types of shell-money each of which has its zone of diffusion. There is above all the cowrie currency zone, which attracts attention particularly because it provides an irrefutable example of borrowing and diffusion through trade and travel which also reveals, in its distinct and excellent details, how such zones sometimes expand, sometimes contract, and how the former extent of the area can be reconstructed out of remnants and traces of all kinds. The cowrie zone, whose

---

*   Schurtz elaborates the concept of "ethnographic zones" in his article "On Ainu Ornamentation" (1896b). The concept describes an area of ethnographic homogeneity. However, it is conceptualized as less internally homogeneous than Adolf Bastian's "ethnological provinces" and as less evolutionary than Friedrich Ratzel's idea of *Kulturkreise*, which was further developed by Leo Frobenius and Fritz Graebner (see Bassi 2023). According to Schurtz (1896b: 250), the concept of the "ethnographic zone" does not offer causal-historical explanations based on assumptions of spatial diffusions. Instead of being understood as directly representing historical relations, the heuristic establishment of a zone of distribution of a "group of specific cultural characteristics or even a single peculiar tool" was seen as a starting point for analysis.

historical development is relatively well understood, can then also shed light on those areas whose conditions we must exclusively deduce from contemporary facts.

One of these more difficult areas is the zone of Melanesian-Micronesian shell-money. The custom of grinding small disks from shells, piercing these, and threading them on strings to use as jewelry and money is found in New Pomerania and New Mecklenburg, on the Solomon Islands and the New Hebrides, in northern and eastern New Guinea, as well as on the Carolines, the Marshall and Gilbert Islands, in scattered traces in the eastern Malay Archipelago, on Fiji, and finally, in earlier times, on the Marianas. The facts that the same shells are not used everywhere,[2] that the technique of production is not the same everywhere, and that, finally, the strings sometimes serve only as ornaments, and sometimes simultaneously as ornaments and money, are not fundamentally relevant to the main point, and we are therefore well justified to group these geographically closely related areas into an ethnographic zone. How, then, is this homogeneity to be explained? We are obviously not dealing with a zone based purely on natural causes, comparable to the zone of fur clothing in the polar regions: snails and shells are found everywhere, and the fact that the material is not the same, that it is not a specific shell found only in the seas of the area, but that the uniformity rather lies in the manner of use, rules out the idea of a simple zoogeographical foundation of the phenomenon. If we do not want to think of the invention of shell-money on the different islands as a purely coincidental and thus highly improbable process, the only remaining option is to assume borrowing and to thereby classify the shell-money into the large group of other ethnographic and linguistic phenomena that point to earlier, livelier relations between the Malay, Micronesian, and Melanesian areas. Some details confirm this. For example, the old shell-money found on Yap is the same as the one formerly used in the Ladrones; that of the Gilbert Islands is found in its characteristic form on New Pomerania, the New Hebrides, the Marshall Islands, and the Carolines; New Pomeranian types of money appear on the mainland of New Guinea. But even if we can thus say that the invention of shell-money originated from a specific place, this does not yet clarify how it spread. Can we assume that a lively trade and migratory movements once took place in the Western Pacific and that at that time the strings of shells, which might have developed as inside-money somewhere, were the common currency used for domestic as well as for the intermediary trade of a larger cultural community, until the latter dissolved and the currency everywhere reverted back to a quintessential inside-money? Or is this picture a mere illusion and the knowledge of shell-money and other cultural institutions only seeped through from island to island very gradually and over long periods of time, without the presence of a common cultural consciousness and thus without shell-money having been used in an external trade on a larger scale? Perhaps a compromise between both views is the most accurate but, in any case, we recognize that it is, with some reservations, correct not to regard the Melanesian and Micronesian monetary systems as purely indigenous formations.

The zone of American shell-money, which is extraordinarily patchy but stretches from the Northwest Coast as well as from the eastern United States down to northern South America, points to, despite its fragmentation, ancient interrelationships for which we observe no shortage of other parallels. Anyone who wishes to venture further into the sea of hypotheses might also search for connections between Micronesian, ancient Chinese, and Northwest American shell-money and would find some support for a cultural area of the North Pacific, especially in the distribution of rod armor;[3] but it is not advisable to use the narrow ground on which we stand for blue-sky thinking and it is particularly important to bear in mind that the forms of Northwest American shell-money bear little resemblance to the Micronesian and Melanesian ones.

We move to a completely different world of ideas when we turn to the remarkable zone of use-money to which most areas of the African Sahel belong, especially those where more stable conditions have not yet been created by the introduction of a cowrie currency. Here, and in a totally different sense than in the case of Pacific shell-money, trade together with state fragmentation are the causes of the prevailing conditions, which no one has described as appropriately as Nachtigal. All small independent territories exhibit the desire to create inside-money but also have to take into account a lively commercial trade, and so it is that everywhere some of the common objects of trade are singled out as money while all others are regarded only as commodities. One thus has a thing in between inside- and outside-money without, however, really achieving a true fusion, which creates extraordinary difficulties for the wholesale trade. The common feature of the entire zone lies precisely in this predominance of use-money. Nachtigal writes the following about the various money substitutes: "Even within the Sahel states, where religion and custom have had a leveling effect, far from the main marketplaces the means of exchange vary significantly from one locality to another. Here cotton strips are demanded, there tobacco, salt, or pepper, there sandalwood or other fragrant woods, here onions, there paper. Here cowrie shells are desired as ornaments but if they are above or below a certain size or if, like most of those used as coin, they are pierced, you could not negotiate a handful of grain for them while elsewhere they would reach a hundred times the value of that. There glass and clay beads are the most commonly accepted valuables but one must know the exact size, pattern, and form, otherwise they are worthless. Here every sheet of paper gives a chicken but you could not buy any other object with it. During my passage through Darfur, sheep could only be bought for amber beads, but the trade was unsuccessful if they were transparent and not milky."[4]

This description proves better than anything that a satisfactory currency can never arise out of pure outside-money, especially if it belongs to the group of use-money; rather, a satisfactory currency develops best on the basis of a solid inside-money that expands its sphere of influence outward. A sudden flood of that commodity that had been elevated to money can at any time plunge each of the small, haphazardly sprung-up money systems of the Sahel into complete confusion. Nachtigal also describes very vividly how laborious it is for the wholesale trade to deal with these petty conditions: "Of the imported commodities of lesser value, a portion is sold wholesale to the shopkeepers and peddlers who take care of retail sales in the marketplaces and provinces; another portion, especially of the items that are acceptable in the large markets, remains in the hands of the foreign merchant to cover his daily needs. Since these items represent the small change of the market, so to speak, the merchant gradually exchanges them for those larger market valuables that provide him with the goods to export to the coast. Thus, they sell small packets of needles, single sheets of paper, strings, glass and clay beads, pieces of amber and coral in exchange for either shells, as these are common in the west as small change, or strips of cotton, as these predominate in the eastern lands, and in turn gradually transform these into Maria Theresa thalers or pieces of cotton cloth, by means of which they finally buy slaves, ivory, and ostrich feathers. The various stages of this exchange are often highly tedious and time-consuming."[5]

We thus have a zone of chaotic entanglement in the Sahel that, however, exhibits a homogeneity with regard to the preference for use-money and the resulting conditions it creates. It is obvious that quite different anthropogeographic aspects are at play here than, for example, in the development of the oceanic shell-money region.

The confusing conditions in the Sahel also explain why the cowrie currency zone has been widening into the Sahel, and why, on the other hand, a connection to the zone of European currency is being prepared through the massive importation of the Maria Theresa thaler.

The African iron-money zone must be understood in yet another way. It is based primarily on natural conditions, namely the iron wealth of Africa, as well as partly on the persistence of African hoe-farming, which produces an even livelier demand for iron goods than war; the fact that hoes and shovels occur as money speaks clearly enough.

We have already noted a few things about the curious zone of ancient pearl-money which certainly deserves a more thorough investigation. Finally, however, attention may be drawn to the moneyless zones of the earth, to which most of South America, Polynesia, the mainland of Australia, and some other, smaller areas belong. It is particularly odd that Polynesia, whose neighboring regions know primitive types of money and especially shell-money, exhibits various imperfect beginnings, materializations of valuable personal property, and so on, but possesses almost nothing that could be reasonably called money. This is in accordance with many other facts that point to a stagnation, or at least a very one-sided development, of culture in Polynesia; the area's poverty corresponds to the absence of ethnographic zones.

CHAPTER 18

Money and Commodity
Conclusion

Looking back at the countless seeds and early beginnings of the monetary system, it becomes clear that defining these things conceptually in a clear-cut way is impossible, inadequate, and consequently misleading. Even the division into ornament- and use-money and further subgroups is crude and only indispensable for a quick overview, just as the labels inside- and outside-money are only collective terms with blurred boundaries.

The large number of types of money originating from external trade should not blind us to the fact that in the development of humanity as a whole it is inside-money, which does not arise from the needs of trade but out of social necessity, that remains triumphant and acquires the most important traits of outside-money through a kind of adjustment. The money of civilized nations is an inside-money brought to the highest level of effectiveness, which, within certain limits, also serves external trade. Since inside-money emerges to fulfill social tasks and outside-money for exchange and commerce, the terms social money and commercial money would perhaps be preferable, if obvious misunderstandings would not prevent us from using these terms.* In this sense,

---

*   Schurtz's retraction of the proposed terms "social money" and "commercial money" illustrates that he understood modern money as an "inside" or "social money" as well, and represents a subtle critique of the then all

light is now also shed on the old dispute about whether money can be simply regarded as a commodity, as Say first resolutely asserted,* or whether it occupies a position of its own.

It is evident that the valuables that are mobilized to fulfill internal social purposes cannot be labeled as commodities, if by commodity we mean something that is purchasable and saleable; a mere change of the owner does not yet stamp an object as a commodity—otherwise, for example, all war loot, flotsam, and so on, would also deserve this name. Even repetitive changes in ownership do not establish the concept of a commodity. Most valuables are tied up within the tribe; they are inalienable or change owners only occasionally, and as a result we cannot speak about a reliable valuation, let alone about a precise measurement of the energy and time spent on the production or procurement of goods: the value of labor and time is only understood with the greatest difficulty by indigenous peoples. Purely subjective appreciations predominate, and what, above all, makes the difference are the delight in specific forms felt by the individual or customarily by the whole tribe, the judgment of others, particularly of the opposite sex, and, finally, superstition which seeks to find all kinds of mystical connections. Once certain types of objects of value have been made transactable for social purposes and have consequently become a measure for all valuable property, they can occasionally also serve to initiate and facilitate the exchange of goods within the tribe. These tasks, however, are only taken over subordinately, and any buying and selling within the tribe appears to the communist views of the original society as something dubious, even profane at first, becoming justifiable only through the influence of external trade. The

---

too common and strict distinction between "premodern" *Gemeinschaften* ("communities") and modern *Gesellschaften* ("societies") set up by Ferdinand Tönnies and Alfred Vierkandt. However, Schurtz's inside-money certainly overlaps with the notion of "social currency" introduced by David Graeber (2009, 2011: 130; 2012; see also Graebner 1910: 205; Breton 2002; Jehu 2014; Keep 2017).

* The French revolutionary liberal economist and businessman Jean-Baptiste Say is considered a precursor to Carl Menger and the Austrian school. Say also elaborated on the idea that money is a "custom" and "not the mandate of authority" by defining it as the "commodity" (1836: 217) that overcomes what was later called the problem of the "double coincidence of wants." For Say, any commodity can become money if it is "acceptable to everybody." The commodity does not need to have an "inherent utility" or represent an underlying value in land or labor (1836: 230, 240–45, 257).

fact that the internal trade within the tribe on the Caroline Islands does not aim to distribute goods evenly but serves purely social purposes is highly characteristic.

It is beyond doubt that the quality of being a commodity, which cannot be disputed in the case of the money of civilized nations, is only brought about by merging inside-money with actual trade- or outside-money. When we use the word commodity, we are thus using a concept that is not as simple and self-evident as it seems and therefore merits a closer look.

Commodities are valuables but not every valuable is a commodity, setting aside the difference between commodities and immovable property for now, which does not apply here. No object is destined to remain a commodity indefinitely: the boots that the cobbler displays in his store are commodities, but when I buy and wear them, they are my personal property and can only become a commodity again under particular circumstances; the apples that I pick and eat from my tree were never commodities like those that I send to the market for sale, and even these are no longer commodities once a buyer has been found. The concept of a commodity is attached to objects only temporarily or at least should not permanently be attached to them according to the wishes of the seller, as might be the case with an unsellable stock that no one wants. That we still use the word "commodity" as if it designates something specific and permanent only happens because trade goods are constantly being produced anew, that is, because the consumed things that lose the quality of commodity are regularly replaced by others of the same kind, which evokes the illusion of permanence. Similar concepts are common in social life when we, for example, speak of the army of a state or of an entire society as something durable and constant even though the individual persons composing the whole constantly change and are renewed.

A commodity, then, is a valuable that has been made transactable and is in the state of transactability,* a valuable meant to be exchanged and traded. Closely related to the concept of commodity is the idea that its transactability should not be continuous, that it should transition into a condition of stasis or be eliminated by complete consumption. How, then, does coined money relate to this definition? That it

---

* We consistently translated *Beweglichkeit*, which literally means "movability" or "motility," as "transactability." Schurtz's idea is closely related to what economic theory later calls "liquidity" but such a rendering would have been too "modern."

originally consists of materials that can become a commodity is correct, its transactability is beyond doubt. However, what sharply distinguishes it from a commodity is the theoretical (even if not actual) infinity of its circulation; complete mobilization is not a mere transitional state for it but essential. Although this mobilization serves trade, it does not necessarily emerge from it, because the valuables made perpetually transactable for social purposes, the actual inside-money, have nothing to do with trade initially, as already mentioned, and conversely, trade goods as such are ill-suited to serve as money. The temporary nature of circulation that is inherent to every commodity paralyzes the transactability of all kinds of use-money and ultimately causes them to lose the competition against ornament-money; despite all attempts to artificially keep them in motion, the mobilized useful goods will always sluggishly fall back to the ground, while the "aesthetic valuables," if one may call them this, stand their ground. The overwhelming number of different use-monies can thus be explained by the futile but repeated attempts to create a permanently useful outside-money. In the end, money made from precious metals triumphs everywhere, because it is better able to perpetually remain in motion compared to all other valuables, and also makes the remaining unwieldy valuables more mobile by inserting itself between them, much like the wheels of a wagon or a cylinder placed below a heavy load allow it to glide more easily over the ground.

The introduction of minted metal-money, by the way, only seemingly puts an end to the attempts to make all valuables transactable. The commercial spirit that created outside-money will continue to strive to mobilize immobile goods, to bring the rigid into a flux, to undermine all that is solid and to draw all valuables into the flow of exchange and trade; the emergence of the credit system, government bonds, and the games of the stock exchange attest to the continuous progress of this development.

But in the face of this flood engulfing the entire world, the internal forces of social life become active; the same forces that, in earlier periods of human history, produced inside-money, a mobile good inconvenient for external trade that exclusively serves the inner life of the social organism, and that have frequently transformed outside-money back into inside-money.

Instead of tying the individual to the perpetual motion of money and purchasable commodities, the goal of these forces is to bind individuals to stable and durable valuables, to the home and hearth. If we still find these opposing powers at work today, just as in the past, we might consider this as the best evidence that the emergence of two original forms [*Urformen*] of money was not mere chance but that these two forms are rather necessary consequences of the laws that set the course for the development of humanity as a whole.

Supplements

As the printing of this treatise unfortunately met an unexpected delay, I would like to append some notes taken partly from recently published studies and partly from older works that I was able to consult recently or whose information I had overlooked.

First and foremost, I have to mention the invaluable observations by Dr. A. Hahl on the shell-money of Northern New Britain published in "Nachrichten über Kaiser Wilhelms-Land, 1897," which offer various crucial insights complementing the reports of other researchers. He mentions, for instance, that the inhabitants of the Gazella Peninsula obtain the shells used for making their money through quite perilous sea journeys to the south side of the island. This shell-money is termed *tabu*; typically, the head of the family is entrusted with all the family's money, and only exceptionally brave warriors (*luluai*) have the right to hold on to their own money themselves. Wealthy men (*uviana*) wield significant influence, although their property does not provide many additional benefits: "Despite the ambitions to become wealthy and achieve higher status, a real distinction in social or political terms among the fellows cannot be said to exist. The dwelling and food of the poorest are exactly the same as those of the wealthiest. The rich man has only one advantage over the poor: he can solicit great power in crucial moments, while the poor man must rely on the support of his own family." An authentic illustration from an area where typical inside-money is prevalent!

Since there is no other measure of value, shell-money is also used for the small-scale trade within the country; canoes can be purchased with it as well, with prices starting from 10 fathoms of *tabu* (equivalent to 25 marks) upwards. Women are bought with *tabu*, and fishing in foreign waters also costs shell-money. The circulation of this money is also partly achieved through the giving of large gifts to visitors during weddings and festivals of the dead. The dying often distribute *tabu* to those surrounding them, apparently to ease their passage to the after-life. Wealthy individuals have a higher status than the poor even in the spirit world. The value ratios for small transactions at the market are as follows:

1 dozen taro	= 1 span of shell-money
1 chicken	= 1/2 fathom of shell-money
60 coconuts	= 1/2 fathom of shell-money
1 rooster	= 1 fathom of shell-money

Loans, pledges, rents, and leases are known.[1]

In the same issue, Vetter also provides some important notes on the conditions in Simbang, especially among the Yabem. Here, circularly curved boar tusks and dog teeth function as money; 160–200 dog teeth correspond to the value of a boar tusk, and a pig can be bought for two boar tusks. The finest boar tusks are heirlooms and never enter circu-lation. The means of exchange for small purchases include red ocher, glass stones (perhaps obsidian) used for shaving, spears, pots, and nets, all of which, except possibly red ocher, are pure use-money. "However, it should be noted that there are no stable prices; the equivalent does not always correspond to the desired item. Prices often depend on the property and reputation of the buyer and the demand and current need of the seller." These are obviously conditions that must arise where the corrective influence of external trade is missing.

The description of communist conditions is excellent: "There is no distinction between rich and poor, no opposition between different classes; no one lives in abundance next to a starving neighbor. Hence, there is no word for rich or poor. Certainly, one person might be more respected than another, his word may carry more weight, and more value may pass through his hands. But no one can enrich himself or enjoy his property alone. If a pig is purchased, the share of the one who paid the most is not larger than that of the one who contributed only a trifle, and even someone who contributed nothing can eat just as much of it. The greatest fame for someone is the testimony that he has distributed everything, and contented himself with little .... Miser is a very grave insult."[2]

With regard to Californian shell-money, it should be added that it especially serves as bride-wealth; among the Karuk, a woman costs between one half to two strings of shell-money, while the Shasta can also give horses instead of strings of shell.[3] The shell-money of the Bubi, "roundly polished and pierced shells," is also mentioned by Baumann,[4] while the Achatina shell-money of Angola is noted by Monteiro.[5] Strung shell-money appears to have originally been widespread even further in the interior of the Congo area, and has been kept as jewelry here and there. I am grateful to Mr. Frobenius in Leipzig for a sample of such money from the Pungo-Andongo region, which is, however, no longer commonly used as a measure of value.

I also owe my gratitude to Mr. Frobenius for some references regarding the use of aggry beads. According to Loyer, the Abouré in Assinie used aggry beads instead of money; they broke them into small pieces, pierced these with the help of a flint, and strung them onto blades of grass.[6] The Leipzig Museum possesses aggry beads from Loango. In Yoruba and Dahomey, they are considered the product or excrement of the rainbow snake—an intriguing parallel to the German fairytale about rainbow cups, the prehistoric bowl-shaped gold coins.

Ling Roth offers a valuation table for the Dayak porcelain vases, which is based on the principle of simply doubling value. Terms including *irun* and *jabir* refer to different types of vases, whose other properties are not relevant here:

1 *irun*	= 2 plates
1 *menukul*	= 2 *iruns*
1 *jabir*	= 2 *menukuls*
1 *panding*	= 2 *jabirs*
1 *alas*	= 2 *pandings*

The value of a plate, which forms the basic unit, is 3–4 pence.[7]

Regarding barter, Karl von den Steinen's remark should be mentioned that trade along the Xingu River is to be seen as an "exchange of gifts of hospitality," whereas exchange or barter as we understand it does not occur. Among the Bororo, arrows almost serve as money; they are, among other things, paid as wages to the girls who occasionally cater to the young men's needs at the "men's house."[8]*

The fact that our German word for money, *Geld*, did not arise out of commercial trading but guides us back to the essence of inside-money, is underlined by Lamprecht's statement that, as late as during the tenth century, *gelt* primarily meant recompense [*Vergeltung*] or substitute [*Ersatz*] but only occasionally actual money.[9]

On fabric-money in Persia, one can consult Polak. Here, shawls "circulate almost like money in commercial transactions", they are a favorite honorific gift among the nobility, and "in every well-to-do household, shawls form a portion of the invested mobile wealth." Being cut into tiny pieces, which in the skilled hands of the Persians can be almost seamlessly put back together, this highly appreciated fabric can even circulate as small change.[10]

As for use-money, coffee beans should be mentioned as well, which, according to Burckhardt, circulated as a substitute for small change in Medina during his time.[11] Also, rubber cubes and rubber balls have, with the boom of the rubber trade in West Africa, often displaced all other means of exchange. In the hinterland of Togo, rubber balls fully function as money and have, in some places, entirely driven out cowrie shells; there are two types of balls, each with a specific size.[12] Rubber cubes now circulate widely along the middle Congo.[13]

Finally I would like to draw attention to Lippert's remarks on priesthood and the monetary economy which I overlooked; he particularly emphasizes how, through the intervention of priests, valuables that would otherwise be destroyed in the cult of the dead are preserved and reintroduced into circulation.[14]

---

* Karl von den Steinen was a notable ethnologist known for his expeditions to the Xingú region of Brazil in the 1880s. His observations and analyses have been much appreciated and were confirmed and updated by a range of more recent ethnological studies of the Alto Xingu. Von den Steinen's notion of seeing "exchange" through the framework of "hospitality" has been analyzed by Heckenberger (2005).

Notes

Chapter 1

1. Andree, *Ethnographische Parallelen und Vergleiche* [221–50].
2. Ilwof, *Tauschhandel und Geldsurrogate.*
3. Lenz, *Ueber Geld bei Naturvölkern.*

Chapter 2

1. Locke already had this useful property in mind when he categorically declared: If anyone exceeds the bounds of moderation and takes more than he needs, he undoubtedly takes something that belongs to others.
2. Strabo, VII, 300 [*Geogr,* 7.3.7].
3. Mariner, *Nachrichten über die Tonga-Inseln,* 75, 236, 562 [Orig.: *An Account of the Natives of the Tonga Islands,* 1:70, 260; 2:350].
4. Pallas, *Historischer Nachrichten über die mongolischen Völkerschaften,* 1:105.
5. Lichtenstein, *Reisen im südlichen Africa,* 1:450; Endemann, "Mittheilungen über die Sotho," 34; Guessfeldt, "Zur Kenntniss der Loango," 210.
6. Röder, *Grundzüge des Naturrechts,* 279 (§154). [Röder as paraphrased in Laveleye, *Primitive Property,* 342.]
7. Bücher, *Die Entstehung der Volkswirtschaft,* 17 [En. transl.: *Industrial Evolution,* 90].
8. Martius, *Von dem Rechtszustande unter den Ureinwohnern Brasiliens,* 41 [Partial English translation in Renouard, "Review," 196]; Chalmers and Gill, *Neuguinea,* 20 [Orig.: *Work and Adventure in New Guinea,* 45].
9. Maltzan, *Drei Jahre im Nordwesten von Afrika,* 3:118.
10. Jung, "Rechtsanschauungen der Eingeborenen von Nauru," 67; Petherick, *Egypt, the Soudan and Central Africa,* 392.
11. On this cf. my essay, "Schädelkultus und Sammeltrieb."

12. Many examples of this in Post, *Afrikanische Jurisprudenz*, 262.
13. Büttikofer, *Reisebilder aus Liberia*, 2:195 [En. transl.: *Travel Sketches from Liberia*, 578].
14. Paulitschke, *Ethnographie Nordost-Afrikas*, 133–34.
15. Martius, *Ureinwohnern Brasiliens*, 23.
16. It is so in Dahomey according to Ellis, *The Ewe-Speaking Peoples of the Slave Coast*, 174; Lafitte, *Le Dahomé*, 95; and among the Afar according to Paulitschke, *Ethnographie Nordost-Afrikas*, 134; Cf. also Hecquard, *Reise an die Küste [von] West-Afrika*, 280 [Orig.: *Voyage sur la côte [de] l'Afrique occidentale*, 391].
17. In Dahomey according to Ellis, *The Ewe-Speaking Peoples*, 173; in Ashanti according to Hutton, *Nouveau voyage dans l'intérieur de l'Afrique*, 297 [Orig.: *A Voyage to Africa*, 326].
18. Ellis, *Polynesian Researches*, 2:375; Pogge, "Bericht über die Station Mukenge," 183.
19. Among the Batak according to Hagen, "Wissenschaftliche Reise an den Toba-See," 344.
20. Semper, *Die Palau-Inseln im Stillen Ocean*, 181 [En. transl.: *The Palau Islands in the Pacific Ocean*, 153–54].
21. Kubary, *Karolinen Archipels*, 9.
22. Papencordt, *Geschichte der vandalischen Herrschaft in Afrika*, 268–69.
23. Hedley, *The Atoll of Funafuti*, 1:54.
24. [Kubary, *Karolinen Archipels*, 2–3.]
25. Codrington, *The Melanesians*, 323; Finsch, *Südsee*, 33.
26. Kubary, *Karolinen Archipels*, 9.
27. Finsch, *Südsee*, 13.
28. Codrington, *The Melanesians*, 326.
29. Rosenberg, *Der malayische Archipel*, 162.
30. Finsch, *Südsee*, 13.
31. Cf. the remarks provided by Rannie, "Among the S.E. Solomons," 58; and more indirectly Codrington, *The Melanesians*, 325; Eckardt, "Die Salomo-Inseln," 377.
32. Köler, *Notizen über Bonny an der Küste von Guinea*, 118.

Chapter 3

1. Kubary, *Karolinen Archipels*, 4; Schmeltz and Krause, *Die ethnographisch-anthropologische Abtheilung des Museum Godeffroy*, 404; Hernsheim, *Südsee-Erinnerungen*, 19.
2. [Finsch, *Südsee*, 597.]
3. Casati, *Zehn Jahre in Äquatoria*, 1:136 [En. transl.: *Ten Years in Equatoria*, 1:144].

4. Cf. amongst others, Hirth, "Ancient Porcelain," 176; Schmeltz, "Ueber einen heiligen Krug von Borneo," 29; Grabowski, "Ueber die 'djawet's'," 121; Bock, *Unter den Kannibalen auf Borneo*, 225 [Orig.: *The Head-Hunters of Borneo*, 198].

5. Niemann, "Volksstammen van Achter-Indië," 346.

6. Boyle, "Schilderungen aus dem Britischen Borneo," 1050 [Orig.: *Adventures Among the Dyaks of Borneo*, 100].

7. Cameron, *Quer durch Afrika*, 2:7 [Orig.: Cameron, *Across Africa*, 2:7].

8. Hassan, *Die Wahrheit über Emin Pascha*, 81.

9. Wilson, *West-Afrika*, 79 [Orig.: *Western Africa*, 113].

10. Mommsen, *Geschichte des römischen Münzwesens*, 408.

11. Heuglin, *Reise nach Abessinien*, 252.

12. Benko, *Die Schiffs-Station der K. und K. Kriegs-Marine in Ost-Asien*, 307; Noetling, "Birmanisches Maass und Gewicht," 40.

13. Hoffmann, "Die Tätowierung," 613.

14. Codrington, *The Melanesians*, 326; Finsch, *Südsee*, 12.

15. Count Tolstoy brilliantly, but very one-sidedly, elaborates on this idea in his text "Money" [Tolstoi, *Geld*; En. transl.: Tolstoy, *What Shall We Do Then?*, 110–64; or "Economics as Deception and Money as Tool to Exploit"].

Chapter 4

1. Stolze and Andreas, *Die Handelsverhältnisse Persiens*, 37.

2. Oppert, *Ein verschlossenes Land*, 132 [En. transl.: *A Forbidden Land*, 147–48].

3. Isert, *Neue Reise nach Guinea*, 64 [En. transl.: *Letters on West Africa and the Slave Trade*, 61]; Andree, *Ethnographische Parallelen und Vergleiche*, 235.

4. Schlegel, "Siamesische und Chinesisch-Siamesische Münzen," 241; Bastian, *Reisen in Siam*, 213–14 [En. transl.: *A Journey in Siam*, 132].

5. Canstatt, *Brasilien: Land und Leute*, 172.

6. Erdmann, "Scherben von dem Weinberge bei Oblath," 148; Virchow, "Bericht über den internationalen prähistorisches Congress," 350.

7. Herberstein, *Notes upon Russia*, 111; Scherer, *Geschichte und gegenwärtiger Zustand des russischen Handels*, 179, 152.

8. Brückner, *Finanzgeschichtliche Studien*, 16–19, 93–105, 177–81.

9. Klemm, *Allgemeine Cultur-Geschichte*, 6:243.

10. Waitz, *Anthropologie der Naturvölker*, 4:101.

11. Ilwof, *Tauschhandel und Geldsurrogate*, 47.

12. Tuckey, *Narrative of an Expedition to Explore the River Zaire*, 119.

13. Andree, *Ethnographische Parallelen und Vergleiche*, 246; Klemm, *Allgemeine Cultur-Geschichte*, 3:320.

14. Codrington, *The Melanesians*, 323; Coote, *The Western Pacific*, 65.

15. Middendorf, *Peru: Beobachtungen und Studien*, 1:463; Napp, *Die Argentinische Republik*, 393 [En. transl.: *The Argentine Republic*, 363]; Moussy, *Confédération argentine*, 2:535–36.
16. Middendorf, *Peru: Beobachtungen und Studien*, 470–71.
17. Petersen, "Gustav Wallis' Reisen in Brazilien," 58; Guthe, "Ausgrabungen bei Jerusalem," 30–31.
18. Rubruk already mentioned Mongolian paper-money, or at the very least, paper notes bearing the stamp of the Mongol Emperor Möngke, which were in circulation in China ("Itinerarium fratris," 329) [En. transl.: Ruysbroek, *The Journey of William of Rubruck*, 201]; Marco Polo, II, 18 [*The Book of Ser Marco Polo*, 1:411].

Chapter 5

1. Meinicke, *Die Inseln des Stillen Ozeans*, 2:48.
2. Parkinson, "Beiträge zur Ethnologie der Gilbertinsulaner," 97.
3. Finsch, *Südsee*, 222–23.
4. Andree, *Ethnographische Parallelen und Vergleiche*, 239.
5. Cooper [*The Mishmee Hills*, 190] in Andree, *Ethnographische Parallelen und Vergleiche*, 240. Animal skulls as house ornaments and symbols of wealth, although not as money, are found among the Bambara (see Caillié, *Voyage à Temboctou*, 2:84) [En. transl.: *Travels Through Central Africa to Timbuctoo*, 1:377].
6. Kubary, *Karolinen Archipels*, 23–24, 6–7.
7. Semper, *Die Palau-Inseln im Stillen Ocean*, 63 [En. transl.: *The Palau Islands in the Pacific Ocean*, 54].
8. Kubary, *Karolinen Archipels*, 23–24, 11.
9. Niblack, *Coast Indians*, 336.
10. For further details, refer to my paper on amulets and charms in the *Archiv für Anthropologie* [Schurtz, "Amulette und Zaubermittel"].
11. Martens, "Conchylien," 70.
12. Isert, *Neue Reise nach Guinea*, 181 [En. transl.: *Letters on West Africa and the Slave Trade*, 131].
13. Lander, *Reise in Afrika*, 1:75 [Orig.: *Journal of an Expedition*, 1:104].
14. Let us here recall the carved scarabs of the ancient Egyptians, which in the opinion of some researchers served only as amulets, while according to others, they served simultaneously as money.
15. On brass coins as amulets [in Vietnam], see Kuntze, *Um die Erde*, 190.
16. Snouck Hurgronje, *Mekka*, 2:166–67 [En. transl.: *Mekka in the Latter Part of the 19th Century*, 1:144].
17. Cooper, *Travels of a Pioneer of Commerce*, 456. As a counterpoint, it may be mentioned that on the Gold Coast, the Irish penny with the harp is

considered a "devil's coin" and is rejected (Duncan, *Reisen in Westafrika*, 1:29) [Orig.: *Travels in Western Africa*, 1:30].

18. Tuckey, *Narrative of an Expedition to Explore the River Zaire*, 115.
19. Büttner, *Reisen im Kongolande*, 91.
20. Cf. for example, Finsch, *Südsee*, 13.
21. Finsch, *Südsee*, 32.
22. Cf. Wilken, "Volken van den Indischen Archipel," 122–23.
23. Hernsheim, *Südsee-Erinnerungen*, 22.
24. Cf. Schurtz, "Schädelkultus und Sammeltrieb."
25. Roth, *The Natives of Sarawak*, 2:142.
26. Meyer, "Der Schädelkultus im ostindischen Archipel," 327.
27. Schleinitz, "Beobachtungen auf Neu-Guinea," 258.
28. Cf. the paper by Merensky, "Waffen, Zauberwürfel und Schmuckkorallen," 542.
29. Boas, "Notes on the Ethnology of British Columbia," 427.
30. Niblack, *Coast Indians*, 336.
31. Cf. my paper in the *Preussische Jahrbücher*, "Die Tabugesetze."
32. Finsch, *Südsee*, 11, 88.
33. Meinicke, *Die Inseln des Stillen Ozeans*, 2:48; Seemann, Viti, 361.
34. Krause, *Die Tlinkit-Indianer*, 185 [En. transl.: *The Tlingit Indians*, 127, fn.27 at 277].
35. According to Morga, *The Philippine Islands*, 303.
36. Mommsen, *Geschichte des römischen Münzwesens*, 171.
37. Curtius, "Über den religiösen Charakter der griechischen Münzen," 466 [En. transl.: "On the Religious Character of Greek Coins," 93].
38. Cf. also Yeats, *The Growth and Vicissitudes of Commerce*, 68.

Chapter 6

1. Mariner, *Nachrichten über die Tonga-Inseln*, 228, 265 [Orig.: *An Account of the Natives of the Tonga Islands*, 1:250, 300]; Ellis, *Polynesian Researches*, 2:371.
2. Werner, *Ein deutsches Kriegsschiff in der Südsee*, 262.
3. On the Duke of York Islands according to Werner, *Ein deutsches Kriegsschiff in der Südsee*, 402.
4. Hedley, *The Atoll of Funafuti*, 1:48. Similarly on neighboring islands.
5. Cibot, "Mémoire sur l'intérêt de l'argent en Chine," 318.
6. Kurz, *Tagebuch des Malers*, 188, 196 [En. transl.: *Journal of Rudolph Friederich Kurz*, 269, 283].
7. Ellis, *Polynesian Researches*, 2:373.
8. Lumholtz, *Unter Menschenfressern*, 213, 245; For gifting festivals of the Maori, see Brown, *New Zealand*, 69.

9. Mariner, *Nachrichten über die Tonga-Inseln*, 239 [Orig.: *An Account of the Natives of the Tonga Islands*, 1:263].

10. [Nansen, *Auf Schneeschuhen durch Grönland*, 295; En. transl.: *Eskimo Life*, 112–13.]

11. Bülow, *Deutsch-Südwestafrika*, 123.

12. Strachey, *Virginia Britannia*, 54.

13. Grandpré, *Reise nach der westlichen Küste von Africa*, 79 [Orig.: *Voyage à la côte occidentale d'Afrique*, 147].

14. Lander, *Reise in Afrika*, 1:85 [Orig.: *Journal of an Expedition*, 1:95].

15. Lander, *Reise in Afrika*, 3:103 [Orig.: *Journal of an Expedition*, 3:115].

16. Müller, *Deutsche Münzgeschichte*, 93.

17. Florenz, "Nihongi," 31, 33.

18. Cf. Andree, *Ethnographische Parallelen und Vergleiche: Neue Folge*, 24–29.

19. Gürich, *Deutsch Südwest-Afrika*, 119.

20. Hecquard, *Reise an die Küste [von] West-Afrika*, 81 [Orig.: *Voyage sur la côte [de] l'Afrique*, 117].

21. Roth, *The Natives of Sarawak*, 1:141.

22. Rosenberg, *Der malayische Archipel*, 351.

23. Allen and Thomson, *Expedition to the River Niger*, 2:202.

24. Lubbock, *The Origin of Civilization*, 354. The property of a deceased native American [Iroquois and Delaware] is also given away; Loskiel, *Geschichte der Mission der evangelischen Brüder*, 82 [En. transl.: *History of the Mission of the United Brethren*, 64].

25. Edelfelt, "Customs and Superstitions of New Guinea Natives," 20. The mother's property is usually given to the daughters (see above, p. 40).

26. Brown, *New Zealand*, 23. In a similar manner, a formal system of extortion (*harai*) [*harahi*] seems to have developed in Japan from initial sacrificial and peace offerings, about which unfortunately only incoherent information is available (cf. Florenz, "Nihongi," 34, amongst others). The following excerpt from a [seventh century] imperial decree seems to prove that it was also connected with the cult of the dead: "Again, there have been cases of men employed on forced labour in border lands who, when the work was over and they were returning to their village, have fallen suddenly ill and lain down to die by the roadside. Upon this the inmates of the houses by the roadside say: 'Why should people be allowed to die on our road?' And they have accordingly detained the companions of the deceased and compelled them to do *harai* (i.e., they plundered them). For this reason it often happens that even if an elder brother lies down and dies on the road, his younger brother will refuse to take up his body for burial" (Florenz, "Nihongi," 35) [En. transl.: Aston, *Nihongi*, 222].

27. Kubary, *Karolinen Archipels*, 22.

Chapter 7

1. Burckhardt, *Reisen in Nubien*, 409 [Orig.: *Travels in Nubia*, 302].
2. Schweinitz, *Deutsch-Ost-Afrika in Krieg und Frieden*, 91.
3. Niblack, *Coast Indians*, 334.
4. Jacobsen, *Reise an der Nordwestküste Amerikas*, 31 [En. transl.: *Alaskan Voyage*, 20].
5. Cf. Parkman, *Die Jesuiten in Nord-Amerika*, 11 [Orig.: *The Jesuits in North America*, xxxv]; Loskiel, *Geschichte der Mission der evangelischen Brüder*, 34 [En. transl.: *History of the Mission of the United Brethren*, 26].
6. Martens, "Conchylien," 68.
7. Gisborne, *The Colony of New Zealand*, 25, 32; Sievers, "Die Arhuaco-Indianer in der Sierra Nevada," 394. The German tribes also exchanged gifts with each other according to Tacitus, *Germania*, chap. 15 [En. transl.: *Ger.* 15].
8. Pasha, *Eine Sammlung von Reisebriefen und Berichten*, 114 [En. transl.: *Emin Pasha in Central Africa*, 116].
9. [Leo Africanus, *Description of Africa*, 3:835.]
10. [Bülow, *Deutsch-Südwestafrika*, 268.]
11. Bosman, *Nauwkeurige beschryving van de Guinese*, sec. 2, 192 [En. transl.: *A New and Accurate Description of the Coast of Guinea*, 404–5].
12. Reichard, "Das afrikanische Elfenbein und sein Handel," 157, 164.
13. Denham et al., *Reisen und Entdeckungen im nördlichen und mittleren Africa*, 546 [Orig.: *Narrative of Travels and Discoveries in Northern and Central Africa*, 2:284].
14. Lander, *Reise in Afrika*, 1:116 [Orig.: *Journal of an Expedition*, 1:136].
15. Pogge, "Die Pogge-Wissmann'sche Expedition," 258.
16. Turner, *Gesandtschaftsreise an den Hof des Teshoo Lama*, 270 [Orig.: *An Account of an Embassy to the Court of the Teshoo Lama*, 273]; Obruchev, *Aus China*, 1:243; these cloths, consecrated by lamas, serve at the same time as offerings, according to Timkowski, *Reise nach China*, 1:78 [En. transl.: *Russian Mission through Mongolia to China*, 66].
17. Venyukov, *Die russisch-asiatischen Grenzlande*, 315.
18. Bock, *Unter den Kannibalen auf Borneo*, 186 [En. transl.: *The Head-Hunters of Borneo*, 163].
19. Venyukov, *Die russisch-asiatischen Grenzlande*, 478–79.
20. Moltke, *Zustände und Begebenheiten in der Türkei*, 294.
21. Im Thurn, *Among the Indians of Guiana*, 271–72.
22. Dobrizhoffer, *Geschichte der Abiponer*, 1:274 [En. transl.: *An Account of the Abipones*, 216].
23. Caillié, *Voyage à Temboctou*, 1:200 [En. transl.: *Travels through Central Africa to Timbuctoo*, 1:134].

24. Serpa Pinto, *Wanderung quer durch Afrika*, 1:223 [En. transl.: *How I Crossed Africa*, 1:242].
25. Eberstein, "Rechtsanschauungen der Kilwa," 172.
26. Büttner, *Reisen im Kongolande*, 110.
27. Caillié, *Voyage à Temboctou*, 2:127 [En. transl.: *Travels through Central Africa to Timbuctoo*, 1:406].
28. Cameron, *Quer durch Afrika*, 1:192, 193, 195 [Orig.: *Across Africa*, 2:224, 225, 228].
29. Reade, *The African Sketchbook*, 2:223.
30. Büttner, *Reisen im Kongolande*, 205.
31. Lander, *Reise in Afrika*, 1:61 [Orig.: *Journal of an Expedition*, 1:75].
32. Marno, *Reise in der Egyptischen Aequatorial-Provinz*, 106.
33. Passarge, *Adamaua*, 218.
34. Reichard, "Das afrikanische Elfenbein und sein Handel," 152–53.
35. Examples in Ilwof, *Tauschhandel und Geldsurrogate*, 36.
36. Duncan, *Reisen in Westafrika*, 1:109, 141 [Orig.: *Travels in Western Africa*, 1:111, 144].

Chapter 8

1. Barth, *Reisen und Entdeckungen in Nord- und Central-Afrika*, 2:396 [Orig.: *Travels and Discoveries in North and Central Africa*, 2:56].
2. Burton, *The Lake Regions of Central Africa*, 2:402, 416.
3. Duncan, *Reisen in Westafrika*, 1:105 [Orig.: *Travels in Western Africa*, 1:106]; Andree, "Aggri-Perlen," 112.
4. Monteiro, *Angola and the River Congo*, 1:110.
5. Lichtenstein, *Reisen im südlichen Afrika*, 2:503; see also Endemann, "Mittheilungen über die Sotho," 35.
6. Grabowski, "Ueber die 'djawet's'," 127.
7. Meyer, *Ostafrikanische Gletscherfahrten*, 92.
8. Büttner, *Reisen im Kongolande*, 195.
9. Nebout, "La Mission Crampel," 39.
10. Golberry, *Reise durch das westliche Afrika*, 1:256 [En. transl.: *Travels in Africa*, 1:304]. In southern New Guinea, varying perceptions regarding exchange and monetary transactions occasionally resulted in bloody conflicts. When a young man wanted to sell feathers to Dr. James and asked for an axe in return, the English traveler offered pearl shells as payment. After the negotiation had failed, the rejected seller initiated an attack, which cost one of the Englishman's companions his life (see Chalmers and Gill, *Neuguinea*, 189) [Orig.: *Work and Adventure in New Guinea*, 221].
11. Smyth, *Aborigines of Victoria*, 1:181.
12. Köler, *Notizen über Bonny an der Küste von Guinea*, 150.

13. Finsch, *Südsee*, 45–46.
14. Kubary, *Karolinen Archipels*, 9.
15. Fischer, "Reise in das Massai-Land," 56.
16. Wilson, *West-Afrika*, 184 [Orig.: *Western Africa*, 246].
17. Müller, "Leben and Treiben in Kamerun," 117.
18. Winterbottom, *Sierra-Leone-Küste*, 226 [Orig.: *Native Africans in the Neighbourhood of Sierra Leone*, 1:173].
19. Köler, *Notizen über Bonny an der Küste von Guinea*, 148.
20. Monteiro, *Angola and the River Congo*, 1:104; Grandpré, *Reise nach der westlichen Küste von Africa*, 88, 96 [Orig.: *Voyage à la côte occidentale d'Afrique*, 182, 211].
21. Rouvre, "La Guinée méridionale indépendante," 418.
22. Schrenck, *Forschungen im Amur-Lande*, 593.

Chapter 9

1. Terrien de Lacouperie's proposed classification into natural, commercial, and industrial money, with its intricate subcategories, appears unusable to me primarily because it disregards the foundational principle of any division into groups, the necessity to begin from a unified perspective [Terrien de Lacouperie, *Catalogue of Chinese Coins*, xx]. In contrast, Dr. Schmeltz's expanded overview of types of money is both useful and praiseworthy (Schmeltz, "Shapes of Currency from Barter to Money," 57).
2. Argensola, *Beschreibung der Molukischen Insuln*, 1515.
3. Morga, *The Philippine Islands*, 285.
4. Pyrard, *Voyage [to] the East Indies*, 1:236–40, 2:429–85.
5. In the *Zeitschrift für die gesamte Staatswissenschaft*, 1854 [Volz, "Geschichte des Muschelgeldes"].
6. Hertz, "Verwendung und Verbreitung der Kauriemuschel."
7. Dalzel, *Geschichte von Dahomy*, xxxv [Orig.: *The History of Dahomy*, xii]; Priestermissionsbund, "Die Missionen," 12.
8. Duncan, *Reisen in Westafrika*, 2:61 [Orig.: *Travels in Western Africa*, 2:68].
9. Lenz, *Timbuktu*, 2:159.
10. Kuntze, *Um die Erde*, 460.
11. Müller-Hess, "Die maledivischen Inseln," 27.
12. Bastian, *Reisen in Siam*, 44, 213 [En. transl.: *A Journey in Siam*, 35, 132]; Benko, *Kriegs-Marine in Ost-Asien*, 306; Bock, *Im Reiche des weißen Elephanten*, 107 [Orig.: *Temples and Elephants*, 131].
13. Scherzer, *Statistisch-commerzielle Ergebnisse einer Reise um die Erde*, 325.
14. Troll, "Reise nach Kaschgar," 309; Rösler, "Ausgrabungen beim Dorfe Artschadsor," 227.
15. In addition to the sources cited by Andree, see in the *Verhandlungen der Berliner Gesellschaft für Anthropologie*: Mannhardt, "Pomerellischen

Gesichtsurnen," 248; Marten, "Verwendung von Conchylien bei verschiedenen Völkern," 156; Virchow, "Ältere Gräber in Livland," 256; Virchow, "Archäologische Reise nach Livland," 377.

16. Klaproth, "Notice sur l'usage des cauries en Chine," 146, 151–54.

17. Marco Polo, book II, chap. 48 [*The Book of Ser Marco Polo*, 2:52–53].

18. Morse, "Currency and Measures in China," 131–33.

19. Rockhill, *Notes on the Ethnology of Tibet*, 718.

20. Leo Africanus, *Beschreibung von Africa*, 485 [*Description of Africa*, 3:825].

21. Cf. Andree, *Ethnographische Parallelen und Vergleiche*, 234.

22. In Morocco, cowries are found as ornaments, as noted by Lenz, "Ausflug von Tanger nach Tetuan," 95. Concerning the export of cowries from Morocco to the Sudan see Winterbottom, *Sierra-Leone-Küste*, 231 [Orig.: *Native Africans in the Neighbourhood of Sierra Leone*, 177].

23. Burton, "The Lake Regions of Central Equatorial Africa," 448.

24. Barth, *Reisen und Entdeckungen in Nord- und Central-Afrika*, 2:395 [English original: *Travels and Discoveries in North and Central Africa*, 2:55–56]; Nachtigal, *Sahárá und Súdán*, 1:690–91 [En. transl.: *Sahara and Sudan*, 2:222–23].

25. D'Escayrac de Lauture, *Die Afrikanische Wüste*, 200 [Orig.: *Le désert et le Soudan*].

26. Petherick, *Egypt, the Soudan and Central Africa*, 397.

27. [Nachtigal, "Handel im Sudan," 315. Direct quote is taken from the very similar version of this paragraph available in the English translation of Nachtigal, *Sahara and Sudan*, 2:224–25].

28. Hartert, "Religion und Lebensweise [in den] Gegenden des Nigergebietes," 436.

29. Isert, Neue Reise nach Guinea, 64 [En. transl.: *Letters on West Africa and the Slave Trade*, 61].

30. Monrad, *Gemälde der Küste von Guinea*, 262.

31. Baumann, "Handel und Verkehr am Congo," 230; Lenz, *Geld bei Naturvölkern*, 18.

32. Wissmann, *Im Innern Afrikas*, 353.

33. Müller, "Reise in Muata-Kumbana," 110.

34. François, *Die Erforschung des Tschuapa und Lulongo*, 49.

35. Nebout, "La Mission Crampel," 14.

36. Johnston, *Der Kongo*, 396 [Orig.: *The River Congo*, 425].

37. Pasha, *Sammlung von Reisebriefen und Berichten*, 112 [En. transl.: *Emin Pasha in Central Africa*, 114]; Stuhlmann, *Mit Emin Pascha ins Herz von Afrika*, 2:182, 194; Herrmann, "Stationen Mwanja und Bukoba," 112.

38. Burton, *The Lake Regions of Central Africa*, 2:419; Lenz, *Timbuktu*, 2:157.

39. d'Albéca, "Voyage au pays des Éoués (Dahomey)," 113.

40. Staudinger, *Im Herzen der Haussaländer*, 618; Nachtigal, *Sahárá und Súdán*, 1:694 [En. transl.: *Sahara and Sudan*, 2:227].

41. Bosman, *Nauwkeurige beschryving van de Guinese*, sec. 2, 206 [En. transl.: *A New and Accurate Description of the Coast of Guinea*, 215].

42. Allen and Thomson, *Expedition to the River Niger*, 1:321.

43. Morse, "Currency and Measures in China," 134. The character for money [in Japanese] means "transformed shell" (Scriba, "Bemerkungen über japanische Gold- und Silbermünzen," 393).

44. Schmeltz, "Shapes of Currency from Barter to Money," 58.

45. Volz, "Geschichte des Muschelgeldes," 105; Klemm, *Allgemeine Cultur-Geschichte*, 3:321; Joest, *Ethnographisches und Verwandtes aus Guayana*, 61.

46. Kubary, *Karolinen Archipels*, 6; Hernsheim, *Südsee-Erinnerungen*, 25. In southeastern New Guinea, mother-of-pearl shells cut into crescent shapes were considered a medium of exchange (Finsch, *Südsee*, 88).

47. See images in Langsdorff, *Reise um die Welt in den Jahren 1803 bis 1807*, plate 11, figs. 4 and 5 [378]; also Whymper, *Alaska*, 245 [Orig.: *Travel [in] Alaska*, 223–24].

48. See Longfellow, *The Song of Hiawatha*, chap. 9 [97].

49. For more details, see, amongst others, Holmes, "Art in Shell of the Ancient Americans"; Hale, "On the Nature and Origin of Wampum," 910–11; Rau, "Ancient Aboriginal Trade in North America"; Waitz, *Anthropologie der Naturvölker*, vol. 3; Stearns, "Rambles in Florida."

50. See Holmes, "Art in Shell of the Ancient Americans."

51. Martens, "Nachträge," 154.

52. Waitz, *Anthropologie der Naturvölker*, 4:306.

53. Finsch, *Südsee*, 45.

54. See Codrington, *The Melanesians*, 323; Guppy, *The Solomon Islands*, 134; Coote, *The Western Pacific*, 146.

55. Kubary, *Karolinen Archipels*, 3.

56. Finsch, *Südsee*, 625, 656.

57. Clerq and Schmeltz, *Nederlandsch Nieuw-Guinea*, 223.

58. Blumentritt, "Die Bubis von Fernando Póo," 27.

59. Martens, "Conchylien," 67.

Chapter 10

1. Kubary, *Karolinen Archipels*, 27.

2. Duncan, *Reisen in Westafrika*, 1:105 [Orig.: *Travels in Western Africa*, 1:106]; Isert, *Neue Reise nach Guinea*, 147, 155 [En. transl.: *Letters on West Africa and the Slave Trade*, 109, 116]; Lander, *Reise in Afrika*, 1:161 [Orig.: *Journal of an Expedition*, 1:180].

3. Allen and Thomson, *Expedition to the River Niger*, 1:121–22.

4. Merensky, "Waffen, Zauberwürfel und Schmuckkorallen der Südafrikaner," 543 [Translated excerpt in Delius et al., *Forgotten World*, 65–67].

5. Endemann, "Mittheilungen über die Sotho," 19.
6. Andree, "Aggri-Perlen," 115; [Tischler, *Eine Emailscheibe von Oberhof*, 23].
7. Finsch, *Südsee*, 343; Coote, *The Western Pacific*, 99.
8. Morgen, *Durch Kamerun von Süd nach Nord*, 43.
9. Casati, *Zehn Jahre in Äquatoria*, 2:46 [En. transl.: *Ten Years in Equatoria*, 2:51].
10. Lichtenstein, *Reisen im südlichen Africa*, 1:456; Petherick, *Egypt, the Soudan and Central Africa*, 368.
11. Maccaulay, "The Seminole Indians of Florida," 529.
12. Meinicke, "Der Archipel der Neuen Hebriden," 342, Finsch, *Südsee*, 222; Coote, *The Western Pacific*, 146.
13. Schomburgk, *Reisen in Britisch-Guiana*, 2:331 [En. transl.: *Travels in British Guiana*, 2:263].
14. Finsch, *Südsee*, 222–23.
15. Codrington, *The Melanesians*, 325, 328. Only a few specific dog' teeth are usable, hence this money's preciousness. Guppy's general remark (*The Solomon Islands*, 134) that "the natives of the Salomon-Islands also occasionally employ as money the teeth of fish, porpoises, fruit-eating bats (Ptero-pidae), and of other animals" seems to indicate that other kinds of tooth-money are in use; however, Guppy's statements about money are often conspicuously short and vague, sometimes even incorrect.
16. Parkinson, "Beiträge zur Ethnologie der Gilbertinsulaner," 97; Mariner, *Tonga-Inseln*, 274 [Orig.: *Tonga Islands*, 1:312–13]; Gordon-Cumming, *At Home in Fiji*, 290; Seemann, *Viti*, 362.
17. "Elk teeth and dentalium shells seem to have some monetary value here (among the Mandan)." Wied, *Reise in das innere Nord-America*, 2:136 [En. transl.: *Travels in the Interior of North America*, 1:353, 340].
18. Waitz, *Anthropologie der Naturvölker*, 5:87.
19. Codrington, *The Melanesians*, 324; Coote, *The Western Pacific*, 99.
20. Harnier, "Reise auf dem Weissen Nil," 132.
21. Marco Polo, II, 37 [*The Book of Ser Marco Polo*, 2:37].
22. Golberry, *Reise durch das westliche Afrika*, 2:322 [En. transl.: *Travels in Africa*, 2:334]; Denham et al., *Entdeckungen im nördlichen und mittleren Africa*, 144 [Orig.: *Discoveries in Northern and Central Africa*, 183].
23. Nachtigal, *Sâhârâ und Sûdân*, 3:36 [En. transl.: Nachtigal, *Sahara and Sudan*, 4:31]; Krapf, *Reisen in Ostafrika*, 1:165.

Chapter 11

1. Golberry, *Reise durch das westliche Afrika*, 1:295 [En. transl.: *Travels in Africa*, 1:347].
2. Lenz, *Timbuktu*, 2:150; Lenz, *Geld bei Naturvölkern*, 27.
3. Werne, *Reise durch Sennaar nach Mandera*, 41.

4.   Schlömann, "Die Malepa in Transvaal," 69; Lenz, *Geld bei Naturvölkern*, 25.

5.   Fischer, "Reise in das Massai-Land," 49.

6.   Burckhardt, *Reisen in Nubien*, 416 [Orig.: *Travels in Nubia*, 307].

7.   Scherzer, *Das wirthschaftliche Leben der Völker*, 662.

8.   Morga, *The Philippine Islands*, 340.

9.   Pyrard, *Voyage [to] the East Indies*, 1:235.

10. Hecquard, *Reise an die Küste [von] West-Afrika*, 235 [Orig.: *Voyage sur la côte [de] l'Afrique occidentale*, 329].

11. See Riley, *Schicksale und Reisen an der Westküste*, 295 [Orig.: *Narrative of the Loss of the American Brig Commerce: Wrecked on the Western Coast of Africa*, 215].

12. Tacitus, *Germania*, chap. 5 [En. transl.: *Ger.* 5].

13. Niebuhr, *Beschreibung von Arabien*, 65 [En. transl.: *Description of Arabia*, 27]; Burton, *Pilgrimage to El-Medinah and Meccah*, 1:34.

14. Nachtigal, *Sahărâ und Sûdân*, 3:36 [En. transl.: *Sahara and Sudan*, 4:72, 85].

15. Kling, "Tagebüchern," 137; Herold, "Gewerbsthätigkeit im Togogebiete," 272; cf. also Büttikofer, *Reisebilder aus Liberia*, 2:89, 224 [En. transl.: *Travel Sketches from Liberia*, 484, 602].

16. Lander, *Reise in Afrika*, 2:69 [Orig.: *Journal of an Expedition*, 2:77]; Wagner, *Handelsverhältnisse in Deutsch-Ostafrika*, 51; Lemaire, *Africaines*, 209.

17. Does, "Nijverheid [in] Bandjarnegara," 50.

18. Schleinitz, "Ethnographische Beobachtungen auf Neu-Guinea," 234.

19. Stolze and Andreas, *Die Handelsverhältnisse Persiens*, 37; Blau, *Commercielle Zustände Persiens*, 114.

20. Cooper, *Travels of a Pioneer of Commerce*, 456.

21. Burton, *Pilgrimage to El-Medinah and Meccah*, 2:110.

22. Maltzan, *Drei Jahre im Nordwesten von Afrika*, 4:55.

23. Moltke, *Begebenheiten in der Türkei*, 49.

24. Lamprecht, *Deutsches Wirtschaftsleben im Mittelalter*, 2:378.

25. Soetbeer, *Edelmetall-Produktion und Werthverhältniss*, 2.

26. Brückner, *Finanzgeschichtliche Studien*, 73.

27. On hacksilver finds, see, among others, Virchow, "Archäologische Reise in der Niederlausitz," 575.

28. Benko, *Kriegs-Marine in Ost-Asien*, 359.

29. Pyrard, *Voyage [to] the East Indies*, 1:61.

30. Sibree, *Madagascar and its People*, 229; Keller, *Reisebilder aus Ostafrika und Madagaskar*, 166.

31. Browne, *Reisen in Afrika, Egypten und Syrien*, 339 [Orig.: *Travels in Africa, Egypt, and Syria*, 290]; Baker, *Die Nilzuflüsse in Abyssinien*, 1:162 [Orig.: *Exploration of the Nile Tributaries of Abyssinia*, 196].

32. In the first half of 1896, six million pieces went to Africa via Trieste and Naples (Hettner's Geographische Nachrichten, "Ausfuhr von Maria-Theresia-Thalern nach Afrika," 699).

33. Andree, *Ethnographische Parallelen und Vergleiche*, 225–30; Rüppell, *Reisen in Nubien, Kordofan*, 139; Cicalek, "Die Währungsverhältnisse der Erde," 459.

34. Bonvalot, *De Paris au Tonkin à travers le Tibet inconnu*, 339 [En. transl.: *Across Thibet*, 2:108].

35. For example in Bamako on the upper Niger according to Boyer, "Voyage au pays de Bamako," 147.

36. Caillié, *Voyage à Temboctou*, 1:391 [En. transl.: *Travels through Central Africa to Timbuctoo*, 1:265].

37. Ramseyer and Kühne, *Vier Jahre in Asante*, 272.

38. Bosman, *Nauwkeurige beschryving van de Guinese*, sec. 1, 74, 82 [En. transl.: *A New and Accurate Description of the Coast of Guinea*, 74, 82].

39. Cameron, *Quer durch Afrika*, 1:275 [Orig.: *Across Africa*, 1:319]. [Schurtz in addition cites "Mouvement Géographique, 1895, 2," which we have not been able to locate, but the reference is likely to Delcommune, "Itinéraire de l'expédition Delcommune au Katanga."]

40. Baumann, "Handel und Verkehr am Congo," 231; [Lenz, *Geld bei Naturvölkern*, 26].

41. Schweinfurth, *Im Herzen von Afrika*, 541 [En. transl.: *The Heart of Africa*, 503].

42. Andree, *Ethnographische Parallelen und Vergleiche*, 242; Köler, *Notizen über Bonny an der Küste von Guinea*, 139; Nachtigal, "Handel im Sudan," 315.

43. Virchow, "Sammlung ethnographischer Gegenstände," 60, 64.

44. Andree, *Ethnographische Parallelen und Vergleiche*, 244; Crawfurd, *History of the Indian Archipelago*, 280; Pyrard, *Voyage [to] the East Indies*, 1:235, also mentions iron coins.

45. Bastian, *Reisen in Siam*, 213 [En. transl.: *A Journey in Siam*, 132].

46. Schlegel, "Siamesische und Chinesisch-Siamesische Münzen," 254.

47. Among the Gilyak according to Schrenck, *Reisen und Forschungen im Amur-Lande*, 594.

48. Müller, *Deutsche Münzgeschichte*, 13, 57; Worsaae, *Dänemarks Vorzeit*, 44.

49. Virchow, "Nachbildungen englischer Münzen durch südafrikanische Eingeborne," 30–32.

Chapter 12

1. See my *Grundzüge einer Philosophie der Tracht*.
2. Hiekisch, *Die Tungusen*, 86.
3. Schoolcraft, *The Indian Tribes on the American Frontiers*, 174; further examples in Andree, *Ethnographische Parallelen und Vergleiche*, 248.

4. Kurz, *Tagebuch des Malers*, 118 [En. transl.: *Journal of Rudolph Friederich Kurz*, 156].

5. Niblack, *Coast Indians*, 334; Krause, *Die Tlinkit-Indianer*, 188–89 [En. transl.: *The Tlingit Indians*, 132].

6. Anderson [*Nachrichten von Island*, 131; En. transl.: *The Natural History of Iceland*, 108] in Andree, *Ethnographische Parallelen und Vergleiche*, 248.

7. Niblack, *Coast Indians*, 335.

8. Cf., amongst others, Mariner, *Nachrichten über die Tonga-Inseln*, 228, 265 [Orig.: *An Account of the Natives of the Tonga Islands*, 1:250, 300]; Ellis, *Polynesian Researches*, 2:371.

9. Stuhlmann, *Mit Emin Pascha ins Herz von Afrika*, 2:194.

10. Bastian, *Expedition an der Loango-Küste*, 1:159.

11. Rockhill, *Notes on the Ethnology of Tibet*, 719; Bonvalot, *Du Caucase aux Indes*, 270 [En. transl.: *Through the Heart of Asia*, 2:46].

12. Florenz, "Nihongi," 17, 20–22, 52.

13. Nachtigal, *Sahârâ und Sûdân*, 1:691 [En. transl.: *Sahara and Sudan*, 2:223].

14. Stüwe, *Handelszüge der Araber unter den Abbassiden*, 113.

15. Golberry, *Reise durch das westliche Afrika*, 1:140 [En. transl.: *Travels in Africa*, 1:174].

16. Schweinitz, *Deutsch-Ost-Afrika in Krieg und Frieden*, 90–91. More detailed information about East African monetary values can be found in Wagner, *Die Verkehrs- und Handelsverhältnisse in Deutsch-Ostafrika*, 50–63.

17. Spiegel, *Erânische Alterthumskunde*, 3:636.

18. 2 Kings 10:22; Job 27:16–17.

Chapter 13

1. Brückner, *Finanzgeschichtliche Studien*, 219–66.

2. [Fichte, *Der Geschloßne Handelsstaat*, 49. En. transl.: *The Closed Commercial State*, 104].

3. Cibot, "Mémoire sur l'intérêt de l'argent en Chine," 305.

4. Crawfurd, *History of the Indian Archipelago*, 280.

5. Keller-Jordan, "Mexico zur Zeit Motezumas," 362.

6. Burckhardt, *Reisen in Nubien*, 323, 435, 630, 643, 656 [Orig.: *Travels in Nubia*, 234, 357, 443, 461, 467].

7. Argensola, *Beschreibung der Molukischen Insuln*, 1124.

8. Edelfelt, "Customs and Superstitions of New Guinea Natives," 14.

9. Haggenmacher, *Reise im Somali-Lande*, 40.

10. Rockhill, *Notes on the Ethnology of Tibet*, 719.

11. Lehmann-Filhés, "Kulturgeschichtliches aus Island," 379.

12. Further details in Ilwof, *Tauschhandel und Geldsurrogate* [30–34, 48, 91].

13. Finsch, Südsee, 565; Finsch, *Samoafahrten*, 58; Rose, "Schutzgebiet der Neu-Guinea-Kompagnie," 89; Semon, *Im australischen Busch*, 357 [En. transl.: *In the Australian Bush*, 329]; Lumholtz, *Unter Menschenfressern*, 97.

14. Schweinfurth, *"Artes Africanae,"* fig. X.

15. Modigliani, *Un viaggio a Nías*, 148.

16. Büttikofer, "Eingeborenen von Liberia," 44 [see: Büttikofer, *Travel Sketches from Liberia*, 499].

17. Ilwof, *Tauschhandel und Geldsurrogate*, 83.

18. Bastian, *Expedition an der Loango-Küste*, 2:18.

19. Batchelor, *The Ainu of Japan*, 29.

20. Henry, *Ling-Nam: Or, Interior Views of Southern China*, 399.

21. Rockhill, *Notes on the Ethnology of Tibet*, 719; Prschewalski, *Reisen in der Mongolei*, 8 [En. transl.: Prejevalski, *Mongolia*, 10]; Obruchev, *Aus China*, 1:38.

22. Dobrizhoffer, *Geschichte der Abiponer*, 1:140 [En. transl.: *An Account of the Abipones*, 82].

23. Nachtigal, *Sahárá und Súdân*, 3:43 [En. transl.: *Sahara and Sudan*, 4:38]; Winterbottom, *Sierra-Leone-Küste*, 232 [Orig.: *Native Africans in the Neighbourhood of Sierra Leone*, 178].

24. See, for example, Barth, *Reisen und Entdeckungen in Nord- und Central-Afrika*, 1:41, 240 [Orig.: *Travels and Discoveries in North and Central Africa*, 1:44, 269].

25. Álvares, *Portuguese Embassy to Abyssinia*, 98, 99, 117.

26. Hildebrandt, "Reisen in den Küstenländern von Arabien und Ost-Afrika," 272.

27. Caillié, *Voyage à Temboctou*, 1:466 [En. transl.: *Travels through Central Africa to Timbuctoo*, 1:316].

28. Nachtigal, *Sahárá und Súdân*, 1:135, 43 [En. transl.: *Sahara and Sudan*, 4:106, 37].

29. Lenz, *Skizzen aus Westafrika*, 81.

30. Marco Polo, II, 38 [*The Book of Ser Marco Polo*, 2:45, 47, 48].

31. Peschel, *Völkerkunde*, 173.

Chapter 14

1. Mommsen, *Geschichte des römischen Münzwesens*, 169; Plutarch, *Lycurgus*, 9 [Schurtz cites the Ancient Greek, *Lykurgos*].

2. Caesar, *Gallic War*, 5.12 [Schurtz cites the Latin, *De Bello Gallico*].

3. Morse, "Currency and Measures in China," 126.

4. Cooper, *Travels of a Pioneer of Commerce*, 453.

5. Such as in Kaur [Senegal] according to Hecquard, *Reise an die Küste [von] West-Afrika*, 143 [Orig.: *Voyage sur la côte [de] l'Afrique occidentale*, 201].

6. Burckhardt, *Reisen in Nubien*, 435 [Orig.: *Travels in Nubia*, 319]; Rüppell, *Reisen in Nubien, Kordofan und dem peträischen Arabien*, 139.
7. Park, *Reise in das Innere von Afrika*, 32 [Orig.: *Travels in the Interior Districts of Africa*, 27].
8. Bibliothek der Geschichte der Menschheit, "Bewohner der Goldküste," 88 [Green, "A Description of Guinea," 654].
9. Wilson, *West-Afrika*, 224 [Orig.: *Western Africa*, 304].
10. Cuny, "Libreville au Cameroun," 339–40.
11. Zenker, "Yaúnde," 63; [Lenz, *Geld bei Naturvölkern*, 24].
12. Schweinfurth, *Im Herzen von Afrika*, 306 [En. transl.: *The Heart of Africa*, 276].
13. Álvares, *Portuguese Embassy to Abyssinia*, 117.
14. Harnier, "Reise auf dem Weissen Nil," 132.
15. Livingstone, *Missionsreisen und Forschungen in Süd-Afrika*, 236 [Orig.: *Missionary Travels and Researches in South Africa*, 197].
16. Reichard, "Das afrikanische Elfenbein," 152; Sigl, "Handelsverkehr von Tabora," 165.
17. Coquilhat, *Sur le Haut-Congo*, 423; Wauters, "La monnaie," 34. Lenz (*Geld bei Naturvölkern*, 25) speaks of "spades or axes about ½ foot long" made by the slaves of the Arabs on their behalf and used to buy slaves. Maybe this refers to hoes.
18. Joest, *Um Afrika*, 221.
19. Dapper, *Beschrijvinge der Afrikaensche gewesten*, 135 [En. transl.: Ogilby, *Accurate Description of the Regions of Aegypt, Barbary, Lybia*, 482].
20. Nachtigal, "Handel im Sudan," 326; Nachtigal, "Sklavenkarawane in Baghirmi," 231.
21. Lichtenstein, *Reisen im südlichen Africa*, 1:456; Paulitschke, *Ethnographie Nordost-Afrikas*, 1:111.
22. Herrmann, "Die Wasiba und ihr Land," 55.
23. [Lenz, *Geld bei Naturvölkern*, 25.]
24. Martens, "Banda, Timor und Flores," 127.
25. Crisp, "An Account of the Inhabitants of the Poggy, or Nassau Islands," 72.
26. Morga, *The Philippine Islands*, 354.
27. Steller, *Lande Kamtschatka*, 320 [En. transl.: *Steller's History of Kamchatka*, 241].
28. Lander, *Clapperton's Last Expedition to Africa*, 117.

Chapter 15

1. Pallas, *Mongolischen Völkerschaften*, 1:196.
2. Codrington, *The Melanesians*, 326; Casati, *Zehn Jahre in Äquatoria*, 1:150 [En. transl.: *Ten Years in Equatoria*, 1:157].

3. Köler, *Notizen über Bonny an der Küste von Guinea*, 139.
4. Krapf, *Reisen in Ostafrika*, 1:165.
5. Caillié, *Voyage à Temboctou*, 1:36 [En. transl.: *Travels through Central Africa to Timbuctoo*, 1:25]. (See also apropros p. 121.)
6. Crawfurd, *History of the Indian Archipelago*, 1:280.
7. Nachtigal, *Sahârâ und Sûdân*, 3:36 [En. transl.: *Sahara and Sudan*, 4:31].
8. Schlömann, "Die Malepa in Transvaal," 69.
9. Schadenberg, "Die Bewohner von Süd-Mindanao," 10, 19, 29.
10. Ehrenreich, "Südamerikanische Stromfahrten," 101.

Chapter 16

1. Oppert, *Ein verschlossenes Land*, 133, 154, 156 [En. transl.: *A Forbidden Land*, 148, 171, 173].
2. Herberstein, *Notes upon Russia*, 1:110.
3. Kubary, *Karolinen Archipels*, 8.
4. Kurz, *Tagebuch des Malers*, 116 [En. transl.: *Journal of Rudolph Friederich Kurz*, 151].
5. Finsch, *Südsee*, 12.
6. Codrington, *The Melanesians*, 325.
7. Coote, *The Western Pacific*, 146.
8. Mollien, *Reise in das Innere von Afrika*, 198 [En. transl.: *Travels in the Interior of Africa*, 190].
9. Stetten, "Das nördliche Hinterland von Kamerun," 34–35.

Chapter 17

1. *Das Augenornament und verwandte Probleme*, 95; "Zur Ornamentik der Aino," 249.
2. Cf. Schmeltz, *Schnecken und Muscheln im Leben der Völker*.
3. Ratzel, *Anthropogeographie*, 2:675–77.
4. Nachtigal, "Handel im Sudan," 325.
5. Nachtigal, "Handel im Sudan," 314.

Supplements

1. Hahl, "Rechtsanschauungen der Eingeborenen [der] Blanchbucht," 71, 74, 72, 79, 84, 85.
2. Vetter, "Papuanische Rechtsverhältnisse," 98, 96, 101.
3. Powers in Westermarck, *Geschichte der menschlichen Ehe*, 393 [Orig.: *The History of Human Marriage*, 392; citing Powers, *Tribes of California*, 247].
4. Baumann, *Eine afrikanische Tropeninsel*, 83.

5. Monteiro, *Angola and the River Congo*, 2:168–69.
6. Loyer, "Kurze Nachricht von einer Seefahrt nach Issini," 457 [En. trans.: Leyden, *Discoveries and Travels in Africa*, 290].
7. Roth, *The Natives of Sarawak*, 2:112.
8. Steinen, *Unter den Naturvölkern Zentral-Brasiliens*, 333, 502–3.
9. Lamprecht, *Deutsche Geschichte*, 3:18.
10. Polak, *Persien. Das Land und seine Bewohner*, 1:153–54.
11. Burckhardt, *Reisen in Arabien*, 587 [Orig.: *Travels in Arabia*, 2:267].
12. According to a report which I owe to Professor O. Schneider in Blasewitz [Verein für Erdkunde zu Dresden, "Versammlung im 35. Vereinsjahre," 26, 32].
13. Lemaire, *Au Congo*, 113.
14. Lippert, *Kulturgeschichte der Menschheit*, 1:33 [En. transl.: *The Evolution of Culture*, 32].

Schurtz's References

Editors' note: The original *Grundriss* lacks a bibliography, so we have added a comprehensive one here which includes the editions cited by Schurtz (in German, English, Latin, Greek, Italian, Spanish, French, and Dutch) and, where available, their translations or English editions, which have been noted in square brackets in the endnotes. For cases where Schurtz mentions an author in his text but does not provide a specific bibliographic reference, we have added a new entry, with the author's surname in bold.

Allen, William, and Thomas Richard Heywood Thomson. 1848. *A Narrative of the Expedition Sent by Her Majesty's Government to the River Niger, in 1841*, vols. 1 and 2. London: Bentley.

Álvares, Francisco. 1881. *Narrative of the Portuguese Embassy to Abyssinia During the Years 1520–1527*. Translated by Lord Stanley of Alderley. London: Hakluyt Society.

Anderson, Johann. 1747. *Nachrichten von Island, Grönland und der Strasse Davis […]* Hamburg: Grund. Translated by Niels Horrebow as *The Natural History of Iceland [...]* (London: Linde, 1758).

Andree, Richard. 1878. *Ethnographische Parallelen und Vergleiche*. Stuttgart: Maier.

———. 1885. "Aggri-Perlen." *Zeitschrift für Ethnologie* 17: 110–15.

———. 1889. *Ethnographische Parallelen und Vergleiche: Neue Folge*. Leipzig: Veit.

Argensola, Bartolomé Leonardo de. 1711. *Beschreibung der Molukischen Insuln; und derer zwischen den Spaniern, Portugiesen und Holländern darum geführten Kriege*, vol. 2. Frankfurt: Rohrlach.

Baker, Samuel White. 1868. *Die Nilzuflüsse in Abyssinien: Forschungsreise vom Atbara zum Blauen Nil und Jagden in Wüsten und Wildnissen*, vol. 1. Braunschweig: Westermann. Originally published as *Exploration of the Nile Tributaries of Abyssinia: The Sources, Supply, and Overflow of the Nile, the Country, People, Customs, etc.* (San Francisco: Case Dewing, 1868).

Barth, Heinrich. 1857. *Reisen und Entdeckungen in Nord und Central-Afrika in den Jahren 1849 bis 1855*, vols. 2 and 3. 5 vols. Gotha: Justus Perthes. English edition published as *Travels and Discoveries in North and Central Africa, Being a Journal of an Expedition Undertaken ... in the Years 1849–1855*. 5 vols. (London: Longman; New York: Harper & Brothers, 1857–1858). [Published in both German and English by Barth. The page numbers are to the first American edition.]

Bastian, Adolf. 1867. *Reisen in Siam im Jahre 1863*. Jena: Costenoble. Translated by Walter E.J. Tips as *A Journey in Siam (1863)* (Bangkok: White Lotus Press, 2005).

———. 1874. *Die deutsche Expedition an der Loango-Küste, nebst älteren Nachrichten über die zu erforschenden Länder*, vols. 1 and 2. Jena: Costenoble.

Batchelor, John. 1892. *The Ainu of Japan: The Religion, Superstitions, and General History of the Hairy Aborigines of Japan*. London: Religious Tract Society.

Baumann, Oscar. 1887. "Handel und Verkehr am Congo." *Revue coloniale internationale* 5 (2): 223–34.

———. 1888. *Eine afrikanische Tropeninsel: Fernando Póo und die Bube*. Vienna: Hölzel.

Benko, Jerolim von. 1892. *Die Schiffs-Station der K. und K. Kriegs-Marine in Ost-Asien: Reisen S. M. Schiffe "Nautilus" und "Aurora" 1884–1888*. Vienna: Gerold.

Bibliothek der Geschichte der Menschheit. 1780. "Bewohner der Goldküste." In *Bibliothek der Geschichte der Menschheit*, vol. 2. Leipzig: Weidmanns Erben. Partly translated and republished in *A New General Collection of Voyages and Travels: Consisting of the Most Esteemed Relations, which have been hitherto Published in any Language [...]*, vol. 2, edited by John Green, 520–732 (London: Astley, 1745).

Blau, Otto. 1858. *Commercielle Zustände Persiens: Aus den Erfahrungen einer Reise im Sommer 1857*. Berlin: Decker.

Blumentritt, Ferdinand. 1893. "Die Bubis von Fernando Póo. Aus den Reise- bzw. Missionsberichten von Don José Valero und P. Joaquin Juanola." *Mitteilungen der Kaiserlich-Königlichen Geographischen Gesellschaft* 36: 23–31.

Boas, Franz. 1887. "Notes on the Ethnology of British Columbia." *Proceedings of the American Philosophical Society* 24 (126): 422–28.

Bock, Carl. 1882. *Unter den Kannibalen auf Borneo: Eine Reise auf dieser Insel und auf Sumatra.* Jena: Costenoble. Originally published as *The Head-hunters of Borneo: A Narrative of Travel Up the Mahakkam and Down the Barito; Also, Journeyings in Sumatra* (London: Low, 1882).

———. 1885. *Im Reiche des weißen Elephanten: Vierzehn Monate im Lande und am Hofe des Königs von Siam.* Leipzig: Hirt. Originally published as *Temples and Elephants: The Narrative of a Journey of Exploration Through Upper Siam and Lao* (London: Low, 1884).

Bonvalot, Gabriel. 1889. *Du Caucase aux Indes à travers le Pamir.* Paris: Plon. Translated by C. B. Pitman as *Through the Heart of Asia: Over the Pamïr to India.* 2 vols. (London: Chapman, 1889).

———. 1892. *De Paris au Tonkin à travers le Tibet inconnu.* Paris: Hachette. Translated by C. B. Pitman as *Across Thibet. Being a Translation of "De Paris au Tonkin à travers le Tibet inconnu."* 2 vols. (London: Cassell, 1891).

Bosman, Willem. 1704. *Nauwkeurige beschryving van de Guinese Goud-, Tand-, en Slave-kust.* Utrecht: Schouten. Translated as *A New and Accurate Description of the Coast of Guinea, Divided into the Gold, the Slave, and the Ivory Coasts* (London: Knapton, 1705).

Boyer, Jean. 1881. "Voyage au pays de Bamako sur le Haut-Niger." *Bulletin de la Société de géographie* 2 (July–December): 123–63.

Boyle, Frederick. 1884. "Schilderungen aus dem Britischen Borneo." *Das Ausland: Wochenschrift für Länder- und Völkerkunde* 38 (44): 1048–52. Excerpts from *Adventures Among the Dyaks of Borneo* (London: Hurst, 1865).

Brown, William. 1845. *New Zealand and its Aborigines: Being an Account of the Aborigines, Trade, and Resources of the Colony [...].* London: Smith.

Browne, William George. 1800. *Reisen in Afrika, Egypten und Syrien.* Weimar: Industrie-Comptoirs. Originally published as *Travels in Africa, Egypt, and Syria: From the Year 1792 to 1798* (London: Cadell, 1799).

Brückner, Alexander. 1867. *Finanzgeschichtliche Studien: Kupfergeldkrisen.* St. Petersburg: Kaiserlichen Akademie der Wissenschaften.

Bücher, Karl. 1893. *Die Entstehung der Volkswirtschaft.* Tübingen: Laupp. Third German edition translated by Samuel Morley Wickett as *Industrial Evolution* (New York: Holt, 1901).

Bülow, Franz Josef von. 1896. *Deutsch-Südwestafrika: Drei Jahre im Lande Hendrik Witboois; Schilderungen von Land und Leute.* Berlin: Mittler.

Burckhardt, Johann L. 1820. *Johann Ludwig Burckhardt's Reisen in Nubien.* Weimar: Industrie-Comptoirs. Originally published as *Travels in Nubia by the late John Lewis Burckhardt* (London: Murray, 1819).

———. 1830. *Reisen in Arabien: Enthaltend eine Beschreibung derj. Gebiete in Hedjaz, welche die Mohammedaner für heilig achten.* Weimar: Industrie-Comptoirs. Originally published as *Travels in Arabia, Comprehending an Account of Those Territories in Hedjaz which the Mohammedans Regard as Sacred.* 2 vols. (London: Colburn, 1829).

Burton, Richard F. 1857. *Personal Narrative of a Pilgrimage to El-Medinah and Meccah,* vols. 1 and 2, 2nd ed. London: Longman.

———. 1859. "The Lake Regions of Central Equatorial Africa, with Notices of the Lunar Mountains and the Sources of the White Nile [...]." *The Journal of the Royal Geographical Society of London* 29: 1–454.

———. 1860. *The Lake Regions of Central Africa: A Picture Exploration,* vol. 2. London: Longman.

Büttikofer, Johann. 1888. "Einiges über die Eingeborenen von Liberia." *Internationales Archiv für Ethnographie* 1: 33–48.

———. 1890. *Reisebilder aus Liberia: Resultate geographischer, naturwissenschaftlicher und ethnographischer Untersuchungen,* vol. 2. Leiden: Brill. Edited and translated by Henk Dop and Phillip Robinson as *Travel Sketches from Liberia: Johann Büttikofer's 19th Century Rainforest Explorations in West Africa* (Leiden: Brill, 2012).

Büttner, Richard. 1890. *Reisen im Kongolande: Ausgeführt im Auftrage der Afrikanischen Gesellschaft in Deutschland.* Leipzig: Hinrichs.

Caesar, Julius. 1853. *C. Julii Caesaris Commentarii de Bello Gallico.* Edited by Friedrich Kraner. Leipzig: Weidmannsche Buchhandlung. English edition translated by W. A. McDevitte and W. S. Bohn as *Caesar's Gallic War* (London: Bohn, 1869).

Caillié, René. 1830. *Journal d'un voyage à Temboctou et à Jenné, dans l'Afrique centrale [...],* vols. 1 and 2. Paris: L'imprimerie Royale. Translated as *Travels Through Central Africa to Timbuctoo; and Across the Great Desert to Morocco, 1824–1828,* vol. 1. London: Colburn.

Cameron, Verney Lovett. 1877. *Quer durch Afrika*, vol. 2. Leipzig: Brockhaus. Originally published as *Across Africa*, vols. 1 and 2 (London: Daldy, 1877).

Canstatt, Oskar. 1877. *Brasilien: Land und Leute*. Berlin: Mittler.

Casati, Gaetano. 1891. *Zehn Jahre in Äquatoria und die Rückkehr mit Emin Pascha*, vols. 1 and 2. Bamberg: Buchner. Translated as *Ten Years in Equatoria and the Return of Emin Pasha*, vols. 1 and 2 (London: Warne, 1891). Original in Italian.

Chalmers, James, and William Wyatt Gill. 1886. *Neuguinea: Reisen und Missionsthätigkeit während der Jahre 1877 bis 1885*. Leipzig: Brockhaus. Originally published as *Work and Adventure in New Guinea: 1877 to 1885* (London: Religious Tract Society, 1885).

Chamisso, Adelbert. 1882. *Chamissos Werke: Gedichte erste und zweite Abteilung [...]*. Edited by Oskar Walzel. Deutsche National-Litteratur 148. Stuttgart: Union Deutsche Verlagsgesellschaft.

Cibot, Pierre-Martial. 1779. "Mémoire sur l'intérêt de l'argent en Chine." In *Mémoires concernant l'histoire, les sciences, les arts, les mœurs, les usages, &c. des Chinois: par les missionnaires de Pékin*, vol. 4, 299–391. Paris: Nyon.

Cicalek, Theodor. 1888. "Die Währungsverhältnisse der Erde." *Deutsche Rundschau für Geographie und Statistik* 10: 455–62, 558–63.

Clercq, Frederik S. A. de, and Johann D. E. Schmeltz. 1893. *Ethnographische beschrijving van de west- en noord-kust van Nederlandsch Nieuw-Guinea*. Leiden: Trap.

Codrington, Robert Henry. 1891. *The Melanesians: Studies in Their Anthropology and Folk-Lore*. Oxford: Clarendon Press.

Cooper, Thomas Thornville. 1871. *Travels of a Pioneer of Commerce in Pigtail and Petticoats: Or, an Overland Journey from China Towards India*. London: Murray.

———. 1873. *The Mishmee Hills: An Account of a Journey Made in an Attempt to Penetrate Thibet from Assam to Open New Routes for Commerce*. London: King & Company.

Coote, Walter. 1883. *The Western Pacific: Being a Description of the Groups of Islands to the North and East of the Australian Continent*. London: Low.

Coquilhat, Camille. 1888. *Sur le Haut-Congo*. Paris: Lebègue.

Crawfurd, John. 1820. *History of the Indian Archipelago: Containing an Account of the Manners, Arts, Languages, Religions, Institutions, and Commerce of its Inhabitants*, vol. 1. Edinburgh: Constable.

Crisp, John. (1799) 1886. "An Account of the Inhabitants of the Poggy, or Nassau Islands, Lying off Sumatra." In *Miscellaneous Papers Relating to Indo-China Reprinted for the Straits Branch of the Royal Asiatic Society*, vol. 1, edited by Reinhold Rost, 66–76. London: Trübner.

Cuny, C. 1896. "De Libreville au Cameroun." *Bulletin de la Société de géographie* 17 (1): 337–65.

Curtius, Ernst. 1870. "Über den religiösen Charakter der griechischen Münzen." In *Monatsberichte der Königlich Preußischen Akademie der Wissenschaften zu Berlin aus dem Jahre 1869*, 465–81. Berlin. Akademie der Wissenschaften. Translated by Barclay V. Head as "On the Religious Character of Greek Coins." *The Numismatic Chronicle and Journal of the Numismatic Society* 10 (1870): 91–111.

d'Albéca, Alexandre L. 1895. "Voyage au pays des Éoués (Dahomey)." *Le Tour du monde*, nouvelle série, 1: 109–16. Republished in *La France au Dahomey* (Paris: Hachette, 1895).

d'Escayrac de Lauture, Stanislas. 1867. *Die Afrikanische Wüste und das Land der Schwarzen am oberen Nil*. Leipzig: Senf. Originally published as *Le désert et le Soudan* (Paris: Dumaine, 1853).

Dalzel, Archibald. 1799. *Geschichte von Dahomy, einem inländischen Königreich in Afrika*. Leipzig: Schwickert. Originally published as *The History of Dahomy: An Inland Kingdom of Africa* (London: Spilsbury, 1793).

Dapper, Olfert. 1676. *Naukeurige beschrijvinge der Afrikaensche gewesten van Egypten, Barbaryen, Libyen, Biledulgerid, Negroslant, Guinea, Ethiopiën, Abyssinie*, 2nd ed. Amsterdam: Van Meurs. Partly translated and republished in *Africa: Being an Accurate Description of the Regions of Aegypt, Barbary, Lybia and Billedulgerid. Collected and Translated from Most Authentick Authors*. Edited by John Ogilby (London: Johnson, 1670).

Delcommune, Alex. 1895. "Itinéraire de l'expédition Delcommune au Katanga, 1891–1892." *Le Mouvement Géographique* 4: 1–6.

Denham, Dixon, Hugh Clapperton, and Walter Oudney. 1827. *Beschreibung der Reisen und Entdeckungen im nördlichen und mittleren Africa in den Jahren 1822 bis 1824*. Weimar: Industrie-Comptoirs. Originally published as *Narrative of Travels and Discoveries in Northern and Central Africa: In the Years 1822, 1823, and 1824*, vols. 1 and 2, 3rd ed. (London: Murray, 1828).

Dobrizhoffer, Martin. 1783. *Geschichte der Abiponer, einer berittenen und kriegerischen Nation in Paraquay [...]*, vol. 1. Vienna: Kurzbek. Translated as *An Account of the Abipones: An Equestrian People of Paraguay*, vol. 1 (London: Murray, 1822).

Does, A. M. K. de. 1893. "Toestand der nijverheid in de afdeeling Band-jarnegara [State of industry in Bandjarnegara district]." *Tijdschrift voor Indische Taal-, Land- en Volkenkunde* 36: 1–112.

Duncan, John. 1848. *Reisen in Westafrika, von Whydah durch das Königreich Dahomey nach Adofudia im Innern: In den Jahren 1845 und 1846*, vols. 1 and 2. Dresden: Arnoldische Buchhandlung. Originally published as *Travels in Western Africa, in 1845 & 1846: Comprising a Journey from Whydah, Through the Kingdom of Dahomey, to Adofoodia, in the Interior*, vols. 1 and 2 (London: Bentley, 1847).

Eberstein, Ernst. 1896. "Ueber die Rechtsanschauungen der Küstenbewoh-ner des Bezirkes Kilwa." *Mitteilungen von Forschungsreisenden und Ge-lehrten aus den deutschen Schutzgebieten* 10: 170–84.

Eckardt, M. 1881. "Die Salomo-Inseln." *Globus: Illustrierte Zeitschrift für Länder- und Völkerkunde* 39 (24): 376–79.

Edelfelt, Erik Gustav. 1892. "Customs and Superstitions of New Guinea Natives." *Proceedings and Transactions of the Queensland Branch of the Ge-ographical Society of Australasia* 7 (1): 9–29.

Ehrenreich, Paul. 1892. "Südamerikanische Stromfahrten. IV. Bei den freien Sambioa." *Globus: Illustrierte Zeitschrift für Länder- und Völkerkunde* 62 (7): 100–106.

Ellis, Alfred Burdon. 1890. *The Ewe-Speaking Peoples of the Slave Coast of West Africa: Their Religion, Manners, Customs, Laws, Languages, &c.* Lon-don: Chapman.

Ellis, William. 1829. *Polynesian Researches, During a Residence of Nearly Six Years in the South Sea Islands*, vol. 2. London: Fisher.

Endemann, Karl 1874. "Mittheilungen über die Sotho-Neger." *Zeitschrift für Ethnologie* 6: 16–66.

Erdmann, Max. 1880. "Scherben von dem Weinberge bei Oblath." *Verhandlungen der Berliner Gesellschaft für Anthropologie, Ethnologie und Urgeschichte* 12: 143–58.

Fichte, Johann Gottlieb. 1800. *Der geschloßne Handelsstaat: Ein philosophi-scher Entwurf als Anlage zur Rechtslehre, und Probe einer künftig zu lie-fernden Politik.* Tübingen: Cotta. Translated by Anthony Curtis Adler as *The Closed Commercial State* (New York: State University of New York Press, 2012).

Finsch, Otto. 1888. *Samoafahrten: Reisen in Kaiser Wilhelms-Land und Eng-lisch-Neu-Guinea in den Jahren 1884 und 1885.* Leipzig: Hirt.

————. 1893. *Ethnologische Erfahrungen und Belegstücke aus der Südsee*. Vienna: Hölder.

Fischer, Gustav A. 1884. "Bericht über die im Auftrage der Geographischen Gesellschaft in Hamburg unternommene Reise in das Massai-Land." *Mitteilungen der Geographischen Gesellschaft in Hamburg, 1882–1883*, 5: 36–99.

Florenz, Karl, trans. and ed. 1889 "Nihongi oder Japanische Annalen. Dritter Teil. Geschichte Japans im 7. Jahrhundert. Buch 25 und 26." In *Mitteilungen der Deutschen Gesellschaft für Natur- und Völkerkunde Ostasiens in Tokio*. Supplement-Heft zu Band V. Yokohama: Meiklejohn. Edited and translated by William George Aston as *Nihongi: Chronicles of Japan from the Earliest Times to A.D. 697*, vol. 2 (London: Kegan Paul, 1896).

François, Curt von. 1888. *Die Erforschung des Tschuapa und Lulongo: Reisen in Centralafrika*. Leipzig: Brockhaus.

Gisborne, William. 1891. *The Colony of New Zealand: Its History, Vicissitudes and Progress*. London: Petherick.

Goethe, Johann Wolfgang von. 1868. *Goethes Werke*, vols. 16 and 23. Stuttgart: Cotta.

Golberry [Golbéry], Sylvain-Meinrad-Xavier de. 1804. *Reise durch das westliche Afrika in den Jahren 1785, 1786 und 1787*, vols. 1 and 2. Paris: Treuttel. Translated as *Travels in Africa, Performed by Silvester Meinrad Xavier Golberry, in the Western Parts of That Vast Continent [...]*, vols. 1 and 2, 2nd ed. (London: Jones, 1808). Original in French.

Gordon Cumming, Constance F. 1881. *At Home in Fiji*, vol. 1. Edinburgh: Blackwood.

Grabowski, F. S. 1885. "Ueber die 'djawet's' oder heiligen Töpfe der Oloh ngadju (Dajaken) von Süd-Ost-Borneo." *Zeitschrift für Ethnologie* 17: 121–28.

Grandpré, Louis de. 1801. *Reise nach der westlichen Küste von Africa in den Jahren 1786 und 1787*. Weimar: Industrie-Comptoirs. Originally published as *Voyage à la côte occidentale d'Afrique: fait dans les années 1786 et 1787, contenant la description des mœurs, usages, lois, gouvernement et commerce des états du Congo [...]*, vol. 1 (Paris: Palais du Tribunal, 1801).

Guessfeldt, Paul. 1876. "Zur Kenntniss der Loango-Neger." *Zeitschrift für Ethnologie* 8: 203–16.

Guppy, Henry Brougham. 1887. *The Solomon Islands and Their Natives*. London: Swan Sonnenschein.

Gürich, Georg. 1891. *Deutsch Südwest-Afrika: Reisebilder und Skizzen aus den Jahren 1888 und 1889 mit einer Original-Routenkarte.* Hamburg: Friederichsen.

Guthe, Hermann. 1882. "Ausgrabungen bei Jerusalem." *Zeitschrift des Deutschen Palästina-Vereins* 5: 7–204.

Hagen, Bernhard. 1886. "Rapport über eine im Dezember 1883 unternommene wissenschaftliche Reise an den Toba-See (Central Sumatra)." *Tijdschrift voor Indische Taal-, Land- en Volkenkunde* 31: 328–83.

Haggenmacher, Gustav Adolf. 1876. *G. A. Haggenmacher's Reise im Somali-Lande, 1874.* Ergänzungsheft zu Petermanns geographischen Mitteilungen 47. Gotha: Perthes.

Hahl, Albert. 1897. "Über die Rechtsanschauungen der Eingeborenen eines Theiles der Blanchbucht und des Innern der Gazelle Halbinsel." *Nachrichten über Kaiser Wilhelms-Land und den Bismarck-Archipel* 13: 68–85.

Hale, Horatio. 1885. "On the Nature and Origin of Wampum." *Report of the British Association for the Advancement of Science*, 54th Meeting: 910–11.

Harnier, Wilhelm von. 1863. "Reise auf dem Weissen Nil, Dezbr. 1860 bis Novbr. 1861." In *Inner-Afrika nach dem Stande der geographischen Kenntniss in den Jahren 1861 bis 1863*, Ergänzungsband II 1862/1863, edited by A. Petermann and B. Hassenstein, 125–41. Mittheilungen aus Justus Perthes' Geographischer Anstalt, Ergänzungsheft Nr. 10. Gotha: Justus Perthes.

Hartert, Ernst. 1886. "Ueber Religion und Lebensweise der Bevölkerung in den von ihm bereisten Gegenden des Nigergebietes, sowie über Handel und Verkehr daselbst." *Verhandlungen der Gesellschaft für Erdkunde zu Berlin* 18: 431–40.

Hassan, Vita. 1893. *Die Wahrheit über Emin Pascha: Die ägyptische Aequatorialprovinz und den Ssudān.* Berlin: Reimer.

Hecquard, Hyacinthe. 1854. *Reise an die Küste und in das Innere von West-Afrika.* Leipzig: Dyk'sche Buchhandlung. Originally published as *Voyage sur la côte et dans l'intérieur de l'Afrique occidentale* (Paris: Bénard, 1843).

Hedley, Charles. 1896. *The Atoll of Funafuti, Ellice Group: Its Zoology, Botany, Ethnology, and General Structure*, vol. 1. Sydney: Australian Museum.

Henry, Benjamin Couch. 1886. *Ling-Nam: Or, Interior Views of Southern China, Including Explorations in the Hitherto Untraversed Island of Hainan.* London: Partridge.

Herberstein, Sigmund von. 1851. *Notes upon Russia: Being a Translation of the Earliest Account of That Country; Entitled Rerum Moscoviticarum Commentarii*, vol. 1. London: Hakluyt Society.

Hernsheim, Franz. 1883. *Südsee-Erinnerungen (1875–1880)*. Berlin: Hofmann.

Herold, Anton Bruno. 1893. "Einheimische Handels- und Gewerbsthätigkeit im Togogebiete." *Mitteilungen von Forschungsreisenden und Gelehrten aus den deutschen Schutzgebieten* 6: 266–80.

Herrmann, [Karl]. 1893. "Bericht des Kompagnieführers Herrmann über die Stationen Mwanja und Bukoba." *Deutsches Kolonialblatt* 4 (1): 111–12.

———. 1894. "Die Wasiba und ihr Land." *Mitteilungen von Forschungsreisenden und Gelehrten aus den deutschen Schutzgebieten* 7: 43–47.

Hertz, John E. 1880. "Ueber Verwendung und Verbreitung der Kauriemuschel." *Mitteilungen der Geographischen Gesellschaft in Hamburg* 11: 14–29.

Hettner's Geographische Nachrichten. 1896. "Ausfuhr von Maria-Theresia-Thalern nach Afrika." *Mittheilungen der Kais. Königl. Geographischen Gesellschaft in Wien* 34: 699.

Heuglin, Theodor von. 1868. *Reise nach Abessinien, den Gala-Ländern, Ost-Sudán und Chartúm in den Jahren 1861 und 1862*. Jena: Costenoble.

Hiekisch, Carl. 1879. *Die Tungusen: Eine ethnologische Monographie*. St. Petersburg: Kaiserlichen Akademie der Wissenschaften.

Hildebrandt, Johann. M. 1874. "Herr Hildebrandt: Uebersicht seiner Reisen in den Küstenländern von Arabien und Ost-Afrika." *Verhandlungen der Gesellschaft für Erdkunde zu Berlin* 1 (2): 269–76.

Hirth, Friedrich. 1888. "Ancient Porcelain." *Journal of the China Branch of the Royal Asiatic Society* 22: 129–202.

Hoffmann, W. I. 1884. "Die Tätowierung und Gesichtsverzierung bei den nordamerikanischen Indianern." *Das Ausland: Wochenschrift für Länder- und Völkerkunde* 57 (31): 612–14.

Holmes, William H. 1883. "Art in Shell of the Ancient Americans." In *Annual Report of the Bureau of American Ethnology to the Secretary of the Smithsonian Institution for 1880–81*, edited by J. W. Powell, 179–305. Washington: U.S. Government Printing Office.

Hutton, William. 1823. *Nouveau voyage dans l'intérieur de l'Afrique, ou relation de l'ambassade Anglaise envoyée, en 1820, au Royaume d'Ashantée*. Paris: Persan. Originally published as *A Voyage to Africa: Including a Nar-*

rative of an Embassy to One of the Interior Kingdoms, in the Year 1820 [...] (London: Longman, 1821).

Ilwof, Franz. 1882. *Tauschhandel und Geldsurrogate in alter und neuer Zeit.* Graz: Leuschner.

Im Thurn, Everard Ferdinand. 1883. *Among the Indians of Guiana: Being Sketches Chiefly Anthropologic from the Interior of British Guiana.* London: Kegan Paul.

Isert, Paul Erdmann. 1790. *Neue Reise nach Guinea und den Caribäischen Inseln in Amerika in den Jahren 1783 bis 1787.* Leipzig: Postum. Edited and translated by Selena Axelrod Winsnes as *Letters on West Africa and the Slave Trade: Paul Erdmann Isert's Journey to Guinea and the Caribbean Islands in Columbia, 1788* (Oxford: British Academy, 1992).

Jacobsen, Johan Adrian. 1884. *Capitain Jacobsen's Reise an der Nordwestküste Amerikas, 1881–1883: Zum Zwecke ethnologischer Sammlungen und Erkundigungen.* Leipzig: Spohr. Translated by Erna Gunther as *Alaskan Voyage, 1881–1883: An Expedition to the Northwest Coast of America* (Chicago: University of Chicago Press, 1977).

Joest, Wilhelm. 1885. *Um Afrika.* Köln: Dumont-Schauberg.

———. 1893. *Ethnographisches und Verwandtes aus Guayana.* Leiden: Trap.

Johnston, Harry Hamilton. 1884. *Der Kongo: Reise von seiner Mündung bis Bolobo.* Leipzig: Brockhaus. Originally published as *The River Congo, from its Mouth to Bólóbó [...]*, 3rd ed. (London: Low, 1884).

Jung, Ferdinand. 1897. "Aufzeichnungen über die Rechtsanschauungen der Eingeborenen von Nauru." *Mitteilungen von Forschungsreisenden und Gelehrten aus den deutschen Schutzgebieten* 10: 64–191.

Keller, Conrad. 1887. *Reisebilder aus Ostafrika und Madagaskar.* Leipzig: Winter.

Keller-Jordan, Henriette. 1889. "Mexiko zur Zeit Montezumas: Nach altspanischen Quellen aus dem Jahre 1691." *Das Ausland: Wochenschrift für Länder- und Völkerkunde* 62 (19): 361–64.

Klaproth, M. Julius. 1834. "Notice sur l'usage des cauries en Chine." *Nouveau journal asiatique* 8: 146–55.

Klemm, Gustav Friedrich. 1844. *Allgemeine Cultur-Geschichte der Menschheit: Die Hirtenvölker der passiven Menschheit*, vol. 3. Leipzig: Teubner.

———. 1847. *Allgemeine Cultur-Geschichte der Menschheit: China und Japan*, vol. 6. Leipzig: Teubner.

Kling, Erich. 1893. "Auszug aus den Tagebüchern des Hauptmanns Kling 1891 bis 1892." *Mitteilungen von Forschungsreisenden und Gelehrten aus den deutschen Schutzgebieten* 6: 105–254.

Köler, Hermann. 1848. *Einige Notizen über Bonny an der Küste von Guinea: Seine Sprache und seine Bewohner.* Göttingen: Dieterichschen Univ.-Buchdruckerei.

Krapf, Johann Ludwig. 1858. *Reisen in Ostafrika, ausgeführt in den Jahren 1837–1855*, vol. 1. Stuttgart: Stroh.

Krause, Aurel. 1885. *Die Tlinkit-Indianer: Ergebnisse einer Reise nach der Nordwestküste von Amerika und der Beringstrasse [...].* Jena: Costenoble. Translated by Erna Gunther as *The Tlingit Indians: Results of a Trip to the Northwest Coast of America and the Bering Straits* (Seattle: University of Washington Press, 1956).

Kubary, Jan Stanislaus. 1889. *Ethnographische Beiträge zur Kenntnis des Karolinen Archipels.* Leipzig: Trap.

Kuntze, Otto. 1881. *Um die Erde: Reiseberichte eines Naturforschers.* Leipzig: Frohberg.

Kurz, Friedrich. 1896. *Aus dem Tagebuch des Malers Friedrich Kurz über seinen Aufenthalt bei den Missouri-Indianern 1848–1852.* Edited by Emil Kurz. Bern: Geographische Gesellschaft von Bern. Translated by Myrtis Jarrell as *Journal of Rudolph Friederich Kurz: The Life and Work of This Swiss Artist* (Fairfield, Wash.: Ye Galleon Press, 1937).

Lafitte, J. (Abbé). 1876. *Le Dahomé: Souvenirs de voyage et de mission*, 4th ed. Tours: Mame.

Lamprecht, Karl. 1885. *Deutsches Wirtschaftsleben im Mittelalter. Statistisches Material, Quellenkunde*, vol. 2. Leipzig: Durr.

———. 1893. *Deutsche Geschichte*, vol. 3. 13 vols. Berlin: Gaertners.

Lander, Richard. 1830. *Records of Captain Clapperton's Last Expedition to Africa*, vol. 1. London: Colburn.

Lander, Richard, and John Lander. 1833. *Reise in Afrika zur Erforschung des Nigers bis zu seiner Mündung*, vols. 1–3. Leipzig: Engelmann. Originally published as *Journal of an Expedition to Explore the Course and Termination of the Niger: With a Narrative of a Voyage Down That River to its Termination*, vols. 1–3 (London: Harpers, 1832).

Langsdorff, Georg H. von. 1812. *Bemerkungen auf einer Reise um die Welt in den Jahren 1803 bis 1807*, vol. 2. Frankfurt: Milmans.

Laveleye, Emile de. 1878. *Primitive Property.* Translated by George Robert Laxon Marriott. London: Macmillan.

Lehmann-Filhés, Margarethe. 1896. "Kulturgeschichtliches aus Island (Schluss)." *Zeitschrift des Vereins für Volkskunde* 6 (4): 373–94.

Lemaire, Charles. 1895. *Au Congo: Comment les noirs travaillent*. Brussels: Bulens.

———. 1897. *Africaines: Contribution à l'histoire de la femme en Afrique*. Brussels: Impr. Scientifique.

Lenz, Oskar. 1878. *Skizzen aus Westafrika*. Berlin: Hofmann.

———. 1880. "Die Lenz'sche Expedition: Ausflug von Tanger nach Tetuan." *Mittheilungen der Afrikanischen Gesellschaft in Deutschland* 2 (2): 67–116.

———. 1884. *Timbuktu: Reise durch Marokko, die Sahara und den Sudan [...]*, vol. 2. Leipzig: Brockhaus.

———. 1895. *Ueber Geld bei Naturvölkern*. Hamburg: Actien-Gesellschaft.

Leo Africanus. 1805. *Johann Leo's des Africaners Beschreibung von Africa*. Translated by Georg Wilhelm Lorsbach, vol. 1. Herborn: Buchhandlung der hohen Schule. Edited by Roberto Brown as *The History and Description of Africa: And of the Notable Things Therein Contained*, vol. 3 (London: Hakluyt Society, 1896).

Lichtenstein, Heinrich. 1811–1812. *Reisen im südlichen Africa: In den Jahren 1803, 1804, 1805 und 1806*, vols. 1 and 2. Berlin: Salfeld.

Lippert, Julius. 1886. *Kulturgeschichte der Menschheit in ihrem organischen Aufbau*, vol. 1. Stuttgart: Enke. Edited and translated by George P. Murdock as *The Evolution of Culture* (New York: Macmillan, 1939).

Livingstone, David. 1858. *Missionsreisen und Forschungen in Süd-Afrika während eines sechzehnjährigen Aufenthalts im Innern des Continents*, vol. 1. Leipzig: Costenoble. Originally published as *Missionary Travels and Researches in South Africa: Including a Sketch of Sixteen Years' Residence in the Interior of Africa* (London: Murray, 1857).

Longfellow, Henry W. 1856. *The Song of Hiawatha*. London: Routledge.

Loskiel, George H. 1789. *Geschichte der Mission der evangelischen Brüder unter den Indianern in Nordamerika*. Leipzig: Barby. Translated as *History of the Mission of the United Brethren Among the Indians in North America* (London: Brethren's Society for the Furtherance of the Gospel, 1794).

Loyer, Gottfried. 1748. "Kurze Nachricht von einer Seefahrt nach Issini auf der Goldküste, im Jahre 1701 [...]." In *Allgemeine Historie der Reisen zu Wasser und Lande, oder Sammlung aller Reisebeschreibungen [...]*, vol. 3, 430–73. Leipzig: Arkstee. Partly translated and republished in *Historical*

Account of Discoveries and Travels in Africa. Edited by John Leyden, vol. 2 (Edinburgh: Constable, 1817). Original in French.

Lubbock, Sir John. 1870. *The Origin of Civilization and the Primitive Condition of Man: Mental and Social Condition of Savages*, 2nd ed. London: Longmans.

Lumholtz, Carl. 1892. *Unter Menschenfressern: Eine vierjährige Reise in Australien.* Hamburg: Actien-Gesellschaft.

Maccaulay, Clay. 1887. "The Seminole Indians of Florida." In *Annual Report of the Bureau of American Ethnology to the Secretary of the Smithsonian Institution for 1883–84*, edited by J. W. Powell, 475–538. Washington: U.S. Government Printing Office.

Maltzan, Heinrich von. 1863. *Drei Jahre im Nordwesten von Afrika: Reisen in Algerien und Marokko*, vols. 3 and 4. Leipzig: Dürr.

Mannhardt, Wilhelm. 1870. "Über die Pomerellischen Gesichtsurnen." *Verhandlungen der Berliner Gesellschaft für Anthropologie, Ethnologie und Urgeschichte* 2: 244–48.

Mariner, William. 1819. *Nachrichten über die Freundschaftlichen, oder die Tonga-Inseln.* Weimar: Industrie-Comptoirs. Originally published as *An Account of the Natives of the Tonga Islands in the South Pacific Ocean [...]*, 2 vols. (London: Murray, 1817).

Marno, Ernst. 1879. *Reise in der Egyptischen Aequatorial-Provinz und in Kordofan in den Jahren 1874–1876.* Vienna: Hölder.

Martens, Eduard von. 1872a. "Ueber verschiedene Verwendungen von Conchylien." *Zeitschrift für Ethnologie* 4: 21–36, 65–87.

———. 1872b. "Nachträge. Verwendung von Conchylien bei verschiedenen Völkern." *Verhandlungen der Berliner Gesellschaft für Anthropologie, Ethnologie und Urgeschichte* 4: 154–56.

———. 1889. "Banda, Timor und Flores." *Zeitschrift der Gesellschaft für Erdkunde zu Berlin* 24: 83–132.

Martius, Karl Friedrich Philipp von. 1830. *Von dem Rechtszustande unter den Ureinwohnern Brasiliens.* München: Lindauer. Partly translated by George Cecil Renouard in "Review." *The Journal of the Royal Geographical Society of London* 2 (1832): 191–227.

Meinicke, Carl Eduard. 1874. "Der Archipel der neuen Hebriden." *Zeitschrift der Gesellschaft für Erdkunde zu Berlin* 9: 275–300, 321–51.

———. 1876. *Die Inseln des Stillen Ozeans: Polynesien und Mikronesien*, vol. 2. Leipzig: Frohberg.

Merensky, Alexander. 1882. "Waffen, Zauberwürfel und Schmuckkorallen der Südafrikaner." *Verhandlungen der Berliner Gesellschaft für Anthropologie, Ethnologie und Urgeschichte* 14: 540–45.

Meyer, Adolf B. 1882. "Der Schädelkultus im ostindischen Archipel und der Südsee." *Das Ausland: Wochenschrift für Länder- und Völkerkunde* 55: 323–28.

Meyer, Hans. 1890. *Ostafrikanische Gletscherfahrten: Forschungsreisen im Kilimandscharo-Gebiet.* Leipzig: Duncker & Humblot.

Middendorf, Ernst W. 1893. *Peru: Beobachtungen und Studien über das Land und seine Bewohner während eines 25-jährigen Aufenthalts*, vol. 1. Berlin: Oppenheim.

Modigliani, Elio. 1890. *Un viaggio a Nías.* Milan: Fratelli Treves.

Mollien, Gaspard Théodore de. 1820. *G. Molliens Reise in das Innere von Afrika nach den Quellen des Senegal und Gambia: Im Jahre 1818 auf Befehl der Französischen Regierung.* Weimar: Industrie-Comptoirs. Translated as *Travels in the Interior of Africa, to the Sources of the Senegal and Gambia [...]* (London: Colburn, 1820). Original in French.

Moltke, Helmuth Karl Bernhard von. 1841. *Briefe über Zustände und Begebenheiten in der Türkei aus den Jahren 1835–1839.* Berlin: Mittler.

Mommsen, Theodor. 1860. *Geschichte des römischen Münzwesens.* Berlin: Weidmannsche Buchhandlung.

Monrad, Hans Christian. 1824. *Gemälde der Küste von Guinea und der Einwohner derselben, wie auch der Dänischen Colonien auf dieser Küste [...].* Weimar: Industrie-Comptoirs. Original in Danish.

Monteiro, Joachim John. 1875. *Angola and the River Congo*, vols. 1 and 2. London: Macmillan.

Morga, Antonio de. 1868. *The Philippine Islands, Moluccas, Siam, Cambodia, Japan, and China, at the Close of the Sixteenth Century.* London: Hakluyt Society. Original in Spanish.

Morgen, Curt von. 1893. *Durch Kamerun von Süd nach Nord: Reisen und Forschungen im Hinterlande, 1889 bis 1891.* Leipzig: Brockhaus.

Morse, Hosea Ballou. 1890. "Currency and Measures in China." *Journal of the China Branch of the Royal Asiatic Society* 24 (1): 46–135.

Moussy, Martin de. 1860. *Description géographique et statistique de la confédération argentine*, vol. 2. Paris: Firmin Didot frères.

Müller, Hans. 1888. "Mueller's Bericht über eine Reise in Muata-Kumbana." In *Im Innern Afrikas: Die Erforschung des Kassai während der Jahre*

1883, 1884 und 1885, edited by Hermann von Wissmann, Curt von Francois, Ludwig Wolf, and Hans Müller, 85–119. Leipzig: Brockhaus.

Müller, Johannes Heinrich. 1860. *Deutsche Münzgeschichte*, vol. 1. Leipzig: Weigel.

Müller, Robert. 1889. "Leben and Treiben in Kamerun." *Das Ausland: Wochenschrift für Länder- und Völkerkunde* 62 (6): 116–25.

Müller-Hess, Walter. 1890. "Die maledivischen Inseln." *Jahresbericht der Geographischen Gesellschaft von Bern* 10: 22–29.

Nachtigal, Gustav. 1873. "Zug mit einer Sklavenkarawane in Baghirmi. II." *Globus: Illustrierte Zeitschrift für Länder- und Völkerkunde* 24 (15): 231–33.

———. 1876. "Handel im Sudan." *Mitteilungen der Geographischen Gesellschaft in Hamburg, 1876–1877*, 305–26.

———. 1879–1881. *Sahărâ und Sûdân: Ergebnisse sechsjähriger Reisen in Afrika*, vols. 1 and 2. 3 vols. Berlin: Weidmannsche Buchhandlung. Translated by Allan G. B. Fisher and Humphrey J. Fisher as *Sahara and Sudan: Kawar, Bornu, Kanem, Borku, Ennedi*, vol. 2. 4 vols. (London: C. Hurst, 1980).

———. 1889. *Sahărâ und Sûdân: Ergebnisse sechsjähriger Reisen in Afrika*, vol. 3. 3 vols. Leipzig: Brockhaus. Translated by Allan G. B. Fisher and Humphrey J. Fisher as *Sahara and Sudan: Wadai and Darfur*, vol. 4. 4 vols. (Berkeley: University of California Press, 1971).

Nansen, Fridtjof. 1891. *Auf Schneeschuhen durch Grönland*, vol. 2. Hamburg: Actien-Gesellschaft. Translated as *Eskimo Life*, 2nd ed. (London: Longmans, 1894).

Napp, Ricardo. 1876. *Die Argentinische Republik*. Buenos Aires: Sociedad Anónima. Translated as *The Argentine Republic* (Buenos Aires: Sociedad Anónima, 1876).

Nebout, Albert. 1892. "La Mission Crampel." *Le Tour du monde* 64 (2): 1–64.

Niblack, Albert Parker. 1890. *The Coast Indians of Southern Alaska and Northern British Columbia*. Report of the United States National Museum for the year ending June 30 1888, 225–386. Washington: U.S. Government Printing Office.

Niebuhr, Carsten. 1772. *Beschreibung von Arabien aus eigenen Beobachtungen und im Lande selbst gesammelten Nachrichten*. Copenhagen: Müller. Translated as *Description of Arabia Made from Personal Observations and Information Collected on the Spot by Carsten Niebuhr* (Bombay: Government Central Press, 1889).

Niemann, G. K. 1895. "Ethnographische Mededeelingen Omtrent de Tjams en eenige Andere Volksstammen van Achter-Indië." *Bijdragen tot de Taal-, Land- en Volkenkunde van Nederlandsch-Indië* 45 (1): 329–53.

Noetling, Fritz. 1896. "Birmanisches Maass und Gewicht." *Verhandlungen der Berliner Gesellschaft für Anthropologie, Ethnologie und Urgeschichte* 28: 40–46.

Obruchev, Vladimir A. 1896. *Aus China. Reiseerlebnisse, Natur- und Völkerbilder,* vol. 1. Berlin: Duncker & Humblot.

Oppert, Ernst Jakob. 1880. *Ein verschlossenes Land: Reisen nach Corea.* Leipzig: Brockhaus. Translated as *A Forbidden Land: Voyages to the Corea* (London: Low, 1880).

Pallas, P. S. 1776. *Sammlungen historischer Nachrichten über die mongolischen Völkerschaften: Erster Teil,* vol. 1. St. Petersburg: Kaiserliche Akademie der Wissenschaften.

Papencordt, Felix. 1837. *Geschichte der vandalischen Herrschaft in Afrika.* Berlin: Duncker & Humblot.

Park, Mungo. 1799. *Mungo Park's Reise in das Innere von Afrika in den Jahren 1795, 1796 und 1797: Auf Veranstaltung der afrikanischen Gesellschaft unternommen.* Hamburg: Hoffmann. Originally published as *Travels in the Interior Districts of Africa [...]* (London: Bulmer, 1799).

Parkinson, Richard. 1889. "Beiträge zur Ethnologie der Gilbertinsulaner." *Internationales Archiv für Ethnographie* 2: 90–106.

Parkman, Francis. 1878. *Die Jesuiten in Nord-Amerika im siebzehnten Jahrhundert.* Stuttgart: Abenheim. Originally published as *The Jesuits in North America in the Seventeenth Century* (Boston: Little, Brown, 1867).

Pasha, Emin. 1888. *Emin-Pascha: Eine Sammlung von Reisebriefen und Berichten Dr. Emin-Pascha's aus den ehemals ägyptischen Aequatorialprovinzen und deren Grenzländern.* Edited by Georg Schweinfurth and Friedrich Ratzel. Leipzig: Brockhaus. Translated by Robert W. Felkin as *Emin Pasha in Central Africa: Being a Collection of His Letters and Journals* (London: Philip, 1888).

Passarge, Siegfried. 1895. *Adamaua: Bericht über die Expedition des Deutschen Kamerun-Komitees in den Jahren 1893/94.* Berlin: Reimer.

Paulitschke, Philipp V. 1893. *Ethnographie Nordost-Afrikas: Die geistige Cultur der Danâkil, Galla und Somâl,* vols. 1 and 2. Berlin: Reimer.

Peschel, Oscar. 1885. *Völkerkunde.* Leipzig: Duncker & Humblot.

Petersen, P. 1887. "Gustav Wallis' Reisen in Brasilien von 1860–1862." *Das Ausland: Wochenschrift für Länder- und Völkerkunde* 60 (2): 58–60.

Petherick, John. 1861. *Egypt, the Soudan and Central Africa*. London: Blackwood.

Plutarch. 1914. *Plutarch's Lives*. Translated by Bernadotte Perrin. Loeb Classical Library. London: Heinemann.

Pogge, Paul. 1884. "Bericht über die Station Mukenge bis Oktober 1883." *Mittheilungen der Afrikanischen Gesellschaft in Deutschland* 4 (3): 179–204.

———. 1885. "Expedition der Gesellschaft: Die Pogge-Wissmann'sche Expedition." *Mittheilungen der Afrikanischen Gesellschaft in Deutschland* 4 (4): 216–65.

Polak, Jakob Eduard. 1865. *Persien. Das Land und seine Bewohner*, vols. 1 and 2. Leipzig: Brockhaus.

Polo, Marco. 1818. *The Travels of Marco Polo, a Venetian, in the Thirteenth Century*. Translated by William Marsden. London: Cox.

———. 1875. *The Book of Ser Marco Polo, the Venetian: Concerning the Kingdoms and Marvels of the East*, vols. 1 and 2. Edited and translated by Henry Yule, 2nd ed. London: Murray.

Post, Albert Hermann. 1887. *Afrikanische Jurisprudenz: Ethnologisch-juristische Beiträge zur Kenntniss der einheimischen Rechte Afrikas*, vol. 1. Oldenburg: Schwartz.

Powers, Stephen. 1877. *Tribes of California*. Vol. 3. Contributions to North American Ethnology. U.S. Government Printing Office.

Priestermissionsbund. 1879. "Die Missionen unter den Negern." *Die Katholischen Missionen: Illustrierte Monatsschrift* 7: 1–24.

Prschewalski, Nikolaj M. 1877. *Reisen in der Mongolei, im Gebiet der Tanguten und den Wüsten Nordtibets: In den Jahren 1870 bis 1873*, 2nd ed. Jena: Costenoble. Translated as Prejevalski [Przhevalsky], *Mongolia, the Tangut Country, and the Solitudes of Northern Tibet, Being a Narrative of Three Years' Travel in Eastern High Asia*, vol. 2. (London: Low, 1876). Original in Russian.

Pyrard, François. 1887–1890. *The Voyage of François Pyrard of Laval to the East Indies, the Maldives, the Moluccas and Brazil*, vols. 1 and 2. London: Hakluyt Society.

Ramseyer, Friedrich August, and Johannes Kühne. 1875. *Vier Jahre in Asante: Tagebücher der Missionare Ramseyer und Kühne aus der Zeit ihrer Gefangenschaft*, 2nd ed. Basel: Verlag des Missionskomptoirs. Translated by Mary Weitbrecht as *Four Years in Ashantee* (London: Nisbet, 1875).

Rannie, Douglas. 1891. "Among the S.E. Solomons." *Proceedings and Transactions of the Queensland Branch of the Geographical Society of Australasia* 6 (2): 54–60.

Ratzel, Friedrich. 1891. *Anthropogeographie: Die geographische Verbreitung des Menschen*, vol. 2, 2nd ed. Stuttgart: Engelhorn.

Rau, Charles. 1873. "Ancient Aboriginal Trade in North America." In *Annual Report of the Board of Regents of the Smithsonian Institution for 1872*, 348–94. Washington: U.S. Government Printing Office.

Reade, William Winwood. 1873. *The African Sketchbook*, vol. 2. London: Smith.

Reichard, Paul. 1889. "Das afrikanische Elfenbein und sein Handel." *Deutsche Geographische Blätter* 12: 132–68.

Riley, James. 1818. *James Riley's Befehlshabers und Supercargo's des Americanischen Kauffahrteischiffs Commerce: Schicksale und Reisen an der Westküste und im Innern von Afrika in den Jahren 1815 und 1816 [...]*. Jena: Schmid. Originally published as *An Authentic Narrative of the Loss of the American Brig Commerce: Wrecked on the Western Coast of Africa [...]*, 3rd ed. (New York: The Author, 1818).

Rockhill, William Woodville. 1895. *Notes on the Ethnology of Tibet: Based on the Collections in the United States National Museum*. Report of the United States National Museum. Washington: U.S. Government Printing Office.

Röder, Karl David August. 1863. *Grundzüge des Naturrechts oder der Rechtsfilosofie. Zweite Abtheilung*, 2nd ed. Leipzig: Winter.

Rose, Fritz. 1893. "Bericht über eine im April und Mai 1892 an Bord S. M. Kreuzer 'Bussard' im Schutzgebiet der Neu-Guinea-Kompagnie ausgeführte Dienstreise." *Deutsches Kolonialblatt* 4 (1): 88–94.

Rosenberg, Hermann von. 1878. *Der malayische Archipel: Land und Leute in Schilderungen, gesammelt während eines dreissigjährigen Aufenthaltes in den Kolonien*. Leipzig: Weigel.

Rösler, Emil. 1894. "Ausgrabungen beim Dorfe Artschadsor (Kreis Dshewanschir, Gouvernement Elisabethpol, Transkaukasien)." *Verhandlungen der Berliner Gesellschaft für Anthropologie, Ethnologie und Urgeschichte* 26: 221–30.

Roth, Henry Ling. 1896. *The Natives of Sarawak and British North Borneo*, vols. 1 and 2. New York: Truslove.

Rouvre, Charles de. 1880. "La Guinée méridionale indépendante: Congo, Kacongo, N'goyo, Loango, 1870–1877." *Bulletin de la Société de Géographie* 20 (2): 401–34.

Rubruk, William of. 1839. "Itinerarium fratris Willielmi de Rubruquis de ordine fratrum Minorum, Anno gratia 1253 ad partes Orientales." In *Recueil de Voyages et de Mémoires publié de la Société de Géographie*, vol. 4, edited by Société de Géographie de Paris, 213–399. Paris: Société de Géographie. Edited and translated by William W. Rockhill as *The Journey of William of Ruhruck to the Eastern Parts of the World, 1253–55, 55th* ed. (London: Hakluyt Society, 1900).

Rüppell, Eduard. 1829. *Reisen in Nubien, Kordofan und dem peträischen Arabien: Vorzüglich in geographisch-statistischer Hinsicht [...]*. Frankfurt: Wilmans.

Say, Jean Baptiste. 1836. *A Treatise on Political Economy; or the Production, Distribution, and Consumption of Wealth*, 4th ed. Translated by C. R. Princep. Philadelphia: Grigg.

Schadenberg, Alex. 1885. "Die Bewohner von Süd-Mindanao und der Insel Samal." *Zeitschrift für Ethnologie* 17: 8–37.

Scherer, Jean Benoît. 1789. *Geschichte und gegenwärtiger Zustand des russischen Handels*. Leipzig: Weygand. Original in French.

Scherzer, Karl von. 1867. *Statistisch-commerzielle Ergebnisse einer Reise um die Erde: Unternommen an Bord der österreichischen Fregatte Novara in den Jahren 1857–1859*. Leipzig: Brockhaus.

———. 1885. *Das wirthschaftliche Leben der Völker: Ein Handbuch über Produktion und Consum*. Leipzig: Dürr.

Schiller, Friedrich. 1805. *Die Räuber*. Tübingen: Cotta.

Schlegel, Gustav. 1889. "Siamesische und Chinesisch-Siamesische Münzen." *Internationales Archiv für Ethnographie* 2: 241–54.

Schleinitz, Georg von. 1877. "Geographische und ethnographische Beobachtungen auf Neu-Guinea, dem Neu-Britannia- und Salomons-Archipel." *Zeitschrift der Gesellschaft für Erdkunde zu Berlin* 12: 230–65.

Schlömann, Hermann. 1894. "Die Malepa in Transvaal." *Verhandlungen der Berliner Gesellschaft für Anthropologie, Ethnologie und Urgeschichte* 26: 64–70.

Schmeltz, Johannes D. E. 1890. "Ueber einen heiligen Krug von Borneo." *Internationales Archiv für Ethnographie* 3: 29–30.

———. 1893. "Shapes of Currency from Barter to Money." *Internationales Archiv für Ethnographie* 6: 56–59.

———. 1894. *Schnecken und Muscheln im Leben der Völker Indonesiens und Oceaniens: Ein Beitrag zur Ethnoconchologie.* Leiden: Brill.

Schmeltz, Johannes D. E., and Rudolf Krause. 1881. *Die ethnographisch-anthropologische Abtheilung des Museum Godeffroy in Hamburg: Ein Beitrag zur Kunde der Südsee-Völker.* Hamburg: Friederichsen.

Schomburgk, Richard. 1848. *Reisen in Britisch-Guiana in den Jahren 1840–1844*, vol. 2. Leipzig: Weber. Edited and translated by Walter E. Roth as *Richard Schomburgk's Travels in British Guiana, 1840–1844*, vol. 2. (Georgetown, British Guiana: Daily Chronicle Office, 1922).

Schoolcraft, Henry Rowe. 1851. *Personal Memoirs of a Residence of Thirty Years with the Indian Tribes on the American Frontiers.* Philadelphia: Lippincott.

Schrenck, Leopold Ivanovich. 1891. *Reisen und Forschungen im Amur-Lande, in den Jahren 1854–1856: Die Völker des Amur-Landes*, vol. 3, 2nd ed. St. Petersburg: Kaiserlichen Akademie der Wissenschaften.

Schurtz, Heinrich. 1891. *Grundzüge einer Philosophie der Tracht.* Stuttgart: Cotta.

———. 1893. "Amulette und Zaubermittel." *Archiv für Anthropologie, Völkerforschung und kolonialen Kulturwandel* 22: 57–65.

———. 1895a. *Das Augenornament und verwandte Probleme.* Abhandlungen der Philologisch-Historischen Klasse der Königlich-Sächsischen Gesellschaft der Wissenschaften. Leipzig: Hirzel.

———. 1895b. "Die Tabugesetze." *Preussische Jahrbücher* 80: 50–61.

———. 1896a. "Schädelkultus und Sammeltrieb." *Deutsche Geographische Blätter* 10 (3): 93–108.

———. 1896b. "Zur Ornamentik der Aino." *Internationales Archiv für Ethnographie* 9: 233–51.

Schweinfurth, Georg. 1874. *Im Herzen von Afrika: Reisen und Entdeckungen im centralen Aequatorial-Afrika während der Jahre 1868 bis 1871*, vol. 1. Leipzig: Brockhaus. Translated as *The Heart of Africa: Three Years' Travels and Adventures in the Unexplored Regions of Central Africa*, vol. 1 (New York: Harper & Brothers, 1874).

———. 1875. *"Artes africanae." Abbildungen und Beschreibungen.* Leipzig: Brockhaus.

Schweinitz, Hans Hermann von. 1894. *Deutsch-Ost-Afrika in Krieg und Frieden.* Berlin: Walther.

Scriba, Julius. 1883. "Bemerkungen über japanische Gold- und Silbermünzen." *Mitteilungen der Deutschen Gesellschaft für Natur- und Völkerkunde Ostasiens* 29 (3): 392–98.

Seemann, Berthold. 1862. *Viti: An Account of a Government Mission to the Vitian Or Fijian Islands in the Years 1860–1861.* London: Macmillan.

Semon, Richard Wolfgang. 1896. *Im australischen Busch und an den Küsten des Korallenmeeres: Reiseerlebnisse und Beobachtungen eines Naturforschers in Australien, Neu-Guinea und den Molukken.* Leipzig: Engelmann. Translated as *In the Australian Bush and on the Coast of the Coral Sea. Being the Experiences and Observations of a Naturalist in Australia, New Guinea and the Moluccas* (London: Macmillan, 1899).

Semper, Karl. 1873. *Die Palau-Inseln im Stillen Ocean.* Leipzig: Brockhaus. Edited by Robert D. Craig and translated by Mark L. Berg as *The Palau Islands in the Pacific Ocean* (Mangilao: Micronesian Area Research Center, University of Guam, 1982).

Serpa Pinto, Alexandre Alberto da Rocha de. 1881. *Serpa Pinto's Wanderung quer durch Afrika vom Atlantischen zum Indischen Ocean durch bisher grösstentheils gänzlich unbekannte Länder, die Entdeckung der grossen Nebenflüsse des Zambesi nach des Reisenden eigenen Schilderungen: Die Büchse des Königs.* Leipzig: Hirt. Translated as *How I Crossed Africa: From the Atlantic to the Indian Ocean, Through Unknown Countries; Discovery of the Great Zambesi Affluents, &c.,* vol. 1 (Philadelphia: Lippincott, 1881). Original in Portuguese.

Sibree, James. 1870. *Madagascar and its People.* London: Religious Tract Society.

Sievers, Wilhelm. 1886. "Die Arhuaco-Indianer in der Sierra Nevada de Santa Maria." *Zeitschrift der Gesellschaft für Erdkunde zu Berlin* 21: 387–400.

Sigl, Alfred. 1892. "Bericht des Stationschefs von Tabora, Lieutenant Sigl, über den Handelsverkehr von Tabora." *Deutsches Kolonialblatt* 3 (5): 164–66.

Smyth, R. Brough. 1878. *The Aborigines of Victoria: With Notes Relating to the Habits of the Natives of Other Parts of Australia and Tasmania,* vol. 1. Melbourne: Government Printer.

Snouck Hurgronje, Christiaan. 1889. *Mekka: Die Stadt und ihre Herren,* vol. 2. Haag: Nijhoff. Translated as *Mekka in the Latter Part of the 19th Century: Daily Life, Customs and Learning of the Moslims of the East-Indian-Archipelago,* vol. 1, 2nd ed. (Leiden: Brill, 2007). Original in Dutch.

Soetbeer, Adolf. 1879. *Edelmetall-Produktion und Werthverhältniss zwischen Gold und Silber seit der Entdeckung Amerika's bis zur Gegenwart.* Ergänzungsheft zu Petermanns geographischen Mitteilungen 57. Gotha: Perthes.

Spiegel, Friedrich. 1878. *Erânische Alterthumskunde*, vol. 3. Leipzig: Engelmann.

Staudinger, Paul. 1891. *Im Herzen der Haussaländer: Reise im westlichen Sudan nebst Bericht über den Verlauf der Deutschen Niger-Benuë-Expedition*, 2nd ed. Oldenburg: Schulze.

Stearns, Robert. E. C. 1869. "Rambles in Florida." *The American Naturalist* 3 (9): 455–70.

Steinen, Karl von den. 1894. *Unter den Naturvölkern Zentral-Brasiliens. Reiseschilderung und Ergebnisse der zweiten Schingú-Expedition, 1887–1888.* Berlin: Reimer. Translated as *Among the Primitive Peoples of Central Brazil*, available as Microfiche in the Human Relations Area File, Bacairi, Category 116, SP7, no. 2.

Steller, Georg Wilhelm. 1774. *Beschreibung von dem Lande Kamtschatka.* Leipzig: Fleischer. Edited by Marvin W. Falk and translated by Margritt Engel and Karen Willmore as *Steller's History of Kamchatka: Collected Information Concerning the History of Kamchatka [...]* (Fairbanks, Alaska: University of Alaska Press, 2003).

Stetten, Max von. 1893. "Das nördliche Hinterland von Kamerun." *Deutsches Kolonialblatt* 4 (2): 34–39.

Stolze, Franz, and Friedrich Carl Andreas. 1885. *Die Handelsverhältnisse Persiens, mit besonderer Berücksichtigung der deutschen Interessen.* Ergänzungsheft zu Petermanns geographischen Mitteilungen 77. Gotha: Perthes.

Strabo. 1857. *Strabo's Erdbeschreibung 3: Buch 6–8.* Edited and translated by Albert Forbiger, vol. 3. Stuttgart: Hoffmann. English edition translated by Horace Leonard Jones as *The Geography of Strabo* (Cambridge: Harvard University Press, 1924).

Strachey, William. (1612) 1849. *The Historie of Travaile into Virginia Britannia: Expressing the Cosmographie and Comodities of the Country, Together with the Manners and Customes of the People.* Edited by R. H. Major. London: Hakluyt Society.

Stuhlmann, Franz. 1894. *Mit Emin Pascha ins Herz von Afrika*, vol. 2. Berlin: Reimer.

Stüwe, Friedrich. 1836. *Die Handelszüge der Araber unter den Abbasiden durch Afrika, Asien und Osteuropa.* Berlin: Duncker & Humblot.

Tacitus. 1868. *Germania.* Stuttgart: Neff. Contained in *Complete Works of Tacitus.* Edited by Alfred John Church, William J. Brodribb, and Lisa Cerrato (New York: Random House, 1942).

Terrien de Lacouperie, Albert. 1892. *Catalogue of Chinese Coins from the Seventh Century B.C. to A.D. 621.* London: British Museum.

Timkowski, Georg. 1825. *Reise nach China durch die Mongoley in den Jahren 1820 und 1821*, vol. 1. Leipzig: Fleischer. Translated as *Travels of the Russian Mission through Mongolia to China, and Residence in Pekin, in the Years 1820–1821* (London: Longman, 1827). Original in Russian.

Tischler, Otto. 1887. *Eine Emailscheibe von Oberhof und kurzer Abriss der Geschichte des Emails [...].* Königsberg: Leupold.

Tolstoi, Leo N. 1890. *Das Geld.* Berlin: Otto Janke. Contained in translation by Leo Wiener of Lev. N. Tolstoy, *What Shall We Do Then?*, 110–64 (Boston: Colonial Press, 1904). Partly republished as "Unknown Classics: Lev N. Tolstóy; Economics as Deception and Money as Tool to Exploit, Illustrated by the Case of the Enslavement of Fiji." *Journal of Banking, Finance & Sustainable Development* 1 (2020): 199–214.

Troll, S. 1893. "Reise nach Kaschgar." *Verhandlungen der Berliner Gesellschaft für Anthropologie, Ethnologie und Urgeschichte* 25: 308–309.

Tuckey, James Hingston. 1818. *Narrative of an Expedition to Explore the River Zaire, Usually Called the Congo.* London: Gilley.

Turner, Samuel. 1801. *Gesandtschaftsreise an den Hof des Teshoo Lama durch Bootan und einen Theil von Tibet.* Berlin: Sprengel. Originally published as *An Account of an Embassy to the Court of the Teshoo Lama, in Tibet: Containing a Narrative of a Journey Through Bootan, and Part of Tibet* (London: Bulmer, 1800).

Venyukov, Mikhail Ivanovitch. 1874. *Oberst Wenjukow: Die russisch-asiatischen Grenzlande.* Leipzig: Grunow.

Verein für Erdkunde zu Dresden. 1898. "Versammlung im 35. Vereinsjahre 1896/7 und 1897/8." *Jahresberichte des Vereins für Völkerkunde zu Dresden* 26: 1–58.

Vetter, Konrad. 1897. "Bericht des Missionars Herrn Konrad Vetter in Simbang über papuanische Rechtsverhältnisse." *Nachrichten über Kaiser Wilhelms-Land und den Bismarck-Archipel* 13: 68–102.

Virchow, Rudolf. 1877a. "Ältere Gräber in Livland." *Verhandlungen der Berliner Gesellschaft für Anthropologie, Ethnologie und Urgeschichte* 9: 255–59.

———. 1877b. "Archäologische Reise nach Livland." *Verhandlungen der Berliner Gesellschaft für Anthropologie, Ethnologie und Urgeschichte* 9: 365–415.

———. 1880. "Bericht über den internationalen prähistorischen Congress in Lissabon." *Verhandlungen der Berliner Gesellschaft für Anthropologie, Ethnologie und Urgeschichte* 12: 333–55.

———. 1886. "Archäologische Reise in der Niederlausitz." *Verhandlungen der Gesellschaft für Erdkunde zu Berlin* 18: 566–96.

———. 1889. "Nachbildungen englischer Münzen durch südafrikanische Eingeborne." *Verhandlungen der Gesellschaft für Erdkunde zu Berlin* 21: 30–33.

———. 1894. "Sammlung ethnographischer Gegenstände aus Russisch- und Chinesisch-Turkestan, Sibirien, der Mongolei und China." *Verhandlungen der Gesellschaft für Erdkunde zu Berlin* 26: 59–64.

Vogelweide, Walther von der. 1864. *Die Gedichte Walthers von der Vogelweide*, 3rd ed. Edited by Karl Lachmann. Berlin: Reimer.

Volz, Wilhelm Ludwig. 1854. "Geschichte des Muschelgeldes." *Zeitschrift für die gesamte Staatswissenschaft* 10 (1): 83–122.

Wagner, Hans. 1896. *Die Verkehrs- und Handelsverhältnisse in Deutsch-Ostafrika*. Frankfurt a. O.: Andres.

Waitz, Theodor. 1864. *Anthropologie der Naturvölker. Die Amerikaner; Ethnographisch und culturhistorisch dargestellt*, vols. 3 and 4. Leipzig: Fleischer.

———. 1865. *Anthropologie der Naturvölker: Die Völker der Südsee; Ethnographisch und culturhistorisch dargestellt*, vol. 5. Leipzig: Fleischer.

Wauters, A. J., ed. 1892. "La monnaie: Unités monétaires indigènes; introduction de la monnaie européenne." *Le Congo illustré* 1: 34–5.

Werne, Ferdinand. 1852. *Reise durch Sennaar nach Mandera, Nasub, Cheli im Lande zwischen dem blauen Nil und dem Atbara*. Berlin: Duncker & Humblot.

Werner, Bartholomäus von. 1889. *Ein deutsches Kriegsschiff in der Südsee*. Leipzig: Brockhaus.

Westermarck, Edward. 1893. *Geschichte der menschlichen Ehe*. Jena: Costenoble. Originally published as *The History of Human Marriage* (London: Macmillan, 1891).

Whymper, Frederick. 1869. *Alaska: Reisen und Erlebnisse im hohen Norden*. Braunschweig: Westermann. Originally published as *Travel and Adventure in the Territory of Alaska: Formerly Russian America [...]* (London: Murray, 1868).

Wied, Maximilian, Prinz zu. 1841. *Reise in das innere Nord-America in den Jahren 1832 bis 1834*, vol. 2. Coblenz: Hoelscher. Translated as *Travels in the Interior of North America* (London: Ackermann, 1843).

Wilken, G. A. 1889. "Iets over de Schedelvereering bij de Volken van den Indischen Archipel." *Bijdragen tot de Taal-, Land- en Volkenkunde van Nederlandsch-Indië* 38 (1): 89–129.

Wilson, John Leighton. 1862. *West-Afrika geographisch und historisch geschildert*. London: Lorck. Originally published as *Western Africa: Its History, Condition, and Prospects* (London: Low, 1856).

Winterbottom, Thomas. 1805. *Nachrichten von der Sierra-Leone-Küste und ihren Bewohnern*. Weimar: Industrie-Comptoirs. Originally published as *An Account of the Native Africans in the Neighbourhood of Sierra Leone [...]*, vol. 1 (London: Whittingham, 1803).

Wissmann, Hermann von, Curt von Francois, Ludwig Wolf, and Hans Müller. 1888. *Im Innern Afrikas: Die Erforschung des Kassai während der Jahre 1883, 1884 und 1885*. Leipzig: Brockhaus.

Worsaae, Jens Jacob A. 1844. *Dänemarks Vorzeit durch Alterthümer und Grabhügel*. Copenhagen: Reitzel.

Yeats, John. 1887. *The Growth and Vicissitudes of Commerce*. London: Philip & Son.

Zenker, Georg A. 1895. "Yaúnde." *Mitteilungen von Forschungsreisenden und Gelehrten aus den deutschen Schutzgebieten* 8: 36–69.

Editors' References

This second bibliography includes all references from the introduction, the image captions, and the editors' annotations. It also offers a more extensive list of Schurtz's works in chronological order.

Abel, Herbert. 1969. "Beiträge zur Geschichte des Übersee-Museums II." In *Veröffentlichungen aus dem Übersee-Museum in Bremen*, vol. 2, 75–81. Bremen: Übersee-Museum Bremen.

Aglietta, Michel. 2018. *Money: 5,000 Years of Debt and Power*. Translated by David Broder. London: Verso Books.

Aglietta, Michel, and André Orléan. 1982. *La violence de la monnaie*. Paris: Presses Universitaires de France.

Akin, David, and Joel Robbins, eds. 1999. *Money and Modernity: State and Local Currencies in Melanesia*. Pittsburgh: University of Pittsburgh Press.

Amin, Samir. 1990. *Delinking: Towards a Polycentric World*. Translated by Michael Wolfers. London: Zed Books.

Athané, François. 2008. "Le don, histoire du concept, évolution des pratiques." PhD diss., Université Paris-Ouest-Nanterre.

Bagehot, Walter. (1848) 1978. "The Currency Monopoly." In *The Collected Works of Walter Bagehot*, vol. 9, edited by Norman St John-Stevas, 235–71. London: The Economist.

Balandier, Georges. (1961) 2018. "Total Social Phenomena and Social Dynamics." Translated by Catherine V. Howard. *HAU: Journal of Ethnographic Theory* 8 (3): 702–708.

———. 1970. *The Sociology of Black Africa: Social Dynamics in Central Africa*. Translated by Douglas Garman. London: Andre Deutsch.

Bassi, Marco. 2023. "From Herder to Strecker: Birth and Developments of the Anthropological Notion of Culture in Germany." In *Histories of Anthropology*, edited by Gabriella D'Agostino and Vincenzo Matera, 127–55. Cham: Palgrave Macmillan.

Bastian, Adolf. 1901. Review of *Urgeschichte der Kultur* by Heinrich Schurtz. *Ethnologisches Notizblatt* 2 (3): 95–103.

Ben Gadha, Maha, Fadhel Kaboub, Kai Koddenbrock, Ines Mahmoud, and Ndongo Samba Sylla, eds. 2022. *Economic and Monetary Sovereignty in 21st Century Africa*. London. Pluto Press.

Birndt, C. F. 1900. "Dr. med. Heinrich Schurtz." *Zeitschrift für Parapsychologie* 27 (November): 653–55.

Bohannan, Paul. 1959. "The Impact of Money on an African Subsistence Economy." *The Journal of Economic History* 19 (4): 491–503.

Bourdieu, Pierre, and Abdelmalek Sayad. 1964. *Le déracinement: la crise de l'agriculture traditionnelle en Algérie*. Paris: Éditions de Minuit.

Brandl, Felix. 2015. *Von der Entstehung des Geldes zur Sicherung der Währung. Die Theorien von Bernhard Laum und Wilhelm Gerloff zur Genese des Geldes*. Wiesbaden: Springer Gabler.

Breton, Stéphane. 2002. "Présentation. Monnaie et économie des personnes." *L'Homme. Revue française d'anthropologie* 162 (2): 13–26.

Briskorn, Bettina. 2000. *Zur Sammlungsgeschichte afrikanischer Ethnographica im Übersee-Museum Bremen, 1841–1945*. Bremen: Übersee-Museum.

Brockhaus. 1897. *Brockhaus Konversationslexikon*, vol. 17, 14th ed. Leipzig: Brockhaus.

Bruhns, Hinnerk. 2006. "Max Webers 'Grundbegriffe' im Kontext seiner wirtschaftsgeschichtlichen Forschungen." In *Max Webers 'Grundbegriffe': Kategorien der kultur- und sozialwissenschaftlichen Forschung*, edited by Klaus Lichtblau, 151–84. Heidelberg: VS Verlag für Sozialwissenschaften.

Brunhoff, Suzanne de. 1976. *Marx on Money*. Translated by Maurice J. Goldbloom. New York: Urizen Books.

Bruns, Claudia. 2008. *Politik des Eros: Der Männerbund in Wissenschaft, Politik und Jugendkultur (1880–1934)*. Cologne: Böhlau.

———. 2009. "Wilhelminische Bürger und 'germanische Arier' im Spiegel des 'Primitiven': Ambivalenzen einer Mimikry an die kolonialen 'Anderen.'" *Comparativ* 19 (5): 15–33.

Burrell, Courtney Marie. 2023. *Otto Höfler's Characterisation of the Germanic Peoples: From Sacred Men's Bands to Social Daemonism*. Berlin: Walter de Gruyter.

Bücher, Karl. 1893. *Die Entstehung der Volkswirtschaft.* Tübingen: Laupp. Third German edition translated by Samuel Morley Wickett as *Industrial Evolution* (New York: Holt, 1901).

———. 1899. Review of *Grundriß einer Entstehungsgeschichte des Geldes* by Heinrich Schurtz. *Historische Zeitschrift* 83: 85–87.

———. 1914. "Volkswirtschaftliche Entwicklungsstufen." In *Grundriss der Sozialökonomik. I. Abteilung; Historische und theoretische Grundlagen. 1. Teil: Wirtschaft und Wirtschaftswissenschaft,* edited by Eugen von Philippovich and Joseph A. Schumpeter, 1–18. Tübingen: Mohr.

Busch, Ulrich. 2003. "Joseph A. Schumpeter's 'Soziologie des Geldes.'" In *Joseph Alois Schumpeter: Entrepreneurship, Style and Vision,* edited by Jürgen Backhaus, 191–202. Boston: Springer US.

Chen, Zhanfeng. 2005. "Cong zhang jiashan han mu zhujian·er nian lüling kan liang zhong huobi yu han chu shehui" [The discussion about two kinds of money in the first Western Han Dynasty and the society reflected by them in The Laws of the Second Year in Zhangjiashan Han bamboo slips]. *Xi'an Dianzi Keji Daxue Xuebao (Shehui Kexue Ban) [Journal of Xi'an University of Electronic Science and Technology: Social Science Edition]* 15 (2): 98–102. DOI: 10.3969/j.issn.1008-472X.2005.02.020.

Codere, Helen. 1968. "Money-Exchange Systems and a Theory of Money." *Man* 3 (4): 557–77.

Cunow, Heinrich. 1900. Review of *Grundriß einer Entstehungsgeschichte des Geldes* by Heinrich Schurtz. *Die Neue Zeit* 1 (18): 569–70.

Dalton, George. 1965. "Primitive Money." *American Anthropologist* 67 (1): 44–65.

Dartevelle, Edmond. 1953. *Les "N'zimbu," monnaie du Royaume du Congo.* Bruxelles: Société Royale Belge d'Anthropologie et de Préhistoire.

Dawson, George M. 1880. *Report on the Queen Charlotte Islands, 1878.* Geological Survey of Canada. Montreal: Dawson.

Delius, Peter, Alex Schoeman, and Tim Maggs. 2014. *Forgotten World: The Stone-Walled Settlements of the Mpumalanga Escarpment.* Johannesburg: Wits University Press.

Desan, Christine A. 2013. "Creation Stories: Myths About the Origins of Money." Public Law & Legal Theory Working Paper Series No. 13–20, Harvard Law School. http://dx.doi.org/10.2139/ssrn.2252074

Dodd, Nigel. 2014. *The Social Life of Money.* Princeton: Princeton University Press.

Dodd, Nigel, and Federico Neiburg, eds. 2019. *A Cultural History of Money in the Age of Empire*, vol. 5. London: Bloomsbury Academic.

Drumm, Colin. 2021. "The Difference that Money Makes: Sovereignty, Indecision, and the Politics of Liquidity." PhD diss., University of California, Santa Cruz.

Ducks, Thomas. 1996. "Heinrich Schurtz (1863–1903) und die deutsche Völkerkunde." PhD diss., Universität Freiburg.

Durkheim, Émile. 1897. "La prohibition de l'inceste et ses origines." *L'Annee sociologique* 1: 1–70.

———. 1901. Review of *Altersklassen und Männerbünde. Eine Darstellung der Grundformen der Gesellschaft. (Classes d'âge et associations masculines. Étude sur les formes fondamentales de la société)* by Heinrich Schurtz. *L'Année sociologique* 6: 316–23.

Eich, Stefan. 2022. *The Currency of Politics: The Political Theory of Money from Aristotle to Keynes*. Princeton: Princeton University Press.

Einzig, Paul. (1949) 1966. *Primitive Money: In its Ethnological, Historical and Economic Aspects*, 2nd ed. Oxford: Pergamon Press.

Emmanuel, Arghiri. 1969. *L'échange inégal: Essai sur les antagonismes dans les rapports économiques internationaux*. Paris: Maspero. Translated by B. Pearce as *Unequal Exchange: A Study of the Imperialism of Trade* (New York: Monthly Review Press, 1972).

Fabian, Johannes. 2000. *Out of Our Minds: Reason and Madness in the Exploration of Central Africa*. Berkeley: University of California Press.

Fage, John D. 1994. *A Guide to Original Sources for Precolonial Western Africa Published in European Languages*, 2nd ed. Madison: African Studies Program, University of Wisconsin-Madison.

Finley, Moses, ed. 1979. *The Bücher-Meyer Controversy*. New York: Arno Press.

Firth, Raymond. 1927. "The Study of Primitive Economics." *Economica* 21: 312–35.

———. 1929. *Primitive Economics of the New Zealand Maori*. London: Routledge.

———. 1972. "Methodological Issues in Economic Anthropology." *Man* 7 (3): 467–75.

Fisher, H. J. 1975. "The Eastern Maghrib and the Central Sudan." In *The Cambridge History of Africa*, vol. 3, edited by John D. Fage and Roland Oliver, 232–330. Cambridge: Cambridge University Press.

Flandreau, Marc. 2004. *The Glitter of Gold: France, Bimetallism, and the Emergence of the International Gold Standard, 1848–1873.* Translated by Owen Leeming. Oxford: Oxford University Press.

Gerloff, Wilhelm. 1940. *Die Entstehung des Geldes und die Anfänge des Geldwesens.* Frankfurt: Klostermann.

———. 1950. *Gesellschaftliche Theorie des Geldes.* Innsbruck: Universitätsverlag Wagner.

Gesell, Silvio. 1916. *Die natürliche Wirtschaftsordnung durch Freiland und Freigeld.* Les Hauts Geneveys: Self-published. Translated by Philip Pye as *The Natural Economic Order* (London: Owen, 1958).

Gingrich, Andre. 2010. "The German-Speaking Countries." In *One Discipline, Four Ways: British, German, French, and American Anthropology*, edited by Fredrik Barth, Andre Gingrich, Robert Parkin, and Sydel Silverman, 61–156. Chicago: University of Chicago Press.

Godelier, Maurice. 1971. "'Salt Currency' and the Circulation of Commodities among the Baruya of New Guinea." In *Studies in Economic Anthropology*, edited by George Dalton, 52–73. Washington: American Anthropological Association.

Gräbel, Carsten. 2015. *Die Erforschung der Kolonien: Expeditionen und koloniale Wissenskultur deutscher Geographen, 1884–1919.* Bielefeld: Transcript.

Graeber, David. 1996. "Beads and Money: Notes toward a Theory of Wealth and Power." *American Ethnologist* 23 (1): 4–24.

———. 2001. *Toward an Anthropological Theory of Value: The False Coin of Our Own Dreams.* New York: Palgrave.

———. 2009. "Debt, Violence, and Impersonal Markets: Polanyian Meditations." In *Market and Society: The Great Transformation Today*, edited by Keith Hart and Chris Hann, 106–33. Cambridge: Cambridge University Press.

———. 2011. *Debt: The First 5,000 Years.* New York: Melville House.

———. 2012. "On Social Currencies and Human Economies: Some Notes on the Violence of Equivalence." *Social Anthropology* 20 (4): 411–28.

Graebner, Fritz. 1910. "Handel bei Naturvölkern." In *Karl Andrees Geographie des Welthandels: eine wirtschaftsgeographische Schilderung der Erde*, edited by Robert Sieger and Franz Heiderich, 149–218. Vienna: Seidel.

Gray, Richard T. 2008. *Money Matters: Economics and the German Cultural Imagination, 1770–1850.* Seattle: University of Washington Press.

Green, Toby. 2019. *A Fistful of Shells: West Africa from the Rise of the Slave Trade to the Age of Revolution.* Chicago: University of Chicago Press.

Gregory, Chris. (1982) 2015. *Gifts and Commodities.* Chicago: Hau Books.

Grierson, Philip. 1978. "The Origins of Money." *Research in Economic Anthropology* 1: 1–35.

Grierson, Philip, Lucia Travaini, and Fitzwilliam Museum. 1986. *Medieval European Coinage: Volume 14, South Italy, Sicily, Sardinia.* Cambridge: Cambridge University Press.

Gurley, John G., and Edward Stone Shaw. 1960. *Money in a Theory of Finance.* Washington, D.C.: Brookings Institution.

Guyer, Jane, ed. 1995. *Money Matters: Instability, Values, and Social Payments in the Modern History of West African Communities.* Portsmouth, N.H.: Heinemann.

———. 2004. *Marginal Gains: Monetary Transactions in Atlantic Africa.* Chicago: University of Chicago Press.

———. 2012. "Soft Currencies, Cash Economies, New Monies: Past and Present." *Proceedings of the National Academy of Sciences* 109 (7): 2214–21.

———. 2013. "On 'The Iron Currencies of Southern Cameroon.'" *Transactions: A Payments Archive* (blog). May 4, 2013. https://transactions.socialcomputing.uci.edu/post/49643279663/on-the-iron-currencies-of-southern-cameroon.

Guyer, Jane, and Samuel M. Eno Belinga. 1995. "Wealth in People as Wealth in Knowledge: Accumulation and Composition in Equatorial Africa." *The Journal of African History* 36 (1): 91–120.

Guyer, Jane, and Karin Pallaver. 2018. "Money and Currency in African History." In *Oxford Research Encyclopedia of African History*, edited by Thomas Spear, 1–29. Oxford: Oxford University Press.

Hann, Chris. 2015. "Jack, Max, Three Karls and Sundry Supporters (the REALEURASIA Pantheon)." *REALEURASIA* (blog). July 21, 2015. https://www.eth.mpg.de/3835023/blog_2015_07_21_01.

Hann, Chris, and Keith Hart. 2011. *Economic Anthropology: History, Ethnography, Critique.* Cambridge: Polity.

Hantzsch, Viktor. 1905. "Schurtz, Camillo Heinrich." In *Biographisches Jahrbuch und Deutscher Nekrolog 1903*, 8: 30–34. Berlin: Reimer.

Hart, Keith. 1986. "Heads or Tails? Two Sides of the Coin." *Man*, New Series, 21 (4): 637–56.

———. 2000. "Comment on Pearson's 'Homo Economicus Goes Native.'" *History of Political Economy* 32 (4): 1017–25. https://johnkeithhart.substack.com/p/comment-on-homo-economicus-goes-native.

———. ed. 2017. *Money in a Human Economy*. New York: Berghahn Books.

Heckenberger, Michael J. 2005. *The Ecology of Power: Culture, Place and Personhood in the Southern Amazon, AD 1000–2000*. New York: Routledge.

Helfferich, Karl. (1903) 1923. *Das Geld*, 6th ed. Leipzig: Hirschfeld. Translated by Louis Infield as *Money* (London: Benn, 1927).

Helleiner, Eric. 2021. *The Neomercantilists: A Global Intellectual History*. Ithaca: Cornell University Press.

Herskovits, Melville J. 1952. *Economic Anthropology*. New York: Knopf.

Hess, Moses. 2004. *Moses Hess: The Holy History of Mankind and Other Writings*. Edited by Shlomo Avineri. Cambridge: Cambridge University Press.

Hildebrand, Bruno. 1864. "Naturalwirthschaft, Geldwirthschaft und Creditwirthschaft." *Jahrbücher für Nationalökonomie und Statistik* 2: 1–24.

Hobsbawm, Eric. 1981. *Bandits*. New York: Pantheon Books.

Hodgson, Geoffrey M. 2001. *How Economics Forgot History: The Problem of Historical Specificity in Social Science*. London: Routledge.

Hogendorn, Jan. 1997. "Money." In *Encyclopedia of Africa South of the Sahara*, edited by John Middleton, 179–83. New York: Scribner's Sons.

Hogendorn, Jan, and Marion Johnson. 1986. *The Shell Money of the Slave Trade*. Cambridge: Cambridge University Press.

Höltz, Joachim. 1984. *Kritik der Geldentstehungstheorien: Carl Menger, Wilhelm Gerloff und eine Untersuchung über die Entstehung des Geldes im alten Ägypten und Mesopotamien*. Berlin: Reimer.

Homer. 1924. *The Iliad*. Translated by A. T. Murray. Loeb Classical Library. Cambridge: Harvard University Press.

Hudson, Michael. 2000. "Karl Bücher's Role in the Evolution of Economic Anthropology." In *Karl Bücher: Theory, History, Anthropology, Non Market Economies*, edited by Jürgen G. Backhaus, 113–38. Marburg: Metropolis.

———. (1972) 2003. *Super Imperialism: The Origin and Fundamentals of U.S. World Dominance*, 2nd ed. London: Pluto Press.

———. 2004. "The Archaeology of Money: Debt versus Barter Theories of Money's Origins." In *Credit and State Theories of Money: The Contributions of A. Mitchell Innes*, edited by L. Randall Wray, 99–127. Cheltenham: Edward Elgar Publishing.

Humphrey, Caroline, and Stephen Hugh-Jones, eds. 1992. *Barter, Exchange and Value: An Anthropological Approach*. Cambridge: Cambridge University Press.

Ingham, Geoffrey. 2004. *The Nature of Money*. Cambridge: Polity.

Jackson, Richard M. 1934. *Journal of a Voyage to Bonny River (1826) on the West Coast of Africa in the Ship Kingston from Liverpool*. Letchworth: Garden City Press.

Jehu [pseud.]. 2014. "Part 1: Some Thoughts on David Graeber, Barter and the Invention of Money." *The Real Movement* (blog). October 22, 2014. https://therealmovement.wordpress.com/2014/10/22/part-1-some-thoughts-on-david-graeber-barter-and-the-invention-of-money/.

Jones, Adam. 1987. *Raw, Medium, Well Done: A Critical Review of Editorial and Quasi-Editorial Work on Pre-1885 European Sources for Sub-Saharan Africa, 1960–1986*. Wisconsin: African Studies Program, University of Wisconsin-Madison.

———. 1991. "'Four Years in Asante': One Source or Several?" *History in Africa* 18: 173–203.

Jones, Gwilym. I. 1963. *The Trading States of the Oil Rivers: A Study of Political Development in Eastern Nigeria*. London: James Currey.

Kaufman, Frederick. 2020. *The Money Plot: A History of Currency's Power to Enchant, Control, and Manipulate*. New York: Other Press.

Keep, Lou [pseud.]. 2017. "Theses on Social Currency." *Sam[]zdat* (blog). February 6, 2017. https://samzdat.com/2017/02/06/brief-theses-on-social-currency/.

Keynes, John Maynard. 1914. "What is Money? By A. Mitchell Innes." *The Economic Journal* 24 (95): 419–21.

———. 1930. *A Treatise on Money: The Pure Theory of Money*, vol. 5. The Collected Writings of John Maynard Keynes, 2nd ed. London: Royal Economic Society.

Kindleberger, Charles P. 1984. *A Financial History of Western Europe*. London: Routledge.

Kipper, Rainer. 2002. *Der Germanenmythos im Deutschen Kaiserreich: Formen und Funktionen historischer Selbstthematisierung*. Göttingen: Vandenhoeck & Ruprecht.

Kiwanuka, M. S. M. 1968. "The Empire of Bunyoro Kitara: Myth or Reality?" *Canadian Journal of African Studies* 2 (1): 27–48.

Knapp, Georg Friedrich. 1905. *Staatliche Theorie des Geldes*. Berlin: Duncker & Humblot. Translated by H. M. Lucas and J. Bonar as *The State Theory of Money* (Abridged. London: Macmillan, 1924).

Knies, Karl. 1885. *Das Geld: Darlegung der Grundlehren von dem Gelde, insbesondere der wirtschaftlichen und der rechtsgiltigen Functionen des Geldes*, 2nd ed. Berlin: Weidmann.

Knight, Frank H. 1941. "Anthropology and Economics." *Journal of Political Economy* 49 (2): 247–68.

Köcke, Jasper. 1979. "Some Early Contributions to Economic Anthropology." *Research in Economic Anthropology* 2: 119–67.

Koppers, P. Wilhelm. 1915. "Die ethnologische Wirtschaftsforschung. Eine historisch-kritische Studie. 5. Die ethnologische Wirtschaftsforschung in der Zeit von 1890 bis zur Gegenwart. (Schluß)." *Anthropos* 10/11 (5/6): 971–1079.

Kopytoff, Igor. 1986. "The Cultural Biography of Things: Commoditization as Process." In *The Social Life of Things: Commodities in Cultural Perspective*, edited by Arjun Appadurai, 64–91. Cambridge: Cambridge University Press.

Kroll, John H. 2008. "The Monetary Use of Weighed Bullion in Archaic Greece." In *The Monetary Systems of the Greeks and Romans*, edited by W. V. Harris, 12–37. Oxford: Oxford University Press.

Krozewski, Gerold. 2022. "Colonial Money in Africa and National Economy-Building in Britain and Germany: Examining Relations of Agency, 1890s–1930s." In *Monetary Transitions: Currencies, Colonialism and African Societies*, edited by Karin Pallaver, 239–63. Cham: Palgrave Macmillan.

Kubary, Jan Stanislaus. 1873. "Die Palau-Inseln in der Südsee." *Journal des Museum Godeffroy* 1 (4): 177–238.

Kula, Witold. 1986. *Measures and Men*. Translated by R. Szreter. Princeton: Princeton University Press.

Kuroda, Akinobu. 2007. "The Maria Theresa Dollar in the Early Twentieth-Century Red Sea Region: A Complementary Interface between Multiple Markets." *Financial History Review* 14 (1): 89–110.

———. 2020. *A Global History of Money*. London: Routledge.

Lagos, Ricardo. 2010. "Inside and Outside Money." In *Monetary Economics*, edited by Steven N. Durlauf and Lawrence E. Blume, 132–36. London: Palgrave Macmillan.

Lasch, Richard. 1906. "Das Marktwesen auf den primitiven Kulturstufen. I." *Zeitschrift für Socialwissenschaft* 9: 619–27.

Laum, Bernhard. 1924. *Heiliges Geld: Eine historische Untersuchung über den sakralen Ursprung des Geldes.* Tübingen: Mohr.

Law, Robin. 2004. *Ouidah: The Social History of a West African Slaving "Port,"1727–1892.* Athens: Ohio University Press.

Lips, Julius E. 1949. *The Origin of Things: A Cultural History of Man.* London: Harrap.

Lotz, Walther. 1894. "Die Lehre vom Ursprunge des Geldes. Eine methodologische Studie." *Jahrbücher für Nationalökonomie und Statistik* 7 (62) (3): 337–59.

———. 1906. "Geld." In *Wörterbuch der Volkswirtschaft in zwei Bänden*, vol. 1, edited by Ludwig Elster, 930–41. Jena: Fischer.

Lowie, Robert Harry. 1920. *Primitive Society.* New York: Bonie and Liveright.

Magnani, Eliana. 2008. "Les médiévistes et le don. Avant et après la théorie maussienne." *Revue du MAUSS* 31 (1): 525–44.

Malinowski, Bronislaw. 1921. "The Primitive Economics of the Trobriand Islanders." *The Economic Journal* 31 (121): 1–16.

———. 1922. *Argonauts of the Western Pacific: An Account of Native Enterprise and Adventure in the Archipelagoes of Melanesian New Guinea.* London: Routledge.

Marees, Pieter de. 1987. *Description and Historical Account of the Gold Kingdom of Guinea (1602).* Edited and translated by Albert van Dantzig and Adam Jones. Oxford: British Academy.

Martino, Enrique. 2018. "Irrationality and Speculation in Finance." *HAU: Journal of Ethnographic Theory* 8 (3): 467–73.

———. 2022. *Touts: Recruiting Indentured Labor in the Gulf of Guinea.* Berlin: De Gruyter.

Marx, Karl. (1859) 1975. "A Contribution to the Critique of Political Economy." In *Marx & Engels: Collected Works*, vol. 29, translated by Salo Ryazanskaya, 257–417. London: Lawrence & Wishart.

Maurer, Bill. 2006. "The Anthropology of Money." *Annual Review of Anthropology* 35 (1): 15–36.

———. 2018. "Primitive and Nonmetallic Money." In *Handbook of the History of Money and Currency*, edited by Stefano Battilossi, Youssef Cassis, and Kazuhiko Yago, 87–104. Singapore: Springer.

Mauss, Marcel. 1914. "Les origines de la notion de monnaie." Communication faite à l'Institut Français d'Anthropologie. *L'Anthropologie* 25 (supplément): 14–19. Republished in *Oeuvres,* vol. 2, edited by Victor Kardy, 106–12 (Paris: Minuit, 1969). Edited and translated by Jerry D. Moore as "The Origins of the Concept of Money." In *Visions of Culture: An Annotated Reader,* 131–35 (Lanham, MD: Rowman Altamira, 2010).

———. (1925) 2016. *The Gift: Expanded Edition.* Translated by Jane Guyer. Chicago: Hau Books.

Meillassoux, Claude. 1964. *Anthropologie économique des Gouro de Côte d'Ivoire: De l'économie de subsistance à l'agriculture commerciale.* Paris: Éditions de l'École des hautes études en sciences sociales.

Melitz, Jacques. 1970. "The Polanyi School of Anthropology on Money: An Economist's View." *American Anthropologist* 72 (5): 1020–40.

Menger, Carl. 1871. *Grundsätze der Volkswirthschaftslehre.* Vienna: Braumüller.

———. 1892. "Geld." In *Handwörterbuch der Staatswissenschaften,* vol. 3, edited by Johann Conrad, 730–56. Jena: Fischer. Translated by C. A. Foley as "On the Origin of Money." *The Economic Journal* 2 (1892): 239–55.

———. (1909) 1936. "Geld." In *The Collected Works of Carl Menger,* vol. 4, edited by The London School of Economics and Political Science, 2nd ed., 1–118. London: Percy Lund.

Mirowski, Philip. 1994. "Tit for Tat: Concepts of Exchange, Higgling, and Barter in Two Episodes in the History of Economic Anthropology." *History of Political Economy* 26 (1): 313–42.

———. 2000. "Exploring the Fault Lines: Introduction to the Minisymposium on the History of Economic Anthropology." *History of Political Economy* 32 (4): 919–32.

Mitchell Innes, Alfred. (1913) 2004. "What Is Money?" In *Credit and State Theories of Money: The Contributions of A. Mitchell Innes,* edited by L. Randall Wray, 14–49. Cheltenham: Edward Elgar.

Mommsen, Theodor. 1863. "Das Geld." *Die Grenzboten: Zeitschrift für Politik, Literatur und Kunst* 22 (I): 381–98.

Müller, Klaus E. 1981. "Grundzüge des ethnologischen Historismus." In *Grundfragen der Ethnologie: Beiträge zur gegenwärtigen Theorie-Diskussion,* edited by Wolfdietrich Schmied-Kowarzik and Justin Stagl, 193–231. Berlin: Reimer.

Ngalamulume, Kalala N. 2011. "Mukenge, Kalamba." In *Dictionary of African Biography*, vol. 4, edited by Emmanuel K. Akyeampong and Henry Louis Gates Jr., 319–21. Oxford: Oxford University Press.

Nkwi, Paul N. 1989. *The German Presence in the Western Grassfields 1891–1913: A German Colonial Account*. Research Report 37. Leiden: African Studies Centre.

Oestermann, Tristan. 2022. *Kautschuk und Arbeit in Kamerun unter deutscher Kolonialherrschaft, 1880–1913*. Cologne: Vandenhoeck & Ruprecht.

Ogundiran, Akinwumi. 2009. "Material Life and Domestic Economy in a Frontier of the Oyo Empire During the Mid-Atlantic Age." *The International Journal of African Historical Studies* 42 (3): 351–85.

Orléan, André. 1992. "The Origin of Money." In *Understanding Origins: Contemporary Views on the Origin of Life, Mind and Society*, edited by Francisco J. Varela and Jean-Pierre Dupuy, translated by Paisley Livingston, 113–43. Dordrecht: Kluwer Academic.

———. 2013. "Money: Instrument of Exchange or Social Institution of Value?" In *Financial Crises and the Nature of Capitalist Money: Mutual Developments from the Work of Geoffrey Ingham*, edited by Jocelyn Pixley and J. C. Harcourt, translated by Geoffrey Ingham, 46–70. London: Palgrave Macmillan.

———. 2014. *The Empire of Value: A New Foundation for Economics*. Translated by M. B. De Bevoise. Cambridge: MIT Press.

———. 2023. "Value and Money as Social Power: New Concepts for Old Questions." *Review of Political Economy* 35 (1): 174–88.

Osterhammel, Jürgen. 1994. "Raumerfassung und Universalgeschichte im 20. Jahrhundert." In *Universalgeschichte und Nationalgeschichten*, edited by Gangolf Hübinger and Ernst Schulin, 51–72. Freiburg: Rombach.

Pallaver, Karin. 2009. "'A Recognized Currency in Beads.' Glass Beads as Money in 19th-Century East Africa: The Central Caravan Road." In *Money in Africa*, edited by Catherine Eagleton, Harcourt Fuller, and John Perkins, 20–29. London: British Museum.

———. 2016. "From Venice to East Africa: History, Uses, and Meanings of Glass Beads." In *Luxury in Global Perspective: Objects and Practices, 1600–2000*, edited by Bernd-Stefan Grewe and Karin Hofmeester, 192–217. Cambridge: Cambridge University Press.

———. ed. 2022. *Monetary Transitions: Currencies, Colonialism and African Societies*. Cham: Palgrave Macmillan.

Parkinson, Richard. 2010. *Thirty Years in the South Seas: Land and People, Customs and Traditions in the Bismarck Archipelago and on the German Solomon Islands*. Edited by B. Ankermann. Translated by John Dennison. Sydney: Sydney University Press.

Parry, Jonathan, and Maurice Bloch. 1989. "Introduction: Money and the Morality of Exchange." In *Money and the Morality of Exchange*, edited by Jonathan Parry and Maurice Bloch, 1–32. Cambridge: Cambridge University Press.

Patnaik, Prabhat. 2009. *The Value of Money*. New York: Columbia University Press.

Pearson, Harry W. 1957. "The Secular Debate on Economic Primitivism." In *Trade and Market in the Early Empires: Economies in History and Theory*, edited by Karl Polanyi, 3–11. Glencoe, Ill.: Free Press.

Pearson, Heath. 2000. "Homo Economicus Goes Native, 1859–1945: The Rise and Fall of Primitive Economics." *History of Political Economy* 32 (4): 933–90.

———. 2010. "Ground between Two Stones: Melville Herskovits and the Fate of Economic Anthropology." *History of Political Economy* 42 (1): 165–95.

Peebles, Gustav. 2011. *The Euro and its Rivals: Currency and the Construction of a Transnational City*. Bloomington: Indiana University Press.

Pietz, William. 2022. *The Problem of the Fetish*. Edited by Francesco Pellizzi, Stefanos Geroulanos, and Ben Kafka. Chicago: University of Chicago Press.

Plenge, Johann, ed. 1919. *Die Stammformen der vergleichenden Wirtschaftstheorie (Aristoteles, Adam Smith, List, Marx, B. Hildebrand, Schönberg, Schurtz, Plenge)*. Essen: Baedeker.

Polanyi, Karl. 1971. "The Semantics of Money Uses. With Appendix on Primitive Money." In *Primitive, Archaic, and Modern Economies: Essays of Karl Polanyi*, edited by George Dalton, 175–203. Boston: Beacon.

Pryor, Frederic L. 1977. "The Origins of Money." *Journal of Money, Credit and Banking* 9 (3): 391–409.

Quiggin, Alison Hingston. 1949. *A Survey of Primitive Money: The Beginnings of Currency*. London: Methuen.

Radkau, Joachim. 2013. *Max Weber: A Biography*. Translated by Patrick Camiller. Cambridge: Polity.

Ratzel, Friedrich. 1894–1895. *Völkerkunde*. 2 vols, 2nd ed. Leipzig: Bibliographisches Institut. Translated by Arthur John Butler as *The History of Mankind*. 2 vols. (New York: Macmillan, 1896–1897).

———. 1903. "Dr. Heinrich Schurtz zum Gedächtnis." *Deutsche Geographische Blätter* 26 (2): 51–61. Republished in *Friedrich Ratzel: Kleine Schriften*, vol. 1, edited by Hans Helmolt, 522–30 (Munich: Oldenbourg, 1906).

Reibig, André. 2001. "The Bücher-Meyer Controversy: The Nature of the Ancient Economy in Modern Ideology." PhD diss., University of Glasgow.

Reulecke, Jürgen. 2001. *"Ich möchte einer werden so wie die…". Männerbünde im 20. Jahrhundert*. Frankfurt: Campus Verlag.

Rey, Pierre-Philippe. 1971. *Colonialisme, néo-colonialisme et transition au capitalisme; exemple de la Comilog au Congo-Brazzaville*. Paris: Maspero.

Richards, Rhys. 2010. "Ceramic Imitation Arm Rings for Indigenous Trade in the Solomon Islands, 1880 to 1920." *Records of the Auckland Museum* 47: 93–109.

Ridgeway, William. 1892. *The Origin of Metallic Currency and Weight Standards*. Cambridge: Cambridge University Press.

Róheim, Géza. 1923. "Heiliges Geld in Melanesien." *Internationale Zeitschrift für ärztliche Psychoanalyse* 9: 384–401.

Rohlfs, Gerhard. 1889. "Geld in Afrika." *Dr. A. Petermanns Mitteilungen aus Justus Perthes' geographischer Anstalt* 35: 187–95.

Roscher, Wilhelm. 1857. *System der Volkswirtschaft: Ein Hand- und Lesebuch für Geschäftsmänner und Studierende*, vol. 1, 2nd ed. Stuttgart: Cotta.

Rospabé, Philippe. 2010. *La dette de vie: Aux origines de la monnaie*. Paris: La Découverte.

Sahlins, Marshall. 1972. *Stone Age Economics*. Chicago: Aldine-Atherton.

———. 1988. "Cosmologies of Capitalism: The Trans-Pacific Sector of 'The World System.'" *Proceedings of the British Academy* 74: 1–51.

Santini, Carlotta. 2018. "Can Humanity Be Mapped? Adolf Bastian, Friedrich Ratzel and the Cartography of Culture." *History of Anthropology Newsletter* 42. https://histanthro.org/notes/can-humanity-be-mapped/.

Schaps, David. 2004. *The Invention of Coinage and the Monetization of Ancient Greece*. Ann Arbor: University of Michigan Press.

Schefold, Bertram. 1996. "The German Historical School and the Belief in Ethical Progress." In *Ethical Universals in International Business*, edited by F. Neil Brady, 173–96. Berlin: Springer.

Schlüter, Otto. 1906. "Die leitenden Gesichtspunkte der Anthropogeographie, insbesondere der Lehre Friedrich Ratzels." *Archiv für Sozialwissenschaft und Sozialpolitik* 22: 581–630.

Schmidt, Mario. 2014. *Wampum und Biber: Fetischgeld im kolonialen Nordamerika. Eine mausssche Kritik des Gabeparadigmas.* Bielefeld: Transcript.

Schmidt, Max. 1920–1921. *Grundriss der ethnologischen Volkswirtschaftslehre,* vols. 1 and 2. Stuttgart: Enke.

Schmoller, Gustav von. 1904. *Grundriss der allgemeinen Volkswirtschaftslehre,* vol. 2. Leipzig: Duncker & Humblot.

Schrader, Heiko. 1980. "The Origin and Meaning of Money: A Discourse on Sociological and Economic Literature." Working Paper 136. Sociology of Development Research Centre, Universität Bielefeld.

Schumpeter, Joseph A. 1954. *History of Economic Analysis.* Edited by Elizabeth Boody Schumpeter. London: Routledge.

———. 1970. *Das Wesen des Geldes.* Edited by Fritz Karl Mann. Göttingen: Vandenhoeck & Ruprecht. Translated by Ruben Alvarado as *Treatise on Money* (Aalten, Netherlands: Wordbridge Publishing, 2014).

———. 1991. "Money and Currency." *Social Research* 58 (3): 499–543.

Schurtz, Heinrich. 1889. *Das Wurfmesser der Neger: Ein Beitrag zur ethnographie Afrika's.* Leiden: Trap.

———. 1890a. "Beiträge zur Trachtenkunde Afrikas; 1. Der Einfluss des Islam; 2. Die europäische Einfuhr; 3. Kleidung als Geld." *Das Ausland: Wochenschrift für Erd- und Völkerkunde* 63: 861–64, 888–92, 910–13.

———. 1890b. *Der Seifenbergbau im Erzgebirge und die Walensagen.* Stuttgart: Engelhorn.

———. 1891a. *Grundzüge einer Philosophie der Tracht.* Stuttgart: Cotta.

———. 1891b. *Die Pässe des Erzgebirges.* Leipzig: Weber.

———. 1891c. "Die Milderung des menschliches Charakters vom Standpunkte der Ethnologie." *Globus* 59/60: 299–303.

———. 1893a. "Amulette und Zaubermittel." *Archiv für Anthropologie, Völkerforschung und kolonialen Kulturwandel* 22: 57–65.

———. 1893b. *Katechismus der Völkerkunde.* Leipzig: Weber.

———. 1893c. *Die Speiserverbote: Ein Problem der Völkerkunde.* Hamburg: Richter.

———. 1895a. *Das Augenornament und verwandte Probleme.* Abhandlungen der Philologisch-Historischen Klasse der Königlich-Sächsischen Gesellschaft der Wissenschaften. Leipzig: Hirzel.

————. 1895b. "Die Tabugesetze." *Preussische Jahrbücher* 80: 50–61.

————. 1896a. "Schädelkultus und Sammeltrieb." *Deutsche Geographische Blätter* 10 (3): 93–108.

————. 1896b. "Zur Ornamentik der Aino." *Internationales Archiv für Ethnographie* 9: 233–51.

————. 1896c. "Einleitung. Entwicklungsgang und Bildungsmittel der Menschheit." In *Das Buch der Erfindungen. Gewerbe und Industrien*, vol. 1, 9th ed., 1–65. Leipzig: Spamer.

————. 1896d. "Das neue städtische Museum für Natur-, Völker- und Handelskunde." *Deutsche Geographische Blätter* 19 (1/2): 66–70.

————. 1897. "Beiträge zur Entstehungsgeschichte des Geldes." *Deutsche Geographische Blätter* 20 (1/2): 1–66.

————. 1898a. *Grundriss einer Entstehungsgeschichte des Geldes.* Weimar: Felber.

————. 1898b. "Wertvernichtung durch den Totenkult." *Zeitschrift für Socialwissenschaft* 1: 41–52.

————. 1898c. "Wirtschaftliche Symbiose." *Zeitschrift für Socialwissenschaft* 1: 899–908.

————. 1898d. Review of *Die Wirthschaft der Naturvölker* by Karl Bücher. *Deutsche Literaturzeitung* 19 (28): 1134–35.

————. 1899. "Anthropologie und Volkswirtschaft." *Zeitschrift für Socialwissenschaft* 2: 734–35.

————. 1900a. *Das afrikanische Gewerbe.* Preisschriften der Fürstlich-Jablonowskischen Gesellschaft der Wissenschaften. Leipzig: Teubner.

————. 1900b. *Urgeschichte der Kultur.* Leipzig: Bibliographisches Institut. The only available translation is in Russian, translated by Ivan Nikitich Smirnov as История первобытной культуры *(Istoriia pervobytnoi kul'tury [History of primitive culture]. Sochinenie Genrikha Shurtsa).* St. Petersburg: Prosveshcheniye.

————. 1900c. "Die Anfänge des Landbesitzes." *Zeitschrift für Socialwissenschaft* 3: 245–55, 352–61.

————. 1900d. "Kairuan." *Deutsche Geographische Blätter* 23: 1–66.

————. 1900e. "Nordafrika." In *Weltgeschichte*, vol. 4, edited by Hans F. Helmolt, 469–550. Die Rändländer des Mittelmeer. Leipzig: Bibliographisches Institut.

————. 1900f. "Schnitzereien der Maori." *Globus* 77: 53–68.

————. 1901a. "Das Basarwesen als Wirtschaftsform." *Zeitschrift für Social-wissenschaft* 4: 145–67.

————. 1901b. "Afrika als Teil der bewohnten Erde." In *Weltgeschichte*, vol. 3, edited by Hans F. Helmolt, 391–574. Westasien und Afrika. Leipzig: Bibliographisches Institut.

————. 1901c. "Westasien im Zeichen des Islams." In *Weltgeschichte*, vol. 3, edited by Hans F. Helmolt, 249–388. Westasien und Afrika. Leipzig: Bibliographisches Institut.

————. 1901d. "Zaubermittel der Evheer." *Internationales Archiv für Eth-nographie* 14: 1–15.

————. 1902a. *Altersklassen und Männerbünde: Eine Darstellung der Grund-formen der Gesellschaft.* Berlin: Reimer.

————. 1902b. "Kolonialmüdigkeit." *Die Grenzboten* 61 (3): 561–65.

————. 1902c. "Die Entstehung der Gesellschaft." *Zeitschrift für Socialwis-senschaft* 5: 454–57.

————. 1902d. "Das Steingeld in Afrika und in der Südsee." *Zeitschrift für Socialwissenschaft* 5: 201–2.

————. 1902e. "Afrikanisches Steingeld." *Globus* 81: 12–13.

————. 1902f. "Die pyrenäische Halbinsel von der iberischen Urzeit an bis zur Seeschlacht von Cavité." In *Weltgeschichte*, vol. 4, edited by Hans F. Helmolt, 469–550. Die pyrenäische Halbinsel. Leipzig: Bibliographisches Institut.

————. 1902g. "Hochasien und Sibirien." In *Weltgeschichte*, vol. 2, edited by Hans F. Helmolt, 117–222. Ostasien und Ozeanien. Leipzig: Bibliographisches Institut.

————. 1902h. "Keimformen der Prostitution." *Zeitschrift für Socialwissen-schaft* 5: 544–45.

————. 1903a. *Völkerkunde.* Leipzig: Deuticke.

————. 1903b. "Santiago de Compostela." *Deutsche Geographische Blätter* 26 (1): 64–70. Originally published in *Die Zeit*, Vienna, March 3, 1903.

————. 1903c. "Die Janitscharen." *Preussische Jahrbücher* 112: 450–79.

————. 1903d. "Türkische Basare und Zünfte." *Zeitschrift für Socialwissen-schaft* 6: 683–706.

Seaford, Richard. 2004. *Money and the Early Greek Mind: Homer, Philosophy, Tragedy.* Cambridge: Cambridge University Press.

Seitz, Emanuel. 2017. "What Is Money?" *Social Analysis* 61 (4): 114–29.

Servet, Jean-Michel, ed. 1984. *Nomismata: État et origines de la monnaie.* Lyon: Presses Universitaires de Lyon.

———. 1998. "Démonétarisation et remonétarisation en Afrique occidentale et équatoriale (XIXe–XXe siècles)." In *La monnaie souveraine*, edited by Michel Aglietta and André Orléan, 290–324. Paris: Odile Jacob.

———. 2001. "Le troc primitif, un mythe fondateur d'une approche économiste de la monnaie." *Revue numismatique* 6 (157): 15–32.

Shell, Marc. 2019. *Wampum and the Origins of American Money.* Champaign: University of Illinois Press.

Shipton, Parker. 1989. *Bitter Money: Cultural Economy and Some African Meanings of Forbidden Commodities.* Washington: American Anthropological Association.

Simiand, François. 1898. Review of *Grundriss einer Entstehungsgeschichte des Geldes (Abrégé d'une histoire des origines de la monnaie)* by Heinrich Schurtz. *L'Année sociologique* 2: 457–59.

Simmel, Georg. 1900. *Philosophie des Geldes.* Leipzig: Duncker & Humblot.

———. (1978) 2004. *The Philosophy of Money*, 3rd enl. ed. Edited by David Frisby. Translated by Tom Bottomore, Kaethe Mengelberg, and David Frisby. London: Routledge.

Smith, Woodruff D. 1991. *Politics and the Sciences of Culture in Germany, 1840–1920.* Oxford: Oxford University Press.

Spread, Patrick. 2022. *Economics, Anthropology and the Origin of Money as a Bargaining Counter.* London: Taylor & Francis.

Steinmetz, George. 2008. *The Devil's Handwriting: Precoloniality and the German Colonial State in Qingdao, Samoa, and Southwest Africa.* Chicago: University of Chicago Press.

Steinmetz, Hans-Dieter. 2009. "Jenseits von Spiritismus und Spiritualismus? Über den Umgang mit mediumistischen Phänomenen in Karl Mays Lebensumfeld." *Jahrbuch der Karl-May-Gesellschaft*, 131–271.

Steuart, James. 1767. *An Inquiry Into the Principles of Political Oeconomy [...]*, vol. 1. Strand: Millar.

Stewart, Pamela J., and Andrew Strathern. 2002. "Transformations of Monetary Symbols in the Highlands of Papua New Guinea." *L'Homme* 162 (2): 137–56.

Stocking, George W. 1991. "Maclay, Kubary, Malinowski: Archetypes from the Dreamtime of Anthropology." In *Colonial Situations: Essays on the Contextualization of Ethnographic Knowledge*, edited by George W. Stocking, 9–74. Wisconsin: University of Wisconsin Press.

Taeuber, Walter. 1945. Review of *Die Entstehung des Geldes und die Anfänge des Geldwesens* by Wilhelm Gerloff. *FinanzArchiv* 10 (2): 461–65.

Tenbruck, Friedrich. 1986. "Max Weber and Eduard Meyer." In *Max Weber and His Contempories*, edited by Wolfgang J. Mommsen and Jürgen Osterhammel, 234–67. London: Routledge.

Thilenius, Georg. 1921. "Primitives Geld." *Archiv für Anthropologie* 18: 1–34.

Thomas, Northcote W. 1901. Review of *Urgeschichte der Kultur* by Heinrich Schurtz. *Man* 1: 125–26.

Thurnwald, Richard. 1923. "Die Gestaltung der Wirtschaftsentwicklung aus ihren Anfängen heraus: Gesichtspunkte und Andeutungen." In *Erinnerungsgabe für Max Weber*, vol. 1, edited by Melchior Palyi, 273–336. Leipzig: Duncker & Humblot.

———. 1932. *Economics in Primitive Communities*. London: International Institute of African Languages and Cultures.

Tucci, Giovanni. 1970. "Origine et développement de la monnaie primitive." *Cahiers Vilfredo Pareto* 8 (21): 17–36.

Tylor, Edward B. 1889. "On a Method of Investigating the Development of Institutions; Applied to Laws of Marriage and Descent." *The Journal of the Anthropological Institute of Great Britain and Ireland* 18: 245–72.

Veblen, Thorstein. 1899. *The Theory of the Leisure Class: An Economic Study of Institutions*. New York: Macmillan.

Vierkandt, Alfred. 1898. Review of *Grundriss einer Entstehungsgeschichte des Geldes* by Heinrich Schurtz. *Zeitschrift für Socialwissenschaft* 1: 479–80.

Vissering, Willem. 1877. *On Chinese Currency: Coin and Paper Money*. Leiden: Brill.

Vogel, Hans Ulrich. 2012. *Marco Polo was in China: New Evidence from Currencies, Salts and Revenues*. Leiden: Brill.

Volckart, Oliver. 2024. *The Silver Empire: How Germany Created its First Common Currency*. Oxford: Oxford University Press.

Wagner, Adolph. 1909. *Sozialökonomische Theorie des Geldes und Geldwesens*. Theoretische Sozialökonomik 2. Abteilung. Bd. 2. Leipzig: Winter.

Wagner-Hasel, Beate. 2011. *Die Arbeit des Gelehrten: Der Nationalökonom Karl Bücher (1847–1930)*. Frankfurt: Campus.

Wallace, Robert W. 1987. "The Origin of Electrum Coinage." *American Journal of Archaeology* 91 (3): 385–97.

Weber, Max. 1922. *Wirtschaft und Gesellschaft*. Grundriss der Sozialökonomik, III. Tübingen: Mohr.

———. 1923. *Wirtschaftsgeschichte*. Berlin: Duncker & Humblot.

———. 1947. *The Theory of Social and Economic Organization*. Translated by Talcott Parsons. New York: The Free Press.

———. 1950. *General Economic History*. Translated by Franklin W. Knight. New York: The Free Press.

———. 1972. *Wirtschaft und Gesellschaft: Grundriß der verstehenden Soziologie*. Tübingen: Mohr.

———. (1905) 2001. *The Protestant Ethic and the Spirit of Capitalism*. Translated by Stephen Kahlberg. New York: Routledge.

———. 2009. *Wirtschaft und Gesellschaft: Entstehungsgeschichte und Dokumente*, vol. I/24 of *Max Weber-Gesamtausgabe*. Edited by Wolfgang Schluchter. Tübingen: Mohr Siebeck.

———. 2019. *Economy and Society: A New Translation*. Translated by Keith Tribe. Harvard: Harvard University Press.

Weiner, Annette B. 1992. *Inalienable Possessions: The Paradox of Keeping-While-Giving*. Berkeley: University of California Press.

Weißenborn, Johannes. 1912. "Heinrich Schurtz." In *Bremische Biographie des neunzehnten Jahrhunderts*, edited by Historische Gesellschaft des Künstlervereins, 452–55. Bremen: Winter.

Wertheimer, Max. 1925. *Drei Abhandlungen zur Gestalttheorie*. Erlangen: Philosophische Akademie.

Wieschhoff, Heinrich A. 1945. *Primitive Money*. University Museum Bulletin. Philadelphia: University of Pennsylvania.

Williamson, John G. 2015. *Karl Helfferich, 1872–1924: Economist, Financier, Politician*. Princeton: Princeton University Press.

Wolf, Eric. 1982. *Europe and the People Without History*. Berkeley: University of California Press.

Wray, L. Randall. 1993. "The Origins of Money and the Development of the Modern Financial System." Working Paper, No. 86, Levy Economics Institute of Bard College.

———. 2014. "Outside Money: The Advantages of Owning the Magic Porridge Pot." Working Paper, No. 821, Levy Economics Institute of Bard College.

Yang, Bin. 2018. *Cowrie Shells and Cowrie Money: A Global History*. London: Routledge.

Yung-Ti, Li. 2003. "On the Function of Cowries in Shang and Western Zhou China." *Journal of East Asian Archaeology* 5 (1): 1–26.

Zelizer, Viviana A. 2004. "Circuits of Commerce." In *Self, Social Structure, and Beliefs: Explorations in Sociology*, edited by Jeffrey Alexander, 122–44. Berkeley: University of California Press.